What Readers Are Saying About

Hidden Solutions All Around You

"Read this book and you will start seeing opportunities that are invisible to your competition. This is a tremendous advantage."

—Barry Burgdorf
Corporate Attorney, Entrepreneur, Strategist

"Dan Castro provides a guidebook for those who want more from life and their business. This in-depth exploration of the psychology of the great innovators in history will kick-start your brain to go places you never dreamed you could go."

—Kevin Ready
Serial Entrepreneur, Author and Contributor to *Forbes* Magazine

"This book is filled with great stories of innovation and entrepreneurship that will inspire you to discover the hidden opportunities that truly are all around you."

—Gary Hoover
Founder of BOOKSTOP, Hoover's, Inc. and Bigwig Games

"Amazing book! It will lead you to many 'aha' moments. After you read it, you will start connecting the dots in new ways."

—Selene Benavides
CFO/COO, National Society of Hispanic MBAs

"I really, really like this book. It hits creativity, innovative thinking, entrepreneurship, and thinking outside the box. Dan Castro nails it."

—Orrin Woodward
New York Times best-selling author of
Launching a Leadership Revolution and *LeaderShift*

"Become the kind of person you read about in this book. This book will shift the way you go about solving problems."

—David Bernert
Zen Restaurants

"This book is really going to help a lot of people overcome financial difficulties and get where they want to be in life."

—Carl Stanley
CEO/Founder of Rising Point Solutions

HIDDEN
SOLUTIONS
ALL AROUND YOU

---✳︎---

*Why Some People Can See Them
and Some Can't*

Beartooth Press
Austin

Beartooth Press
7800 Shoal Creek Blvd.
Suite 100N
Austin, Texas 78757

First Edition

Publisher's Cataloging-in-Publication
(Provided by Quality Books, Inc.)

Castro, Daniel R., 1960-
    Hidden solutions all around you : why some people can
see them and some can't / Daniel R. Castro.
    pages cm
    Includes bibliographical references and index.
    LCCN 2014903166
    ISBN 978-0-9914564-0-6

    1. Creative ability. 2. Entrepreneurship.
    I. Title.

BF408.C37 2014   153.3'5
                        QBI14-600013

Book design by Janice Benight

page 1 image source istockphoto, © Zakai
page 338 image source istockphoto, © Rawpixel

Manufactured in the United States of America

"Here is Edward Bear, coming downstairs now,
bump, bump, bump
on the back of his head, behind Christopher Robin.

It is, as far as he knows, the only way of coming downstairs,
but sometimes he feels that there really is another way,
if only he could stop bumping a moment
and think of it."

—A.A. MILNE
Winnie-the-Pooh

To all those who were born to walk alone.

Misunderstood.

Reprimanded as children for coloring outside the lines.

Rejected by their peers.

They were mocked, ridiculed, and scorned.

They were considered weird.

Yet, they continued to follow their own path,

blazing trails through dark jungles,

surging forth into the heat of a battle they could not win

when everyone told them they were crazy,

and emerged from the fight,

beat up,

filthy,

bloody,

but joyous

with the heart of the enemy in their teeth.

—Daniel R. Castro

CONTENTS

PART THREE

Now Look Around You   219

Acknowledgments

I would like to say a heartfelt thank you to the following people who gave of their time and brain cells to pour over my manuscript and provide valuable feedback and insights. Because of you, this book is what it is.

Selene Benavides

David Bernert

Barry Burgdorf

Laura Fowler

Mark LaSpina

Robert "T-Ray" Manley

Kevin Ready

Christopher R. Webb

Orrin Woodward

Rose Castro

Heather Mauel

MANY THANKS!

Daniel R. Castro

PART ONE

The Eye of the Brain

How Far Will Your Arrow Fly?

The next time you are tempted to say, "I'm out of options. I'm defeated. There is nothing left that I can do," step outside on a clear, starry night. Look up. Recall that at one point in time, humans believed that all that existed was that which we could see with our own eyes. The earth, the sun, the moon, and a sea of stars.

As you look up at the stars, single out one star among all you can see. Focus on it. Zoom in on it with your mind's eye. Now mentally transport yourself to it and stand on it in your very own specially designed space suit. Look deep into space. Deeper. Into the inky black night. Isolate the darkest spot in the night sky.

Now let your mind wander through *that* dark spot to the furthest edge of space you can imagine. Stand there at that edge and reach out your hand. What do you feel?

While standing at that edge, pull out an imaginary arrow from your quiver and notch it in your imaginary bow and draw back on the string. Let the arrow fly. How much deeper into space can it fly? Will it hit anything, or will it keep flying forever?

If it hits something, go stand on that something and let fly another arrow.

Until *it* hits something.

Then go stand on that something and do it again . . . and again . . . and again.

Then you will know that even with the most powerful telescopes we have sent into outer space, we have seen but a fraction of all that exists.

Who knows what exists beyond the reach of our most powerful arrow? Beyond our most powerful telescopes?

Who knows what possibilities exist beyond that which we can *see* or even imagine? You see, every day scientists, anthropologists, oceanographers, and astronomers discover things that *were there all along*, but which we simply never saw.

Do you really think the options you are considering right now are really the *only* options that exist?

When you contemplate the vastness of the universe who are YOU to say, *I am out of options*?

—DANIEL R. CASTRO

CHAPTER 1

---------- -‹‹‹◆›››- ----------

The Question Is Why?

I n the early 1960s, in the City of Schertz, a small rural town outside of San Antonio, Texas there lived a young Hispanic woman named Rosie Gutierrez. Rosie was poor, but she wanted more than anything to put her children through college so that her children would not have to grow up poor like her. She prayed with all her heart to find a way to earn enough money to put them through college. One day, she got up off her knees and wiped her tears with her apron. Then, she looked outside her window and *saw* what she had never seen before. She saw a huge pile of trash in the neighbor's yard. Yes, the *trash had always been there*. But on this day, she saw something she had never seen before, she *saw* a problem that needed a solution. On that day, Rosie made what would turn out to be a life-changing decision: She offered to carry the trash to the dump for a dollar. She piled all the trash into the trunk of her car and carried it away. This was a dirty, thankless job, but it was sorely needed in that community. Back then, the City of Schertz did not have municipal trash pick-up. Everyone was on their own. Other neighbors began asking for her services as well. She became very busy doing what no one else would do.

Her operation began to grow larger than she had expected. She saved half the money and used the other half to supplement her husband's meager income. She soon saved enough money for a down payment on a used pickup truck and eventually bought an even bigger truck. After a time, she had to hire help.

One day, the City took bids on a contract for municipal trash pickup. Rosie submitted a bid and to her surprise won the contract. She beat out all of the national and statewide garbage haulers to get this contract. Eventually, she had her own fleet of industrial-size garbage haulers that bore the name Gutierrez in bold letters on their sides. In this case, one man's trash literally became a woman's treasure. This woman *made a decision* to use all her available resources and do whatever it took to achieve her objective. She believed in something bigger than herself. She was focused, not on money, but on a purpose bigger than herself—putting her kids through college. This purpose, coupled with her faith, mobilized all the forces within her and allowed her to see what no one around her saw.

Throughout your life you have heard the saying, "one man's trash is another man's treasure." Indeed, the stories of simple men and women rising from rags to riches are now so commonplace that, unless there is sex or violence involved, they bore us. History is filled with them. Coco Chanel was a poor orphan girl raised by nuns. Ralph Lauren grew up poor in the Bronx, the son of an impoverished Russian immigrant. Andrew Carnegie's father brought him to the United States with only the clothes on his back. Oprah Winfrey was abused as a child and raised in poverty. Tyler Perry was so poor he had to live on the streets while he was working on his first play. Howard Schultz, the founder of the Starbucks empire grew up poor in Brooklyn.

The question of *how* they did it has been answered over and over in their biographies and autobiographies, articles and interviews. Movies have been made about them. But one question few, if any, people ask is *why*. *Why* were they able to do it? *Why* were they able to see the opportunities and solutions that were invisible to others? From a purely biological point of view, we all have essentially the same kinds of brains and the same kinds of eyeballs.

Yet Rosie saw what everyone around her missed. She saw treasure where others literally saw trash. But why? The "how" is interesting. The "why" is profound.

What gave Rosie this rare, mysterious ability to see the incredible opportunity that was invisible to everyone else around her? Whenever I ask people this question, they always give the standard answers: (1) positive thinking; (2) shifting the lens through which you view the world; (3) shifting your paradigm; (4) hard work; (5) perseverance;

(6) the law of attraction; and (7) other similar philosophies. Entire libraries of those kinds of books already exist.

But I have met too many people over the years who did all of those things and they still lost their jobs, their homes, their cars, and had to file bankruptcy—due to no fault of their own. They did everything right. They went to the right colleges, got the right degree, went to work for the right company, and worked hard all their lives. They are honest, intelligent, hard-working people. They checked all the right boxes, went to the right churches, temples and synagogues. Joined the right clubs and networking groups.

But due to circumstances beyond their control, they got "downsized" or they hit the "glass ceiling" where they could climb no higher. Some of them lost their spouses or children to a terminal illness, or a car accident. If I were to tell these people, "Listen, all you need to do is adjust your attitude and start being more positive," they would punch me. If I said, "Here's a list of daily affirmations to tape to your bathroom mirror and repeat them every day," this book would be the same as all the others.

When the storm winds of chaos are whirling all around you, when you are at the lowest point of your life, what you really need is a real-world, tangible, concrete solution you can take to the bank. You need to see the answer to your prayers riding over the horizon like a white knight coming to rescue you at just the right moment. That's what we all secretly want, crave, and need. That's why I wrote this book.

I conducted seven years of research into the lives of people who see solutions that are invisible to others. This book explains in depth *why* it is that some people can see the solutions that are in plain sight, and some can't. This book is not just a collection of amazing stories of innovators and entrepreneurs who went from rags to riches, who turned trash into treasure, who overcame extreme obstacles to make their dreams come true. It is much more than that. This is the first book that attempts to explain exactly *why* some people are able to see solutions that are invisible to everyone else. It also explains how *you* can become one of those people.

But first, I must ask you a question. Do you believe the solution to the problem you are facing *already exists*?

✳

THINGS TO PONDER

+ The "how" is interesting. The "why" is profound.

+ You are about to discover *WHY* one-hundred people can be looking at the same pile of trash and only one of them see treasure.

✳

CHAPTER 2

Can You Believe in Something You Cannot See?

During the gold rush days in Colorado, a man named R.U. Darby and his uncle went west in search of gold. With only a pick and a shovel, they dug and dug until they finally struck the shiny gold ore. But they needed specialized machinery to bring the gold to the surface. They quietly buried their small mine and went back east to Williamsburg, Maryland and told a few relatives and neighbors of their find. They convinced them to invest and loan them the money they needed to buy the equipment and had it shipped to the mine.

They brought up the first car of ore and shipped it to the smelter. The results showed that there was indeed gold in that mine. A few more cars of this gold would pay their debts and then they could start reaping enormous profits. But then tragedy struck. The vein of gold disappeared. They searched and searched—desperate to pick up the vein again. But no luck. They continued drilling in vain and after a few more weeks of frustration, they gave up. They sold the machinery to a junk man for a few hundred dollars and took the train back home.

In the meantime, the junk man called a mining engineer to look at the mine. The engineer took some calculations and concluded that the project had failed because the owners were not familiar with "fault lines." The junk man took over the drilling and found the vein of gold within three feet of where the Darbys had stopped drilling! The mine turned out to be one of the biggest gold mines ever discovered in Colorado.

Why would the Darby's have given up when they were so close? The surface level answer is because they could not find the vein of gold. But the real answer lies beneath the surface. They gave up because they had stopped *believing*. Moreover, their beliefs were based on sound logic. The evidence seemed to support their beliefs. After searching, and searching, and searching, they could not find the vein of gold anywhere. They were tired, and running low on cash. But if they had truly *believed* there was a mountain of gold within their reach, they could have found a way to hire an engineer just like the junk man did, right? Surely they had enough cash to dig three more feet, right? If the Darbys had *kept believing*, it would have prompted their brain to come up with the creative solutions they needed to achieve their wildest dreams.

Throughout history, scientists, legendary entrepreneurs, and innovators believed in things that could not be seen, touched, smelled, heard or tasted. They believed in solutions no one else could see. Solutions that *they alone* knew existed. Solutions that became obvious only after these entrepreneurs and innovators pulled back the curtain. In fact, it turns out, this ability was their best kept secret. Do you have the ability to believe in something you cannot see?

The most important factor that determined whether the seeker found the solution was, first and foremost, whether he *believed* it existed. You will not begin to look for something *in earnest* unless you truly believe it exists. It's like when you can't find your car keys, but you know they are somewhere in the house because you could not have driven home without them. You will not stop searching until you find them because you *know for sure* they are somewhere in the house. It takes *that* kind of belief. If you don't have that kind of belief, you will never invest the right amount of time, energy, and brain cells into trying to find the solution.

Just like the car keys, everything you want, and everything you need is somewhere in the world around you. And it's closer than you think. All you have to do is develop the ability to sense it, feel it, see it, and hear it. But first, you have to *believe* it. Belief gives birth to passion. Passion gives birth to action.

The saying "necessity is the mother of invention" has been around a long time. But it is only partially true. The Darbys had a great "necessity." But the necessity alone yielded no solution. Many people throughout history have been in desperate need of a solution, but never found one. You see, necessity may be the mother of invention, but she still needs a father to plant a seed in her. Belief is the *father* of invention. Belief is the most powerful generator of ideas the world has ever known. Belief energizes you to keep looking for solutions, to keep hoping when everyone else has given up. It motivates you. It inspires you. It gets you out of bed in the morning. It keeps you up late at night. It drives you to keep turning over stones until you find the right answer.

But, what about the people who believed with no logical reason to believe, and no tangible clue in the first place to inspire that belief? We call them unrealistic fools, lunatics, delusional, and neurotic. And yes, some of them were. But some of those crazy people, who believed with only a hunch to go on, changed the history of the world.

In the U.S. Army, the Rangers, an elite fighting force, are required as part of their training to go through rigorous survival exercises in which they must eat bugs and leaves and suffer extreme physical conditions. This training teaches them that there is always a solution to their problem somewhere nearby. It builds confidence, layer by layer, and ingrains well-worn paths and patterns in their brains that they follow instinctively if they ever encounter a similar situation in real life. They come to *believe* that, even when they are in grave danger, there might be alternatives to death, if they choose to exercise them. This *belief* allows them to see potential sources of food, shelter and weapons that others might not see.

On June 2, 1995, Captain Scott O'Grady's F-16 was shot down by a Bosnian Serb surface-to-air missile while trying to enforce the NATO no-fly zone over Bosnia. He was hunted and shot at by the Serbs, but he escaped and survived for six days behind enemy lines by eating grass, leaves, and ants and collecting rainwater to drink. He was ultimately rescued in a harrowing mission. In his book *Return With Honor*, Captain O'Grady relates two stories that were constantly on his mind while he was evading capture and trying to survive.

The first story was about a man who was stranded eight days in the Arizona desert without food or water. He lost 25 percent of his body weight from lack of water. This is normally fatal. His blood was so thick that his lacerations could not bleed. The man had made every mistake in the book. He survived not because of his training or survival skills, but because of his will to live. He simply refused to die.[1]

The second story was about a civilian pilot who was forced to land on a frozen lake in Canada when his engine failed. He was not hurt. He saw a wooded shoreline approximately two hundred yards away, which was a *potential* source of food and shelter. He started off across the lake and made it halfway, but not knowing what he would encounter when he got to the woods, he lost hope and returned to the plane. When he arrived at the plane, he smoked a cigar, took a pistol out and shot himself in the head. Less than twenty-four hours later, a rescue team came upon his body. Was it the circumstances that determined his fate or an internal decision that there was no hope?

These two stories kept reminding Captain O'Grady that he must keep believing and keep hoping against hope that he would survive and be rescued. It gave him the motivation and the energy to keep struggling no matter what—and it worked. Captain O'Grady survived and became a national hero. The decision behind his decision was to *believe* and keep trying. This belief allowed him to *see* and *hear* options that kept him alive until he was rescued.

The U.S. Military has learned what the rest of us need to learn: the most dangerous and daunting circumstances alone cannot defeat us. Our circumstances need help from *us* in order to prevail. The problem itself is never the real problem. It's what we *believe* about the problem that determines the outcome of any given situation. You can literally turn your fate around by learning to respond properly in any given situation. But first you have to make a conscious decision to *believe* that you can survive and prosper. This belief will help you *see* that there are other viable options to defeat. Then you've got to make a decision to pursue them.

The power of belief is what gave Columbus the courage to dedicate his whole life to finding a route to the East by traveling in the opposite direction. It's what gave the Wright Brothers the ability to conceive of and create the first successful manned flight. Without this ability,

Steve Jobs could not have come up with iTunes, the iPod, the iPhone, or the iPad. Without it, Mark Zuckerberg could not have come up with Facebook. Without it, the internet would not exist. Cell phones would be a fantasy. Texting would be a joke. Flying 500 mph at 30,000 feet above the earth in a hunk of metal that weighs 975,000 pounds would be sheer lunacy.

Unless Alexander Graham Bell actually believed it was possible to transmit understandable words over a pair of wires we would have no telephones or cell phones. If Benjamin Franklin and Thomas Edison had not truly believed that the bolts of lightning we see in the sky could be captured and placed into a small glass bulb, we could not command the power of electricity today with the flick of a switch. Indeed Benjamin Franklin's belief was so strong that he was willing to risk being killed by a lightning strike. Belief is not a feeling. It is a choice. True belief commands action. Is your belief that strong?

Anthropologists and biologists tell us there is very little that separates us from the great apes.[2] The ability to believe in things we cannot see as though they are real is one of the most important things that separates us from the animals. This is the same ability that allows us to think in terms of concepts. It's what gives us the ability to use words. It's what gives us the ability to count from zero to three.

Did you know that you will never see the numeral zero in nature? For thousands of years, the Western numeric system had no zero in it.[3] The reason was because in Western philosophy there was no such thing as *nothing*.[4] This was only possible in Eastern philosophy where nothingness was not only possible, but was actually deeply rooted in the culture. It was in India where the concept of zero as a number was born. Without the number zero, there would be no modern mathematics, no algebraic equations, no calculus, no modern science. The number zero did not arrive in Western culture until 1200 A.D. when an Italian mathematician named Fibonacci started using it in his calculations.

And yet, despite the fact that you cannot see the number zero in nature, you believe in it. You use it to balance your checkbook. You use it to count your change at the supermarket. It is as real as your own eyeballs, but it only exists because it is a tool *we created* to help organize our world.

The ability to believe in things we cannot see as though they are real is what gives us the ability to intuit the right answer even though we cannot yet prove it. For example, the quest to discover what matter is ultimately made of has haunted humans since the time of the ancient Greeks. For thousands of years, scientists believed that the atom was the smallest building block of nature and, therefore, could not be split. It was the Greeks who came up with the word "atom" which means "unsplittable."

But, as every grade school child now knows, the atom is not the smallest building block of nature. After physicists were finally able to see inside the atom, they found even tinier subatomic particles called neutrons, protons, electrons, photons, gluons, fermions, hadrons, bosons, and quarks. However, no physicist has ever *actually seen* any of these subatomic particles. They exist beyond the level of our sensory perception. We only know they exist because we can see their effects. When physicists came to this realization, they were faced with a first-time anomaly in science. Everything about classical physics requires, for its legitimacy, that each conclusion be based on that which can be seen, touched, weighed, and measured. But for the first time, physicists had to admit they were dealing with a *non-sensory* experience of reality. We only know these subatomic particles exist because we can observe the consequences of their existence. All we have is indirect, circumstantial evidence.

Actually, the most startling thing was not what these researchers found, but what they did *not find*. Between these subatomic particles there was *nothing*. Early physicists, Ernest Walton, Ernest Rutherford, and John Cockcroft were shocked to discover that an atom consists almost entirely of empty space. In fact, physicists found that these subatomic particles are so tiny and the space between them so vast that they compared them to finding flies in a cathedral.[5] To this day, physicists still have no idea what is holding these particles together. So, they simply call it "energy."

Arthur Koestler describes it this way:

> The chair on which I sit seems a hard fact, but I know that I sit on a nearly perfect vacuum. The wood of the chair consists of fibres, which consist of molecules, which consist of atoms, which are miniature solar systems with a central nucleus and electrons for planets. ..... [I]t has become an accepted truism among physicists that the sub-atomic structure of any object, including the chair I sit on, cannot be fitted into a framework of space and time. Words like 'substance' or 'matter' have become void of meaning.[6]

All physicists agree that the only thing that gives the chair you are sitting on the illusion of substance, solidity, and matter is the fact that tiny, and as of yet invisible, subatomic particles are constantly vibrating with energy. It is both profound and frightening. Everything we can see is made of stuff we cannot see.

Long before these subatomic particles had been discovered, Einstein had already intuited the same conclusion. He even came up with a very simple mathematical equation to explain it. Einstein instinctively believed that mass (that which you can see, touch, and measure) is made up of energy (that which you cannot see or touch). You have undoubtedly seen this formula many times in your life. $E=mc^2$. The mass of an object is equal to a certain amount of energy. Subatomic particles can be spontaneously generated from pure energy, and can vanish into pure energy.[7]

The most significant factor that drove the earliest nuclear physicists forward was the undying *belief* that a solution existed. They were up against an impenetrable obstacle that was thousands of years old—the belief that the atom could not be split. This belief was so well ingrained into scientific culture that it even made up the definition of the nouns they used. Nevertheless, they persisted, believing against all logic that something "unsplittable" could, in fact, be split.

The ability to believe in things we can't see is truly a gift. It is one of the things that makes us uniquely human.

> ***I have heard articulate speech produced by sunlight.***
> ***I have heard a ray of sun laugh, cough and sing.***
>
> —ALEXANDER GRAHAM BELL

In quantum physics, mass does not exist at any specific place or time. Matter simply equals energy in motion. Perhaps this is why every spiritual leader who ever lived taught the futility of clinging to tangible things. They are merely an illusion. The more we try to hold onto them, the more they seem to slip through our fingers like soap bubbles.

It actually takes more faith to believe that what you can see is all that exists than it takes to believe that what you cannot see is real.

> *Through faith we know that what can be seen*
> *is made of things that cannot be seen.*
> —HEBREWS 11:3 (NIV)

Whatever problem you are facing, whether in business or in your personal life, I can tell you from the historical record that you will not overcome it unless and until you *choose to believe,* as an act of your will, that a solution exists—a solution that you may not *yet* be able to see, hear, taste, touch, or smell. A solution that all your friends and even the experts may tell you does not exist and can never exist. Like the number zero. Like the invisible stuff that holds subatomic particles together.

But how do you choose to believe in something that you cannot yet see? How do you keep believing when all evidence is to the contrary? How do you know you are not being completely foolish? If you let them, the heroes and legends in this book will show you how. Innovators and entrepreneurs have a different definition of "faith" than most. Faith is believing in something that you cannot see—and accepting the responsibility for bringing it into the world you *can see.* You will see many examples of it in this book.

> *Alice laughed. "There's no use trying," she said;*
> *"One can't believe impossible things."*
>
> *"I daresay you haven't had much practice," said the Queen.*
> —LEWIS CARROLL
> *Through the Looking Glass*

Will you stand with the heroes and legends that have come before you and *choose to believe* in something you cannot see, and act like it exists, and keep acting like it exists until you actually bring it to pass through sheer hard work, determination, creativity, and innovation? Only those who see beyond the limits of their own eyes can ever reach beyond the limits of their own grasp.

If you are surrounded by naysayers, you are in good company. The greatest entrepreneurs, scientists, explorers and innovators were all told the same thing by the experts in their respective fields. "You're nuts. That's insane. Are you crazy?" This was the resounding chorus that preceded most great discoveries and accomplishments in history. Indeed, some of these people were just *this side* of crazy. But that is the kind of crazy that changes lives. It is the kind of crazy that carries you on its shoulders before the throngs of people shouting "Victory!" in your honor through the streets of your home town. It is the kind of crazy to which monuments are built, about which bestsellers are written, and about which movies are made. It's the kind of crazy that changed the history of the world. Are you crazy enough to believe a solution exists—even though you can't see it yet? Are you crazy enough to act as though it is so real that your actions and beliefs alone can will it into existence? If you are, then come with me, walk with me, journey with me on an adventure from which you will never return to the world as you know it.

Here's To The Crazy Ones. The misfits. The rebels.
The trouble-makers. The round pegs in the
square holes. The ones who see things differently.
You can quote them, disagree with them, glorify, or vilify them.
About the only thing you can't do is ignore them.
They're not fond of rules, and they have
no respect for the status-quo.
Because they change things.
They push the human race forward.
And while some may see them as the crazy ones,
we see genius.

Because the people who are crazy enough
to think they can change the world
are the ones who do.

—Steve Jobs
Apple, Inc.'s "Think Different"
Ad Campaign, 1977

THINGS TO PONDER

+ Everything you want, and everything you need is somewhere in the world around you. And it's closer than you think.

+ It takes more faith to believe that what you can see is all that exists than it takes to believe that what you cannot see is real.

+ The problem itself is never the main problem. It's what we believe about the problem that is the problem.

+ Only those who can see beyond the limits of their own eyes can reach beyond the limits of their own grasp.

CHAPTER 3

Are There Ideas in the Air?

Is it really possible that the solution to the problem you are facing already exists? Is it possible that there are solutions free floating in the air, waiting to land on the right brain at just the right geographic spot on the planet at just the right point in time? The evidence may surprise you. The historical record shows that the following life-changing inventions/discoveries were achieved by separate people working independently on separate parts of the globe at around the same time.

- **Light Bulb:** Joseph Swan, and Thomas Edison independently invented the light bulb at around the same time. (1860–1879)

- **Paper:** The Mayans and the Chinese each separately, and independently, developed paper around the same time. (105 A.D.–300 A.D.)

- **The Rise of Agriculture:** The Chinese and the Mesopotamians independently developed agriculture around the same time. (6500 B.C.)

- **Telephone:** Elisha Gray and Alexander Graham Bell each independently discovered the telephone at around the same time. (both in 1876)

- **Writing:** The art of writing was developed independently by three ancient cultures: (1) the Chinese in Asia; (2) the Quipu in South America; and (3) the Sumerians in ancient Mesopotamia. (4000 B.C.)

- **Photography:** Louis Daguerre and Henry Talbot both independently invented photography at around the same time. (1835–1839)

- **Telegraph:** Joseph Henry and Samuel Morse each separately invented the telegraph at around the same time. (1831–1837)

- **Airplane:** Both Samuel Pierpont Langley and the Wright brothers independently invented the airplane at around the same time. (1903–1914)

- **Phonograph:** Charles Cros and Thomas Edison invented the phonograph independently at around the same time. (1877–1878)

- **Color Photography:** Louis Ducos du Hauron and James Maxwell each independently discovered color photography at around the same time. (1861–1869)

- **Splitting the Atom:** In the 1930s, a team of British scientists were working on splitting the atom. At the same time, an independent team of German scientists were doing the same thing. James Chadwick, Ernest Rutherford, John Douglas Cockroft and Earnest Thomas Sinton Walton split the atom in England in 1932. Otto Han and Fritz Strassman split the atom in Germany in 1938.

- **Race to the Moon:** The Americans and the Russians each separately and independently developed the ability to fly a man to the moon at the same time. (1961–1969) (The first man in space was Yuri Alekseyevich Gagarin—1961; The first man to walk on the moon was Neil Armstrong—1969).

- **Social Networking:** Mark Zuckerberg invented Facebook at around the same time that Tom Anderson invented MySpace. (2003–2004)

- **Calculus:** Isaac Newton and Gottfried Leibniz independently invented calculus at around the same time. (1665–1684)

- **Telescope:** Hans Lippershey, James Metius, and Zacharias Jansen each independently invented the telescope around the same time. (1608)

- **Oxygen:** Joseph Priestley and Carl Wilhelm Scheele each discovered the molecules that make up oxygen at around the same time. (1773–1774)

- **Logarithms:** John Napier, Henry Briggs, and Joost Burgi each independently invented logarithms at around the same time. (1614–1620)

- **Sunspots:** Kepler, Galileo, Christoph Scheiner, Johannes and David Fabricus, and Thomas Harriott each independently discovered sunspots at around the same time. (1610–1612)

- **Electricity:** Thomas François D'Alibard and Benjamin Franklin each independently captured electricity at around the same time. (1750–1752)

- **Thermometer:** Cornelis Drebbel, Robert Fludd, Galileo Galilei, and Santorio Giuseppe Biancani each independently invented the thermometer at around the same time. (1592–1638).

- **Steam Engine:** Thomas Savery, Thomas Newcomen, and James Watt each independently created the steam engine at around the same time. (1700–1769)

- **Steamboat:** James Watt, John Fitch, and Robert Fulton each independently created a steamboat at around the same time. (1769–1807)

- **Internal Combustion Engine:** Nicéphore Niépce, François Isaac de Rivaz, Samuel Brown, Sadi Carnot, Samuel Morey, William Barnett, Eugenio Barsanti, Felice Matteucci, and Pietro Benini each independently created an internal combustion engine at around the same time. (1807–1857)

- **Two Stroke Engine:** Dugald Clerk and Karl Benz each independently created a two stroke engine at around the same time. (1878–1879)

- **Molecular Theory:** Amedeo Avagadro and John Dalton each independently came up with the theory of molecules at around the same time. (1803–1811)

- **Typewriter:** Christopher Latham, Pellegrino Turri, Giuseppe Ravizza, Henry Mill, William Austin Burt, and Francisco João de Azevedo each independently created a typewriter at around the same time. (1714–1861)

- **Anesthesia:** Crawford Long and William Morton each independently discovered anesthesia for use in surgery around the same time. (1842–1846)

- **Electric Motor:** Michael Faraday, Anyos Jedlik, William Sturgeon, Emily and Thomas Davenport, Zenobe Gramme, and Frank Julian Sprague each independently created an electric motor at around the same time. (1821–1886)

- **Radioactivity:** Henri Becquerel and Sylvanus Thompson each independently discovered radioactivity at around the same time. Becquerel went public with the announcement just a few days before Thompson. (1896)

- **Communication Satellites:** John Pierce and Arthur Clarke each separately and independently conceived of the idea of transmitting sound by radio waves through satellites orbiting the earth. (1944–1954) Although Pierce is primarily credited with the idea, he did not consider himself to be the creator of the idea. He said the idea was floating "in the air."[8]

- **Higgs Boson Particle:** In 1964, Peter Higgs and François Englert each separately and independently discovered the existence of the particle that is referred by sensationalists as the "God Particle" because it explains how the most elementary particles inside of an atom obtained their mass. The existence of this particle was confirmed in March 2013. In October 2013, they were awarded the Nobel Prize in physics.

As far back as 1922, William Ogburn and Dorothy Thomas had already identified no less than one hundred and forty-eight major scientific discoveries that were made by separate people working independently and on different parts of the globe—at around the same time.[9]

This historical record raises the question—is it possible that there really are some ideas "in the air?" If there really are some ideas "in the air" waiting to be snatched up by the right person at the right time in history, why can't that person be you?

"Ideas in the air" are like radio waves. Radio waves are part of the electro-magnetic field that exists all around you all the time.[10] It is the same stuff that exists in the "empty space" between the planets. In reality, there is no such thing as empty space. Cosmologists and physicists have confirmed that there exists a powerful electromagnetic field that is constantly vibrating, flowing and connecting the entire universe.[11]

That same electromagnetic field is what allows you to listen to the radio.[12] All radio waves vibrate at a different rate, called frequencies.[13] Right now, in the air all around you, are flowing the sounds of music, people talking, people laughing, and carrying on in far-away places you have never been to and may never go. They exist in the room where you sit right now—whether you can hear them or not.[14] You can only hear them—if you have a receiver, a tuner, and an amplifier/speaker. The receiver is an antenna. The tuner is simply a small coil of wire that looks like tiny Slinky.[15] Once you turn on the receiver, and tune in to the right frequency, suddenly that tiny coiled wire captures the invisible and unheard sounds. The amplifier/speaker increases the volume and allows you to hear them.

It is a fairly simple system that is so basic, it was discovered in the late 1800s.[16] Your brain works the same way. In order to "receive" the ideas in the air, you have to have your antenna up all the time. This means you have to be deliberately, consciously scanning your environment constantly for ideas that are relevant to your task. To capture new ideas, you have to make a *new choice* about what is relevant. Then you have to adjust your "tuner" (your focus) to isolate and hone in on those newly relevant ideas. Then you have to turn on your "speakers," which requires that you carry around a journal, a small notebook, or a digital recorder in which to record those ideas as they come to you. This allows you to go back and reflect on them over and over (to amplify them in your head) until they produce fruit.

These are the basic steps to capturing the ideas "in the air" all around you. Throughout this book, you will see many examples of people who either saw or *did not see* a solution that was right in front of them depending on whether they thought it was relevant to the task at hand. Be watching for them. Relevance is a critical factor. What you choose to be relevant determines whether you can see it or not.

To be fair, there are certain discoveries and inventions that cannot come to fruition until the right point in history—when the foundations of previous discoveries and inventions have been laid. For example, Facebook could not have been created until the internet had been created. The internet could not exist until computers were invented. Electronic computers could not exist without the invention of the transistor and the vacuum tube. The vacuum tube could not exist without the discovery and capturing of electricity. In addition, the gas powered engine could not exist until we found a way to distill gas from oil.[17] The cell phone could not exist until the telephone had been invented. The telephone could not exist until the telegraph had been invented. Arthur Koestler explains it this way:

> If you put kitchen salt into a glass of water until the water is saturated and will dissolve no more salt, and suspend a thread with a knot at its end in the solution, then after a while a crystal will form round the knot. The shape and texture of the knot are irrelevant; what matters is that the liquid has reached saturation point, and that a core has been provided round which it can start to crystalize.[18]

Some solutions, innovations, discoveries and inventions cannot be realized until the base of knowledge and technology have saturated the environment so much that the next logical step is the crystallization of an idea that seems to have never existed before. Yet the particles necessary for that idea to be born already exist—free floating in the air. It then becomes easy for the right person in the right place at the right time to connect those particles in new and different ways.

It is as though all the available knowledge of the universe has been organized, categorized, and dispersed slowly over time by some divine hand parsing out nuggets of truth here and there at certain points in history. Otherwise, humans would have gone from cave dwellers to moon walkers in just a few years. Koestler accurately points out:

> "If progress had been continuous and organic, all that we know, for instance, about the theory of numbers, or analytical geometry, should have been discovered within a few generations after Euclid."[19]

Innovation, knowledge, and discovery are not evenly distributed along an orderly time-line, or among the various cities and continents on the planet. There were long dark periods of history where few, if any, new discoveries were made. There appeared to be a mysterious fog hiding what was right in front of us until just the right time in history at the right geographical coordinates on the planet. Then several people saw it at the same time, and the race was on. Examples of this include the race to split the atom, the race to create the atomic bomb, the race to achieve manned flight, and the race to the moon.

There are periods of history and geographical locations on the planet that appear to be hot spots of creativity where ideas, knowledge, science, art, sculpture, literature, and poetry seemed to explode out of thin air and into our consciousness. The centers of creativity at various points in history were Athens in 500–400 B.C., Alexandria in 300 B.C., Rome in 200 B.C. to 300 A.D., the Han Dynasty in China from 250 B.C. to 220 A.D., the Islamic world from the 8th century to 1258, Florence in the Renaissance, Venice in the 15th century, Paris, London and Vienna in the 19th century, Hollywood and New York in the 20th century, and the Silicon Valley in 21st century.

For example, from the 1400s through the 1600s there was an explosion of knowledge and thought throughout Europe whose ripple effects were so strong they could be felt literally around the globe. Johannes Gutenberg invented the printing press in 1439. It was only because of the printing press that Marco Polo's famous book *The Wonders of the World* found its way into the hands of a young and impressionable Christopher Columbus. He was so fascinated by what he read, he swore that one day he would find an alternative route to the riches of India and China.

Christopher Columbus was born in 1451—just one year before Leonardo da Vinci. Michelangelo was born in 1475. Nicolaus Copernicus was born in 1473. Johannes Kepler was born in 1571. Galileo was born in 1564. On October 31, 1517, Martin Luther nailed his *Ninety-Five Theses* to the door of the Wittenberg church in Germany. By this single act, he declared the freedom of thought of the individual from the constraints and restrictions of the dictatorial Catholic Church. This new found freedom of thought opened the door to the Age of Reason and the scientific revolution, which we are still experiencing to this day. But for this freedom, every time you got sick, you might still believe God was somehow mad at you.

While Leonardo da Vinci was busy coming up with the earliest mechanical drawings of flying machines, bicycles, scuba diving suits, submarines, tanks, machine guns, exploding cannon balls, and dissecting human bodies to discover the inner workings of our biology, Christopher Columbus was discovering new worlds in which all these ideas would eventually take root and prosper. While Leonardo da Vinci was busy painting the *Mona Lisa* and *The Last Supper*, Michelangelo was busy painting the Sistine Chapel, carving the *Pietà* and carving the famous statue of *David* out of a solid block of marble.

In England, Shakespeare (1564–1616) was busy writing *Romeo and Juliette, Macbeth* and, *The Tempest*, while John Milton (1608–1674) was busy writing *Paradise Lost* and Edmund Spencer (1552–1599) was busy writing the *Faerie Queen.*

Just a few years later, Kepler (1571–1630), Galileo (1564–1642) and Newton (1642–1727) were unlocking the keys to the universe. As historian Serge Bramly explains, "Nature was yielding up her secrets, slowly giving way; she was a treasure chest full of riches, just beginning to open."[20] Coincidentally, Johannes Kepler was born almost one hundred years after Copernicus was born. Newton was born exactly a hundred years after Copernicus died. Galileo died in the year Newton was born.

Alexander Fleming, who accidentally discovered the power of the *penicillium* mold to cure bacterial infections, had this to say in his speech as he was accepting the Nobel Prize in medicine, "Penicillin started as a chance observation . . . It may be that while we think we are masters of the situation we are merely pawns being moved about on the board of life by some superior power."[21]

In fact, many of the discoveries that changed the world were discovered by chance. However, chance discoveries would not be possible unless some mind sharpened by years of study had been in the right place at the right time to observe the solution magically opening like the pedals of a flower. Louis Pasteur said, "In the field of observation, chance favors only the prepared mind." Joseph Henry whose work in electromagnetism made Samuel Morse's invention of the telegraph possible, explained that, "The seeds of great discoveries are constantly floating around us, but they only take root in minds well prepared to receive them."[22]

> *Luck is where preparation meets opportunity.*
> —VINCE LOMBARDI

I believe we are living at that point in history where "the air" is more saturated with knowledge, innovation, creativity, and technology than it has ever been in the history of the human species. As a result, new ideas are crystallizing at a much faster rate than they ever have in the history of mankind. There is "low hanging fruit" everywhere—if you will but reach up and grab it. If you don't reach up and grab it, you can be assured that someone else will. Yes, there really are ideas, solutions, innovations, discoveries and inventions hanging in the air all around you—all the time. Is your brain prepared to observe them, to catch them in action, to peel back the layers, to unfold them, to explain them, and to share them with the world?

When I was a first-year attorney, I hung the words of the famous Carthaginian General Hannibal on my wall, "We will either find a way or make one." That was my motto. I truly believed that there was no legal problem for which I could not find the solution. But over the years, I changed up that quote to make it my own, and today I have these words hanging up over my desk, "There is no such thing as a problem without a solution."

Over the years, as the problems of life have surfaced, some routine, some critical, and some life-threatening, I have always found the words *"There is no such thing as a problem without a solution"* to be true. I have used these words to console many clients who were faced with legal upheavals and financial stress that threatened to destroy their lives. Throughout my life, I can say that, without exception, no matter what problem I was facing, there was always a solution which eventually presented itself. I may not have always liked the solution, but there was always a solution. There are no impossible situations in life, only difficult decisions waiting to be made.

Aaron Ralston was dying of starvation and dehydration in the remote Blue John Canyon in Utah because his arm was caught under a giant boulder and he couldn't get it out. He had been there for several days without food or water, and he was starting to hallucinate and pass out. He had a solution, but he did not like it. Eventually, he did what he did not want to do. He hacked off his arm with a dull pocket knife. It saved his life. There is always a solution—even though you may not like it. Eventually, Ralston wrote a best-selling book about his experience. He was interviewed on all the major talk shows, and a movie was even made about his experience. He ended up a multi-millionaire. All because he was willing to accept a solution that really sucked.

A few years ago, I went backpacking in the Amazon jungle. In the first 100 yards, my indigenous guide had identified at least ten things that could either kill me or severely injure me. And I was going to be in the jungle for an entire week! Every day, he identified yet another spider, snake, mosquito, ant, leaf, fish, tiny frog, tree bark, bat guano, or parasite that could kill me or change my life for the worse forever. Yet somehow, right around the corner, was some root, feather, leaf, tree sap, or mud mixture that could cure me of whatever I was suffering. After a while, I said, "Hey, does that seem kinda weird to you, that every time you show us something that can kill or maim us, there is always something nearby that can cure us?" He laughed and said,

"How do you think my ancestors survived in the jungles for thousands of years without modern medicine or doctors?" Then he told me his grandfather lived to be 98 years old and never left the jungle. I was dumbfounded.[23]

Standing right there, hot and sweaty, in the middle of the Amazon jungle, I had a startling realization. The universe simply cannot exist in a state of imbalance. Isaac Newton explained it in the Third Law of Physics: "For every action, there is an equal and opposite reaction." The ancient Chinese philosophers discovered this universal balance several thousand years before Newton. They called it *yin* and *yang*. In quantum physics, we know that for every negatively charged particle, there is a positively charged particle. The universe seemed to be shouting, "Dan! You're right! The world cannot exist in a state of imbalance. Therefore, there is *no such thing* as a problem without a solution!" The greatest thinkers in history understood this, and *this* was their greatest secret.

While Edison was busy trying to create a good storage battery that could store electricity for longer than just a few minutes, he told a friend, "I don't think Nature would be so unkind as to withhold the secret of a *good* storage battery if a real earnest hunt for it is made. I'm going to hunt."[24] He instinctively *knew* there was no such thing as a problem without a solution, or he would not have kept looking. In the late 1890s Edison successfully created a long lasting, commercially viable lead acid battery, an alkaline electrolyte battery, and an iron-nickel battery.

In 1910, telephonic technology was still in its infancy. When you made a phone call, the sound of your voice got weaker and weaker the further away the other person was. This would not suffice if AT&T was going to unite the nation from one end to the other. Researchers at AT&T were desperately trying to find a way to amplify sound waves so they could be transmitted successfully across long distances. They referred to these amplifiers as "repeaters," but they had not been invented yet. Frank Jewett who worked at AT&T once wrote, "Did we know how to develop such a repeater? No. Why not? Science hadn't yet shown us the way. Did we have any reason to think that she would?

Yes!"[25] This undying belief is what kept Jewett's team of researchers plunging forward until they indeed found a way. The answer was the vacuum tube, which was ultimately replaced by the transistor, and then the semiconductor.

Isaac Newton, the ancient Chinese philosophers, Thomas Edison, Frank Jewett, the laws of physics and quantum physics, and the experience of the Amazonian Indians over the last several thousand years seem to cry out—*the universe cannot exist in a state of imbalance*! In order for the universe to remain in balance, for every problem there *must be* a solution. Indeed, every problem has within it the seeds of its own solution.

> ***Seek and you will find.***
> —Matthew 7:7 (NIV)

All things ultimately resolve toward harmony and peace. No matter how much turmoil and strife you may be experiencing right now, one day there will be peace because the situation will be resolved. All things will ultimately be resolved. You just can't see it or feel it in your gut right now.

Over the last twenty-five years, I have been involved in many multi-million dollar lawsuits that saw armies of lawyers on both sides of the dispute fighting and agonizing over issues that have now long been resolved and almost completely forgotten. Their stories are relegated to the dusty book shelves of law libraries and electronic databases. The only people who read them today are law students because they are forced to do so in order to graduate, and lawyers who are paid hundreds of dollars per hour to do so.

Even the most horrific and devastating wars in human history came to an end at some point, and all we have is the memories of them. Eventually, flowers blossom out of the soil where blood once covered the ground. Where once there were the sounds of bombs blasting and machine gunfire, all you hear is birds singing. The universe ultimately resolves all conflict. All things tend toward resolution and peace.

Whenever a situation develops to its extreme, it turns around and slowly becomes its opposite. The further East you go the closer you get to the West. Day always becomes night. Night always becomes day.[26]

All things tend toward balance. All things tend toward resolution.

The next logical question then is—If there really are solutions all around you, why aren't you seeing them?

✳

THINGS TO PONDER

+ There is no such thing as a problem without a solution.

+ There are ideas and opportunities "in the air" all around you.

+ To capture the ideas "in the air," all you have to do is adjust your tuner (your focus) by making a *new choice* about what is relevant, and deliberately, consciously concentrating on it every day.

+ Suddenly, ideas you never knew existed will start magically appearing before your very eyes.

✳

----‹‹‹◆›››----

CHAPTER 4

Why Do We Look Without Seeing?

How many times have you been looking right at an object and not seen it? Wives tell me that husbands are the worst at this. See if this conversation sounds familiar?

> *Setting: The wife is eating popcorn while watching a movie.*
>
> **Wife:**   Honey, can you please get me the salt?
>
> **Husband:** Sure, where is it?
>
> **Wife:**   Right there on the counter, next to the fridge.
>
> **Husband:** Ok, I'm standing in front of the counter, right next to the fridge. It's not here.
>
> **Wife:**   Yes, it is. I put it there this afternoon.
>
> **Husband:** No, it's not.
>
> **Wife:**   Yes, it is!
>
> **Husband:** Nooooooo . . . . it's not!

This dialogue continues for a few minutes until the wife gets up off the couch, marches to the counter and grabs the salt, which is right in front of him. Has anything like this ever happened to you? It happens to me all the time.

Behavioral psychologists and neurobiologists discovered long ago that we as humans can be looking right at a physically concrete, very tangible object and not see it. Laurence Gonzales has studied why

accidents happen in the wilderness among hikers, kayakers and moun-
taineers. In his profound work, *Deep Survival,* Gonzales explains why
otherwise intelligent people miss obvious warning signs that could
have prevented the accident and fail to see obvious escape routes
and sources of food and shelter. Gonzales explains that, because of
how the brain works, if we are searching the house for a *red* hardback
edition of *Moby Dick,* we are not likely to see a *blue* hardback copy of
Moby Dick even though it is staring us in the face. Our mind literally
filters out things we are not expecting to see.

Most people assume that they simply see what is there and that they
do so by merely opening their eyes and looking. However, psychologists
have concluded that we are blind to many objects in our daily experience, which may be in plain sight. Psychologists Arien Mack and Irvin
Rock call it "looking without seeing," or "inattentional blindness."

My own experience with this happened when I returned home
from a trip to New York City. After finding my car in the airport parking lot, my next challenge was to find the parking meter ticket that
would tell the parking attendant how many days to charge me for. It's
a tiny piece of paper and I normally toss it in the center console of my
car with all the other stuff that sits in the center console. So, that's
where I looked. I found loose change, paper clips, fingernail clippers,
pens, highlighters, dental floss, a pocket knife, a comb, receipts and
who knows what else. But no parking meter ticket. *I must have put it in
my wallet.* Sometimes I write down the number of the parking section
I'm in on the meter ticket and stick it in my wallet so I don't have to go
through the entire five acre parking lot looking for my car. My wallet
was stuffed fat with my business cards, other people's business cards,
driver's license, credit cards, State of Texas Bar card, pictures, long
distance calling cards, a Sam's card, cash and handwritten reminders
of things to do. But no parking meter ticket.

I searched the center console again, slower this time. Nothing.
I decided to take more serious measures and pulled everything out
of my wallet and spread it out on the passenger seat. As I was going
through this pile, one piece of paper at a time, something blew into my
face from the air conditioner, which was blowing full blast. It felt like

a bug was dancing on my nose. I reached up to swat it and discovered that it was a tiny piece of paper. It was the parking meter ticket! *What the *#@!?* I stared at it in disbelief. Then I busted out laughing.

I remembered I had stuck the parking meter ticket in the very center of the steering wheel where the seams come together so that it would stick out horizontally and point right at me when I sat down in the car. The point was to try to save myself the regular hassle I go through every time I return home from a trip—trying to find the stupid parking meter ticket. But even when it was literally staring me in the face, I couldn't see it. The air conditioner had to make it fly up and hit me on the nose! Why? Because I was not expecting it to be there. I expected it to be somewhere else. My mind had literally filtered it out.

Arien Mack and Irvin Rock explain that:

> Almost everyone at one time or another has had the experience of looking without seeing and of seeing what is not there... During these moments, even though our eyes are open and the objects before us are imaged on our retinas, we seem to perceive very little, if anything.[27]

To confirm this fact, psychologist R.F. Haines conducted an experiment in which researchers asked commercial airline pilots to fly a simulated plane into a landing. As they began to descend for the landing, the computer put another airplane right in the middle of the runway where they were supposed to land. Many pilots tried to land the plane anyway instead of pulling up. Why is that? Haines explains that our minds tend to filter out things that we weren't expecting so that *reality becomes consistent with our expected model of the world.*

When my book editor read this chapter, she concluded that this must also be why it is so difficult to proofread your own letters and reports. You know what the document is *supposed to say* and your mind filters out all of the errors. That's why you need someone else to proofread your work.

Most people say "I'll believe it when I see it." But psychiatrists and behavioral psychologists tell us that the opposite is *more true.* Most people see only the things they have already previously chosen to believe. We don't look for information to inform us. We look for information to *affirm* us. The more the new information threatens our world view, the less likely we are to believe it. We tend to overlook, ignore or discount real tangible, concrete evidence when it goes against our beliefs. Entrepreneurs and innovators are different. They tend to focus on and believe in things they cannot see. They can do this because they see with their heart, not with their eyes.

If you feel bad because you keep missing opportunities and solutions that are all around you, take comfort. You are not alone.

THINGS TO PONDER

+ We don't look for information to inform us. We look for information to affirm us.

+ We tend to overlook, ignore or discount real, tangible, concrete evidence when it goes against our beliefs.

+ The brain filters out things we are not expecting to see.

CHAPTER 5

Why Do Even Experts
Miss the Obvious?

In 1830, the Comanche Indians were still the masters of their domain in the great plains of the middle of what is now the United States. They consistently defeated everyone who crossed their path, and dared to enter their territory, including the Utes, the Apaches, the Arapahos, the Spaniards and the French. The white pioneers from the East were next, and the Comanches were winning that war too.[28] Because their land was being invaded, they felt their attacks on white settlements in their territory were just.

The invaders who came into their domain were at a huge disadvantage because they were still using the old, single-shot, black powder muskets that they had been using since the Revolutionary War. In order to defend themselves, they had to fill a small cotton patch with black powder, form it into a ball, ram it down into the barrel of the gun, cock the gun, raise it up to their shoulder, aim it, and then fire it. Pistols had to be fired much the same way. During the time it took to do this, a skilled Comanche warrior could launch at least five arrows into the soldier or his horse, and ride away swiftly on his Spanish bred Mustang—the swiftest horse on the prairie.

Around this same time, a 16-year-old boy named Samuel Colt carved a new type of weapon out of a piece of wood and later had it made into a real gun. It was a .36 caliber, five-chambered revolving pistol with an octagonal barrel and a concealed trigger that dropped down when the gun was cocked. It could shoot five rounds in a matter of seconds. It was the world's first revolver.

There was only one problem. No one wanted it. The U.S. government could see no practical use for it. Colt's fledgling manufacturing plant went bankrupt in 1842, and he spent the next five years in poverty.

It wasn't until 1846 that a band of ruffians without discipline, uniforms, officers, protocol, or a hierarchy came to see the usefulness of this new weapon. As historian S.C. Gwynn puts it:

> They wore whatever pleased them. Sometimes that meant colorful Mexican serapes and wide-brimmed sombreros. Sometimes fur hats, bobtailed coats, or dirty panamas. Often it meant head-to-toe buckskins or bits and pieces of buffalo robes. Some went about naked to the waist, wearing the equivalent of Indian breechcloths over leggings. Many were large, physically imposing men with thick, brawny arms, long hair, and full beards. They had names like "Big Foot" Wallace (who was truly huge, and a savage fighter), "Alligator" Davis (because he had wrestled one to a draw on the Medina River), and "Old Paint" Caldwell (because his skin was so mottled it looked like peeling paint). They were just this side of brigands and desperados. They were not whom you wanted to pick a fight with in a frontier saloon.[29]

This band of misfits would later become known as the Texas Rangers. Using this newly created weapon, the Texas Rangers were the first group of white men to see any kind of success in fighting the Comanches. Texas Ranger Samuel Walker and Samuel Colt later collaborated to improve the Colt revolver into a .44 caliber pistol with six cylinders and nine inch barrel that was as deadly as any rifle up to 100 yards. It was like carrying a cannon on your hip. Colt became one of the richest men in the country.

Why couldn't the U.S. government see the usefulness of this new weapon? The seat of the government was back East where things were civilized and cultured. Gentlemen walked about in felt hats and polished shoes. Women wore silk dresses, corsets, and carried frilly parasols. They were not clawing and scratching out a subsistence living in the hard earth of an unexplored wilderness. They were not being attacked and killed in their homes on a regular basis. This was during the relative calm between the Revolutionary War and the Civil War. For the most part, America was at peace. The Colt Revolver was simply not relevant back East.

The tendency of humans to be blind to the obvious benefits of a great invention is not an isolated incident. Elisha Gray actually invented the telephone before Alexander Graham Bell, but he put it on a shelf and let it sit for months because he could see no useful purpose for it. His own patent attorney told him the device was a "mere curiosity." You may wonder how someone could have invented a revolutionary device and not have seen the importance of it. The reason Gray could not see the importance of what he had created is because he was actually trying to create something else. He was trying to solve the problem of sending more than one telegraph at a time on the same electrical wire. This was called "multiplexing."

In the process of trying to come up with a way to send multiple telegraph messages at one time, he found a way to send different musical notes over a wire and have them be reproduced at the other end. If he could send musical notes over a wire, then why not voice? The reason Gray was blind to the value of what he created is because the solution did not look like *what he was expecting* it to look like. What he found did not appear to be relevant to his objective.

Bell saw what Gray could not see because he was looking for something different than Gray. Gray was a consummate "tinkerer" whose myopic focus was fixated on the thing itself. In contrast, Bell was not focused exclusively on the machine itself, but on finding all possible ways to help people communicate. He was focused more on improving people's lives. That's the difference between a technician and an entrepreneur. Bell was just an ordinary school teacher, but he could see what the great inventor Gray could not. He saw something different than what Gray saw because *he was looking for something different.*

Before you are too harsh on Gray, consider this. Once Alexander Graham Bell obtained his patent on the telephone,[30] he could not persuade any corporation of its value. Bell offered to sell his telephone patent to Western Union for $100,000. Western Union turned him down flat. The leading industry journal, *The Telegrapher*, wrote an article saying the telephone had "no direct practical application." Neither Western Union nor the leading industry journal could see the incredible opportunity that was right in front of their eyes—even after someone had demonstrated it to them.

In the process of inventing the light bulb, Thomas Edison created a "direct current" system as a means to provide electricity to the masses. At the time, he had a young unknown apprentice named Nicola Tesla who was also experimenting with ways to bring electricity to the masses. While working for Edison, Tesla invented "alternating current" and tried to persuade Edison of its benefits. Edison ignored the invention as an inferior product. Frustrated because Edison would not listen to him, Tesla resigned and began looking for investors who would help him start his own electric company. He found George Westinghouse. Together, Tesla and Westinghouse brought electricity to the World's Fair in Chicago in 1893, and won the lucrative bid to distribute electricity to the entire northeastern seaboard from the most powerful electrical generator at the time, the Niagara power plant.

Westinghouse also bought the patent to the transformer, which allowed electricity to be delivered over long distances quicker, and then "stepped down" so it could be used safely in people's homes.

This was a better solution than Edison's "direct current" because direct current loses strength over long distances. If you are using direct current, you have to build a lot more power plants because each one has to be very close to the neighborhood it serves. This solution was much more expensive than alternating current, which can serve a much greater area with only a few power plants.

European engineers had offered to sell Edison their alternating current transformer patent. But Edison turned it down believing in the superiority of his own system. He was too close to his own invention to see that there was a better system out there. He was blinded by his own success. In the race to power America, the alternating current system won out because it was a much cheaper way to deliver electricity to the masses. To this day, it is alternating current that is now being delivered to every household in America.

Thomas Edison also invented the *precursor* to the vacuum tube, but could not see any practical use for it. William Preece and John Ambrose Fleming took Edison's technology and created the vacuum tube. It was the vacuum tube that made the first computers possible.

Chester Carlson was working at a patent office duplicating documents by drawing them each by hand. He knew there had to be a better way. He considered George Eastman's photographic process which used a film emulsion to make photos. But it was too chemical intensive, too messy, and too slow. He needed a "dry reproduction" process.

Carlson solved the problem by creating a positively charged plate. When he passed negatively charged dust particles over it in a specific pattern, they naturally attached themselves to the metal plate in the same pattern. The first successful photocopy was made in 1938. But Carlson could not persuade the corporate giants of his day of the value of his device. IBM, General Electric, RCA, and all other major corporations turned Carlson down when he asked them for investment capital to fund the manufacture of the device.

Finally, a small struggling maker of photographic supplies became interested. Their sales had hit a slump. They had nothing to lose. They took a chance. They named the device after the Greek word "xeros" for dry, and "graphos" for writing. The Xerox copier was born!

After World War II, the British invited Henry Ford to Germany and asked him to take over the Volkswagen automobile plant and all related patents. Ford turned down the opportunity because he could not see any value in it.[31]

William L. Gore had been working at DuPont for 17 years. He was trying to find new commercial uses for Teflon, which was owned by DuPont. Working out of the basement of his house, he discovered that Teflon could be made into strands to form a very strong and water resistant fabric. But, when he tried to convince DuPont of the amazing qualities and characteristics of this new fabric, DuPont rejected the idea. So, Gore resigned and decided to make the fabric on his own—in that same basement.[32]

His first employees lived in his house in lieu of wages. These early employees slept in the basement and set up a production line in the backyard. They often raided Bill's kitchen for any cooking equipment that they could adapt for manufacturing. Gore patented the fabric and called it *GoreTex*.[33] This amazing fabric is now used in thousands of medical devices and human "patches" because the body does not reject it. Why could DuPont not see the value of a product that was made from a product they already owned? They failed to see it because it did not look like anything they were expecting to see. DuPont told Gore it was in the polymer business, not in the clothing business.

In 1869, a chemist named Robert Chesebrough heard of the amazing healing properties of a waste product that came from the process of pumping oil out of the ground.[34] The waste product was a slippery black paraffin type substance they called "rod wax." Rod wax was a nuisance because it clogged up the works and had to be continuously cleaned off. But the workers noticed that whenever the rod wax accidentally smeared over a cut, scrape, or blister, the wounds healed amazingly fast. Chesebrough took a bucket of the rod-wax back to his lab and distilled it to clean away the impurities. The resulting product was a very light colored jelly which he called "petroleum jelly."

Chesebrough tested the product by scraping and cutting his own body and applying the petroleum jelly to some of the wounds but not to others. Sure enough, the wounds to which he applied the jelly healed much faster than the wounds to which he did not apply the jelly. Convinced of its healing powers, Chesebrough put it in jars and tried to sell it to doctors and pharmacists. But they rejected it outright. It didn't look like any healing product they had ever seen. He even tried giving it to them to create demand, but to no avail.

Chesebrough then decided to bypass the so called experts by giving away free samples to the masses. Whenever customers ran out of the miracle jelly, they went to their doctors and pharmacists and demanded more. Now the doctors and pharmacists had to buy the product from Chesebrough. Today, you may know the product by its brand name *Vaseline*.

Many years later, medical studies have shown that Vaseline has no medicinal effect, nor any effect on the blistering process. Petroleum jelly's effectiveness in accelerating healing stems from its sealing effect on cuts and burns, which inhibits germs from getting into the wound and keeps the injured area supple by preventing the skin's moisture from evaporating. People today use petroleum jelly for many common ailments, including chapped hands and lips, toenail fungus, nosebleeds, diaper rash, chest colds, and even to remove makeup or stains from furniture. In the first part of the 20th century, petroleum jelly was also popular as a hair pomade. During World War II, a type of petroleum jelly was often included in life raft survival kits because it made an effective sunscreen against ultraviolet rays. Today, petroleum jelly is a common ingredient in most skin lotions and cosmetics.

But in the early years, why were those whose sole job was to heal the injured so blind to the value of this product? One reason is because it came from someone outside of the industry, a person not schooled in the healing arts. The second reason is it did not look, smell, or act like any healing product they had ever seen or were expecting to see.

From the 1960s to the late 1980s, the Digital Equipment Corporation (DEC) was one of the leading manufacturers of business computers, software and peripherals. With annual sales of $14 billion, it was the second largest computer company in the world, second only to IBM. While Bill Gates and Steve Jobs were tinkering in their garages with personal computers, Ken Olson, the founder of DEC, was publicly declaring that there was no need for personal computers in the home.[35] DEC should have been the first to see the huge opportunity that lay before them in the realm of personal computers. DEC was blind to this opportunity because they were suffering from "myopia." Like Elisha Gray, they were focusing solely on the gadgets they were already good at making rather than on the needs of their customers. The net result was the same—obsolescence.

In the 1700s, paper was made from very expensive hemp, linen and cotton. It was a very precious commodity because it was so expensive and difficult to make. In 1719, there was a shortage of paper due to a lack of the raw materials needed to make it. René Antoine Ferchault was a French Naturalist who took a random walk through the woods one day. He found an old abandoned wasp nest. He took it home and peeled back the layers one layer at a time and discovered it was made of a very delicate paper-like substance. He went back to the woods and observed many wasps building their nests using wood pulp which they had first digested in their abdomens with enzymes. Something in his mind went "click." It was then that it occurred to him that paper could be made from wood pulp using chemicals.[36]

In 1800, Matthias Koops began manufacturing paper from wood pulp using Ferchault's recipe. But he couldn't convince people that paper made from wood pulp was as high in quality as paper made from hemp, linen, and cotton. The people of the day were blind to the benefits of the much less expensive paper. His business went under. It wasn't until the early 1900s when major newspapers started looking for a cheaper and more efficient source of paper that commercial paper mills began manufacturing paper from wood pulp—the same kind of paper we know today.

How many people over the last several thousand years have walked through the woods and seen an old abandoned wasp nest? Why was it that no one before Ferchault discovered that all we had to do was learn from the wasp in order to make paper efficiently and cost effectively?

Ray Kroc had absolutely no education, experience or training in the fast food business. He was merely a salesman peddling malted milk shake mixers. But he saw potential that Mac and Dick McDonald could not see. He bought out the McDonald brothers and took their operation global. Why did the McDonald brothers not see the tremendous potential of their own business? You owe thanks to Ray Kroc for every Happy Meal you've ever bought for your kids.

Why did it take an outsider with no experience, education or training to turn over the next rock and find the gems that were right under their feet? The original founders were so focused on the day to day headaches of running a business, and trying to make ends meet that they could not see past making payroll this month. What was relevant was making sure they ordered enough hamburger patties for next week. What was relevant was whether their teenage cashier would show up for work tomorrow.

There are probably thousands of such struggling mom and pop businesses all around you right now. It often takes an outsider to see the big picture. It often takes an outsider to come up with creative, innovative ideas for growing the business. It takes a fresh influx of intellectual capital. It takes someone with grandiose, almost delusional, larger than life dreams to come in, take over, and propel the operation to the next level. Entrepreneurs are not experts at finding something new. They are experts at finding things hidden in plain sight.

In about 1986, two teenage boys moved to Austin, Texas as immigrants with their single mother. Their mother went there on a student visa because she was looking for a better way of life. It was a typical story repeated thousands of times throughout the history of America. They spoke not a word of English. But they somehow survived their high school years in Austin, Texas. They experienced culture shock because of all the technology that was so freely available to the average teenager here. Personal computers, cell phones, the internet, wi-fi, video games—all luxuries the average Mexican teenager cannot afford, but that the average American teenager takes for granted.

They worked hard in school and eventually Roy found himself in medical school, and Bertrand in the business school at the University of Texas. In the middle of their educational process, Roy came up with an idea of selling pre-paid debit cards to illegal immigrants. He knew that most illegal immigrants did not have bank accounts because banks required a social security number. He knew that millions of new immigrants (legal and illegal) were storing cold, hard cash at home in coffee cans, under the mattress, and in old cigar boxes. He knew that they were at risk of robbery and theft at every turn. He knew they could not buy goods and services on the internet because they did not have credit cards. He knew they could not buy gas at a gas station unless they went inside and paid the cashier in cash first.

So, Roy and Bertrand, both in their twenties, started approaching banks and credit unions with their idea of selling pieces of plastic the size of a credit card. The idea was that anyone could walk into a convenience store or bank and give the cashier a wad of cash and walk out with a magnetic card that digitally contained that same amount of cash. The Sosa brothers sold the plastic cards for $10 each, and charged a $1 surcharge for each transaction made with that card. It was brilliant.

But at bank after bank they were laughed at and shown the door. Roy and Bert had no experience, education or training in the financial services industry. No credibility. No authority. No reputation to precede them. No cash. The banks told them, "These people don't have any money!" You see, to a bank, if you don't have a social security card and a bank account, you don't exist. But Roy and Bertrand knew better. They knew that new immigrants (legal and illegal) across the United States were sitting on billions of dollars in cash. They also knew that there were millions of natural born American citizens who had bad credit and could not get credit cards. This meant they could not do something as basic as renting a car, buying airline tickets, or buying tickets to the theater on the internet. But with a prepaid debit card, they could rent cars, and buy anything they wanted on the internet.

Finally, one day, someone said "yes" and the Sosa brothers started selling pre-paid debit cards at one of those "cash a check" places on the poor side of Austin. They were working out of a one bedroom apartment with only $750 between them. They called their company NetSpend. Word began to spread. In their first year, the Sosa brothers sold over a million cards. Within five years, people all over the country were spending over a billion dollars per year with these little pieces of plastic.

Soon enough, guess who caught notice? The big banks. They began to play the game as well, but not until the Sosa brothers had such a huge head start that they were firmly entrenched. Eventually, the Sosa brothers sold their business for hundreds of millions of dollars.

By the time they were 28 and 32 years old, the Sosa brothers were each multi-millionaires. Today they are actively investing in other young start-up businesses through a company called MPower Labs. They saw an opportunity that the big banks were blind to. But why were the big banks blind to this opportunity? They should have been the first to see it. They were the experts in providing financial services. They were blind to the opportunity because they didn't see that a problem existed at all. The solution the Sosa brothers presented was irrelevant to the banks. The Sosa brothers saw a solution no one else saw because they first *saw a problem* no one else saw.

It turns out that this is one of the best held secrets of entrepreneurs throughout the ages. Entrepreneurs don't look for money. They look for problems that need solutions. When you start identifying problems that are not on the radar screen of the "big boys," suddenly new information that is already "in the air" all around you starts becoming very relevant. When you start focusing on this new relevant information, you will start seeing problems and solutions that are invisible to others. Innovators and entrepreneurs see solutions that no one else sees, in part, because they see problems that no one else sees.

You may think you're running out of money. But you're not. You're running out of problems to solve. Start solving problems that no one else is solving and people will chase you down, and tackle you and beg you to solve their problems too. If you want to get ahead in business, stop looking for money, and start looking for very real problems that no one else sees, and start solving them.

The birthplace of revolutionary ideas is not a brilliant solution waiting for a problem, but a wicked, nasty problem begging for a solution. Before you can start seeing the solutions that are all around you, you have to start seeing the problems that are right in front of you—*in a new way*. You have to start recognizing problems that no one else thinks are problems. We rarely find affirmative statements of truth or knowledge from wandering around in nature. Instead, nature provides riddles to be solved. Enlightenment and knowledge come when we search for and discover the answers to these riddles.

Many of the most revolutionary changes in business and technology were created, not because the creator saw a solution no one else saw, but because they saw a problem no one else saw. IBM and Compaq did not see a problem with the way they sold computers until Michael Dell came along and showed the world there was a better way. Likewise, television was good enough. Why would anyone want to watch homemade videos on the Internet? Email was good enough. Why would anyone want to connect through Facebook or Twitter? The big box retail stores did not see that there was a problem with the way they sold retail goods until *Amazon* and *eBay* came along and provided better goods at lower prices. Film based cameras were good enough. Why would anyone need a digital camera? No one knew there was a problem with how we purchased and listened to music until Steve Jobs gave us the iPod and iTunes. Entrepreneurs don't strike while the iron is hot. They strike when everyone else thinks the iron is cold.

If I had asked my customers what they wanted,
they would have said a faster horse.

—HENRY FORD

In 1930, Galvin Manufacturing Corporation introduced the Motorola radio. The first commercially successful car radio. In 1936, the founder, Paul Galvin took a trip to Europe and did not like what he saw. He became convinced that Hitler was going to start a war. He sent his assistant, Don Mitchell, to a military base in Wisconsin (Camp McCoy) to find out how the army communicated information to its troops in the field. He discovered that the Army was still communicating the same way it did in WWI, using strung wire from the front line to the command posts. It was in that moment that Galvin saw a problem that was invisible to others. Once the problem was firmly fixed in his brain, he could start scanning his environment for possible solutions. The solution he saw was something that did not exist.

In his mind's eye, he envisioned a radio that was small enough to fit in a car fitted with a radio transmitter and a power unit packaged into a nice little box so someone could hold it and communicate with the command post without strung wire. Then he created it. By the time Hitler invaded Poland, Motorola was ready. Motorola made the SCR536, the famous "walkie-talkie" of WWII. Galvin saw what no one else could see because he wasn't looking in the same place everyone else was looking. Seeing solutions no one else sees starts with seeing problems no one else sees. Galvin wasn't aiming at where the duck was now. He was aiming at where the duck *was going to be.*

A good hockey player plays where the puck is.
A great hockey player plays where the puck is going to be.

—WAYNE GRETZKY

In 1947, at Bell Labs in New Jersey, John Bardeen, Walter Brattain, and William Shockley invented the first transistor. The transistor replaced the vacuum tube for regulating the flow of electricity. It also acts as a switch for electronic signals. The original purpose of the transistor was for use in tiny hearing aids.

At that time, radios were still using vacuum tubes, which were huge. As a result, the radios of the day were as large as your modern day TV. But an unknown engineer from Japan named Akio Morita wondered if he could miniaturize the radio—if only he could replace the vacuum tubes with transistors. Bell Labs laughed when Akio Morita asked if he could use the transistor to power radios. Keep in mind, Morita was taking a huge risk. There were no throngs of people in the streets begging for pocket held radios. After two years of experiencing rejection after rejection, eventually Western Electric agreed to license the transistor to Morita.[37]

In 1955, Morita sold his first transistor radio in Japan. For the first time in history, people could now carry music around in their pockets. A few short years later, during the 1960s, Rock-n-Roll music was invading the planet, and people's appetite for music was becoming voracious. The pocket held radio took off. Morita branded his pocket held radio the Sony, based on the Latin word for sound "sonus." Sony sold hundreds of millions of its transistor radios all over the world.

In 1979, Sony introduced the world to the Sony Walkman, a pocket held device that did nothing more than play cassette tapes filled with your favorite music. It too was a smash success, selling millions all over the world. Then came the Discman, which played digital music on a disc.

The next logical step for Sony would have been to create something like the iPod and iTunes. But Sony was asleep at the wheel, basking in its own success, focusing on making more products, faster, cheaper, and more efficiently. Then along came Steve Jobs who gave us the iPod and iTunes, making the Sony pocket radio and the Walkman obsolete overnight. But Apple's expertise was in computers, not radios, digital recorders or any kind of music player. Why didn't Sony see the iPod and iTunes before Apple did? Sony was asking "How can we make a better Discman?" instead of "How can we make it easier for people to listen to music?"

It's never enough to do more of what you are doing, or to do it better, cheaper, faster or more efficiently. While you are busy tinkering with improving your product, someone else is busy making your product obsolete. While you are busy making a better can opener, someone else is working on making a can that opens itself. Are you so busy focusing on what you do well that you can't see the next evolutionary step in the market?

✳ THINGS TO PONDER

+ Entrepreneurs are not experts at finding something new. They are experts at finding things hidden in plain sight.

+ Seeing solutions no one else sees starts with seeing problems no one else sees.

+ You may think you're running out of money. But you're not. You're running out of problems to solve.

+ The birthplace of revolutionary ideas is not a brilliant solution waiting for a problem, but a wicked, nasty problem begging for a solution.

+ While you are busy tinkering with improving your product, someone else is busy making your product obsolete.

+ Strike when everyone else thinks the iron is cold.

+ If you're shooting at ducks, don't focus on where the duck is now. Focus on where it is going to be.

CHAPTER 6

——— ·«‹◊›»· ———

Does the Brain Have Its Own Eye?

There are plenty of animals whose eyesight is better than ours. Bald eagles have incredible vision. They have two foveae, or centers of focus, that allow them to see forward and sideways at the same time. Bald eagles are capable of seeing fish in the water from several hundred feet above, while soaring, gliding or while flapping. The sharpness of an eagle's vision is four times that of a person with perfect vision. If an eagle could read, it could read a newspaper from fifty yards away. The eagle can spot a rabbit or a mouse almost a mile away. That means that an eagle flying at an altitude of 1,000 feet over open country can spot prey over an area of almost three square miles.

Dragonflies have the largest compound eyes of any insect, each containing up to 30,000 facets. The eyes cover most of the insect's head, resembling a motorcycle helmet. Each facet within the compound eye points in a slightly different direction and perceives light emanating from only one particular direction in space, creating a mosaic of partially overlapping images. It's like a human having 10,000 to 30,000 photoreceptors spread out across the retina. As a result, dragonflies can see in all directions at the same time. The spherical field of vision means that dragonflies are still watching you after they have flown by. But dragonflies also have an additional visual enhancement. If you've ever worn polarized sunglasses, you have an idea of what a dragonfly sees all the time. They view the world through a polarizing filter.

Despite the fact that many other creatures have better eyesight than humans do, humans still have greater ability to see things that other animals cannot. Humans have the ability to *see patterns*, to link cause with effect, to ask the question *why*, and to *see concepts*. But why? What gives us this ability?

If we define intelligence as the ability to perceive the environment and respond appropriately to it, then each cell in our body is an intelligent being.[38] Each cell is imbued with intent and purpose. Each one selects an appropriate response designed to favor growth and reject pain and toxins. Each cell is capable of learning, and then remembering what it learned.[39]

A single cell organism actually eats, digests, breathes, and excretes waste matter. It senses where food is and propels itself to that location. It recognizes toxins and predators and initiates escape maneuvers and communicates with other cells to save its own life. Single celled creatures even have a "brain" and a memory. But contrary to popular belief, the brain is not in the nucleus. When cell biologists take a microscopic pipette and suck out the nucleus of a cell, the cell will actually live for one or two months. It will continue to ingest food, metabolize it, secrete waste, breathe, communicate with other cells, and respond actively and appropriately to its environment.[40] It will eventually die, but only because the nucleus is what causes the cell to reproduce the amino acids from which the cell is made.

It turns out that the "brain" of the cell is its membrane, which is seven millionths of a millimeter thick. Before the development of the electron microscope, scientists weren't even sure if a cell had anything holding it together, or whether it was just a soupy mix of cytoplasm that held itself together like Jello. However, we now know that each cell has a membrane that is three layers thick. The membrane is considered the "brain" of the cell because it can sense the presence of opportunity or danger in the environment and act appropriately by adjusting its shape and size, and by moving towards or away from that external stimulus.[41] The membrane also acts as a filter that allows only things that are beneficial into the cell. The membrane is also able to filter out what is not beneficial to the cell because *it knows the difference*. When you remove the membrane of a cell, it becomes comatose and dies because it can no longer respond to stimulus from the environment. In fact, this is how penicillin kills bacteria. It destroys the membrane.[42] In that sense, it is the membrane that gives the cell the ability to interact intelligently with its environment.

The net result of more *awareness* is a greater ability to respond appropriately to external stimuli. This ability increases the ability to survive. Cells have found a way to become smarter. When the size of the cell has reached a critical mass, it cannot expand the surface area of its membrane any more. So, the cell does the most logical thing. It starts banding together with other similar cells to form colonies so that they can expand their surface area, increase their *awareness*, and respond even more appropriately to external stimuli.

Famous bacteriologist Robert Koch first discovered the tendency of single celled organisms to form colonies in 1876 when he noticed that a slice of old potato left on a bench was covered in spots of different colors.[43] He examined the different spots under a microscope and discovered that all the mirco-organisms in each spot were identical, but clearly different from those in the other spots. The different types of bacteria had formed colonies that were each unique.

There are certain advantages to banding together. A colony of cells has a greater *awareness* of its environment and a greater ability to absorb nutrients, and repel invaders. The greater the *awareness* an organism has of its environment, the greater its chances of survival.

In fact, Nobel Prize winner Alexander Fleming actually used the tendencies of bacteria to colonize to his advantage. Fleming had a practice of systematically collecting various types of bacteria in petri dishes for the purpose of letting them colonize. Then he would try different substances on them to see what might be effective in retarding their growth or killing them. It was this process that led him to the discovery of penicillin—the first pharmaceutical antibiotic in the world.

Recently, a group of cell biologists at the University of Minnesota conducted an experiment with Brewer's yeast, a single celled organism, to determine if cells would clump together to form cooperative colonies. At the conclusion of the experiment, the scientists observed multi-cellular clusters that were similar in nature. The cells in each cluster began to cooperate with each other, and when the cluster reached a critical size, some cells died off in a process known as *apoptosis* to allow offspring to be "born" and separate. The offspring then reproduced, but only after they attained the size of their "parents." Astounded by this observation, one of the scientists, Will Ratliff, concluded that cells cluster, cooperate, make sacrifices for the common good, and adapt to change.[44]

As the size and complexity of these cell-communities grows, it makes sense to assign certain tasks to specialized groups of cells whose only job is to perform specialized tasks. In this way, those specialized groups of cells can perform those tasks more effectively and efficiently than others. Some cell biologists believe that the joining together and cooperation of single celled organisms is ultimately what led to the development of plants and animals. Some people believe that cells began forming specialized colonies that became the bodily organs such as the liver, the spinal cord, the heart, the kidneys, and ultimately . . . the human brain. Each cell retains a "memory" of its specialized purpose in its DNA so that they always know their specialized tasks from the very beginning. A cell's genes are the "physical memories of the organism's learned experiences."[45]

Most pop-psychologists commonly divide the human brain into two parts, the right hemisphere and the left hemisphere.[46] This is because those two parts are the most obvious to the uninformed eye. However, neurologists and neurobiologists more accurately describe the brain as a *triune brain,* which has three distinct layers, one encircling the other. Each layer has a unique function.

At the very top of the spinal cord there is a small bit of swelling like a soft squishy marble. Every mammal and every reptile has this part of the brain. It is called the *pons.* The *pons* is often referred to as the reptilian brain because for fish, snakes and frogs, this is all the brain there is. It controls basic bodily functions that happen automatically without you thinking about them, like the heartbeat, and breathing.

Surrounding the *pons* like the spirals of a conch shell, is the *limbic system.* It consists of the amygdala, the hippocampus, the thalamus, and the pineal gland. The limbic system is often referred to as the mammalian brain because all mammals have it. The limbic system is the seat of the emotion. The limbic system is what gives us the ability to feel raw emotion. It generates the hormones that cause us to feel passion, anger, love, joy, and happiness. Every time you "fall in love" the limbic system is to blame. Every time you get jealous, the limbic is at the core. Every time you feel anger or hatred, the limbic system is responsible. It is because you have a limbic system that you are able to bond with your dog, your cat, and even your new born baby. When you have that feeling of longing in your soul for your lover, you can thank your limbic system. Without it, you would feel nothing. The limbic system is also responsible for the fight or flight reaction. For example, snakes are the mortal enemies of rhesus monkeys. However, a rhesus monkey whose limbic system has been destroyed or removed will show absolutely no signs of fear when in the presence of a live snake.

Surrounding the limbic system is the neocortex. A few mammals have a thin neocortex, such as cats, dogs, monkeys, dolphins, whales, and elephants. The neocortex is what gives mammals the ability to reason and make decisions that are not purely instinctive. It's why you can teach your dog to fetch, sit, and roll over. It is also why you can watch Shamu perform tricks at Sea World. It is why mammals, not reptiles, are used to perform tricks at the circus.

Many animals know how to use tools. Bottlenose dolphins in Shark Bay Australia use marine sponges in their beaks to stir up the ocean bottom to uncover prey. Otters use stones as a hammer to crack abalone shells. The diving bell spider actually spins a "diving bell" out of silk which creates a bubble of air that it uses to breathe under water. It is more sophisticated than the man-made Aqualung because as the spider uses up oxygen, the silk bell actually diffuses oxygen from the surrounding water to replenish the oxygen inside. Orangutans, chimpanzees, elephants, crows, and octopuses have all been seen using tools.

They know how tools work, but not *why* they work. No other animal has the ability to make tools for the sole purpose of making other tools. Humans can see not only the pattern, but the reason for the pattern. It is the neocortex, not our eyeballs, that give us the ability to see things that other animals can't. Humans have the thickest and most highly developed neocortex of all.

One of the earliest pieces of tangible evidence that primitive humans began to recognize patterns is the fossilized jaw bone of a deer-like creature on which the phases of the moon were carved. But why would early humans want to record the phases of the moon? No other animal does this. Once we learned to link cause and effect, we could anticipate certain events and make plans.[47] We could predict when the herds would migrate. We could actually see it in our mind's eye. We also knew when the tides would come in. We knew when to launch our ships. We knew when to plant. We knew when to harvest. We began to *see* that there is order hidden beneath the disorder. We had suddenly created order out of chaos. It should come as no surprise that, in the book of Genesis, the very first thing God did was banish chaos and bring order to a universe that otherwise had no form or meaning.

The neocortex gives us the ability to organize our world according to what is "good" and "bad" for us. The neocortex gives us the ability to ask *why*. It gives us the ability to say to ourselves, "When I do *this*, good things happen. When I do *that*, bad things happen."

Before Adam and Eve became consciously aware of things in their external world that were either *good* or *bad* for them, the first thing that happened is that they became "self-aware." Genesis tells us that their "eyes were opened" and they suddenly knew they were "naked." But this passage could not have been referring to Adam and Eve's physical eyeballs because there is no indication that they were blind. Accordingly, Genesis could only have been talking about the internal eye—the eye of the brain. It was as much a neurological awakening as it was a spiritual awakening.[48]

No other animal that we know of is consciously aware that it is "naked." That word itself is a sort of pejorative term that casts judgment on the natural human condition. Humans now had a conscious awareness of themselves. The eye of the brain had been opened. They could now look upon themselves as an "external watcher." When the neocortex blossomed to the point of awakening it gave us an awareness of ourselves and our state of being. We could suddenly see things no other animal could see. We could see ourselves. Indeed, with the awakening of the neocortex came the ability to create an ideal state of existence that we could never attain—and then punish ourselves for not attaining it. No other animal has this ability.

We could even observe our own thoughts and feelings. This is what gives you the ability to look inward and say "I'm feeling sad today" or "I'm feeling happy today." It's what gives you the ability to have a conversation with a friend, and at the same time be observing yourself having that conversation and contemplate the effect of your words on the listener. The neocortex allowed us the ability to *self-reflect* and *self-correct*.

The neocortex also gives us the *ability to see* (like a third party observer) our primal urges and make a conscious decision whether to follow them or not. Our primal instincts never really go away. Oftentimes, they override our intelligence and we end up doing things we later regret.

Regardless of how logical and rational we try to be as humans, our mammalian brain is constantly in the background trying to assign meaning to any new external stimuli we encounter. This is a survival instinct we cannot turn off. We are always subconsciously asking three questions: (1) Will it hurt me? (2) Will it benefit me? (i.e. can I eat it?) (3) Can it help me grow my tribe? (i.e. can I mate with it?)

In fact, I have often witnessed my little white puff-ball of a dog going through these same three stages when he encounters something new. Upon seeing a giant pumpkin in the neighbor's yard one Halloween, he instinctively jumped back and growled. Then he circled the pumpkin suspiciously. Then he got closer and sniffed it thoroughly. Then he tried to hump it.

Our instincts are not always correct, but they give us a huge advantage when we are trying to figure out what will make us feel good and what could kill us. Whenever we hear the sound of a loud gunshot behind us, our bodies jump before we have a chance to figure out why. Upon further investigation, we may discover that it was just a door slamming. But our body's initial reaction could have just saved our lives.

Yes, the brain has its own eye—an eye you can open and close just like your regular eyes. Your ability to see hidden solutions and opportunities can also be exercised and developed.

It is amazing that a single celled organism is aware of its surroundings and responds appropriately to sources of food and sources of danger. The greater its awareness, the greater its ability to respond appropriately. When this happens, the cell becomes stronger, healthier, and begins to multiply. Likewise, we behave more intelligently when we become more aware of our surroundings and respond appropriately. When we do this, we become stronger, wealthier, and our income begins to multiply. To the outside world, it looks like we are more intelligent than others. But we're not. We have simply learned to increase our awareness of solutions and opportunities and respond accordingly.

Even though the brain has its own eye, many people go through life with the brain's eye half shut. They simply act out their primal urges, making irrational decisions, blindly stumbling into the same problems over and over, ignoring the solutions that are all around them. However, there is a better way. Opening the eye of the brain means developing a heightened state of awareness of things that already exist. Once you do this, you will begin to see both the problem and the solution—*the solution that was there all along.* So how do you open the eye of the brain?

✳ THINGS TO PONDER

+ Greater intelligence = Greater awareness.

+ The net result of more awareness is a greater ability to respond appropriately to external stimuli.

+ The greater your ability to respond appropriately to external stimulus, the greater your chances of surviving, advancing your tribe, and prospering.

+ When you learn to open the eye of the brain, you will begin to see solutions and opportunities that were there all along.

✳

PART TWO

Opening the Eye of the Brain

CHAPTER 7

Can You Enhance Your Sense of Awareness?

When my dad passed away, I started listening to salsa music because it reminded me of him. I listened to it everywhere. In my car. At home. At the office. At that time, unbeknownst to me, someone who worked for me turned out to be an experienced salsa dancer. Whenever she came into my office and heard the music, she would say, "Hey, that's bachàta. That's meréngue. That's chá-cha. That's classic salsa." Then she would demonstrate the basic steps for each genre. Up until then, I had no idea that there were four sub-genres of salsa. It all sounded the same to me. Until I finally decided to take salsa dancing lessons.

After around six months of taking salsa lessons, whenever a song came on, I could hear the difference in the beat and I could identify whether it was bàchata, meréngue, chá-cha, or classic salsa. But more importantly, my body could *feel* the difference in the beat. My body would naturally move differently to each different type of music. I also learned to identify the sound of each individual instrument in the band. In most salsa bands, there are at least ten different instruments. The most obvious ones are the loud ones, the guitar, the horns, the timbàle, and the conga. The less obvious ones are the clàve (a pair of sticks), the cowbell, and the bongos. The clàve and the cowbell are only used intermittently, and are usually buried somewhere deep in the heart of the song. But today, when I hear a salsa song, I can also hear *each individual beat* of the clave and the cowbell. More recently, I can also hear the very specific rhythm of the bongos.[49]

What amazes me is that before I took salsa lessons, each of those instruments was creating sound waves that were actually landing on my eardrums. *But I could not hear them.* Nor could I distinguish the difference in the beats of the various genres. Now I could hear everything. Nothing about the biology of my eardrum had changed. Only my brain had changed. It had developed a heightened awareness for the beat of the song, and the sound of each individual instrument. Now I can hear things that other people do not hear. But I didn't suddenly develop super-sonic hearing. I just made a different choice about what was *relevant,* and my brain is now attuned to it.

I have spoken with Marines who served in Afghanistan and Iraq who said that even in the heat of battle, when they fired their M-4's, they could actually hear the springs and the mechanisms in the guns making pinging sounds over the loud gunshots and bombs exploding all around them. This doesn't mean they have super-human hearing. They simply have a heightened awareness. Some people would call this *hyper*-awareness.

Criminologist David Klinger interviewed hundreds of police officers for his book *Into the Kill Zone.* In it he describes what it feels like to be in this state of heightened awareness. Your brain literally slows down time and isolates sights and sounds that you wouldn't normally see or hear. In one particular story, the officer describes what he saw and heard during a gun battle when an aggressor was threatening to kill another officer named Dan.

> He looked up, saw me, and said, "Oh, *#@*!" Not like "Oh, *#@*!" I'm scared." But like "Oh, *#@*! now here's somebody else I gotta kill"—real aggressive and mean. Instead of continuing to push the gun at Dan's head, he started to try to bring it around on me. This all happened real fast—in milliseconds—and at the same time, I was bringing my gun up. Dan was still fighting with him, and the only thought that came through my mind was "Oh, dear God, don't let me hit Dan." I fired five rounds. My vision changed as soon as I started to shoot. It went from seeing the whole picture to just the suspect's head. Everything else just disappeared. I

didn't see Dan anymore, didn't see anything else. All I could see was the suspect's head.

I saw four of my rounds hit. The first one hit him on his left eyebrow. It opened up a hole and the guy's head snapped back and he said, "Ooh," like, "Ooh, you got me." He still continued to turn the gun toward me, and I fired my second round. I saw a red dot right below the base of his left eye, and his head kind of turned sideways. I fired another round. It hit on the outside of his left eye, and his eye exploded, just ruptured and came out. My fourth round hit just in front of his left ear. The third round had moved his head even further sideways to me, and when the fourth round hit, I saw a red dot open on the side of his head, then close up. I didn't see where my last round went. Then I heard the guy fall backwards and hit the ground.[50]

This story is amazing because the officer seems to have acquired slow motion laser like vision. How is it possible to see your bullets at the actual moment they connect with the head of your target? How is it possible to see a "red dot" upon impact—which could only have appeared for a split second before things got really gory?

But this phenomenon is not limited to people in a combat situation. Michael Jordan describes many instances where in the heat of a basketball game, time slowed down and the basketball hoop literally became a giant hoop in his brain, which even from well beyond the three point line, he simply could not miss. Here's how Michael describes it. "The basket appears to be six feet across. How can I miss a basket that large? The nine other players on the court seem to be moving in slow motion. I know exactly what everyone's going to do even before they know."

In March 2014, LeBron James scored a career high 61 points against the Charlotte Bobcats. Here's how he described it, "The basketball felt small as a golf ball. The basket looked as wide as the ocean. It was a surreal experience."

Some people would say this is the result of thousands of hours and many years of practice and being in the "heat of the moment" basketball situations hundreds of times over the course of his career.

But how do you explain it when it happens to a 17-year-old autistic kid in a typical high school basketball game? Jason McElwain was only a 5'6" tall. He was a "high functioning" autistic kid who tried out for the basketball team at Greece Athena High School near Rochester, New York. He didn't make it. But his love for the game compelled him to stay on as team manager, passing out towels and water to the other players.

On February 17, 2006, in the very last game of his senior year, the coach asked him to suit up for the varsity team. He was determined to give Jason a chance to play. With three minutes and forty six seconds left in the game, Jason got the ball and launched it at the basket beyond the three point line. It was an air ball. The coach sat on the bench and put his head in his hands and said, "Dear God, please. Just let him get a basket." Then a miracle happened. Jason started connecting. He hit a three point shot. The crowd went wild! Then he hit another. Then another. Then another. In that last three minutes forty-six seconds, he scored twenty points. He was 6 for 10 from three point range. He was 7 for 13 overall. He was the leading scorer for the entire game. Asked to explain his success, all Jason could say was, "The basket was like this big ole huge bucket. It was huge! I couldn't miss." It was the one and only game Jason ever played in. But he saw the basketball hoop the exact same way Michael Jordan did.[51]

This means that *anyone* can put themselves into a heightened state of awareness. I have interviewed hundreds of serial entrepreneurs in my research for this book. The following response from David Bernert, part owner of the Zen chain of restaurants is typical of what all of them told me: "Dan, I don't understand why people moan and groan about not having enough money. Everywhere I go, I see opportunities to start new businesses all around me." Then they rattle off all the businesses they would love to start—if they only had the time.

One such entrepreneur is Gary Hoover. Gary found success when he originated the "big box" bookstore concept. Up until he came along, most book stores were smallish and sandwiched between other retail stores inside the old traditional enclosed malls. Hoover started a chain of bookstores called BOOKSTOP, which were absolutely cavernous inside. When Barnes & Noble eventually offered to buy the company for $41.5 million dollars, the BOOKSTOP chain became the corner-stone of the Barnes & Noble empire.

Hoover also started a business information company, which became Hoovers Inc., operator of Hoovers Online. Hoovers Online maintains a database of 66 million companies and 85 million people who work for those companies. Its purpose is to help businesses know more about the businesses and the key players to which they are sell-ing. It is the Webster's dictionary of businesses.

Eventually, the company went public, and then was sold to Dun & Bradstreet for $117 million. Hoover eventually became the first Entre-preneur in Residence at the McCombs School of Business at the Uni-versity of Texas in Austin.

Hoover explained to me that quite often students would come to his office with a business idea in their heads, or struggling to find an idea. Hoover says that they couldn't see the opportunities that were all around them. "All the opportunities are all right under their noses and they can't even see them," he says. "They come in and say 'I want to start the next Facebook,' or 'I want to develop a cell phone app,' but on the way to my office, they tripped over the carpet, and it never occurred to them to create carpet that stays down."

Within four weeks of Hoover's appointment at the University of Texas, he had already come up with six business ideas, all of which served students and faculty. All of which if they worked on the U.T. campus, could be duplicated at universities nationwide. They all solved already existing problems.

One such problem was that Hoover himself had to park a half-mile away from his office. The University of Texas is home to approxi-mately 100,000 students, faculty, and staff. Competition for parking is fierce. There was a three year waiting list to get a parking spot in the garage closest to his own office. "If you're old, and fat, and you have to carry a lot of books, and it's pouring down rain, it's a real problem," Hoover says. "The bus system is too inefficient because these huge lumbering buses can only go down a few main thoroughfares. They never actually reach everywhere the students and faculty need to go."

Within a few weeks of his arrival, Hoover conceived of an electric vehicle "jitney" type service that would carry people through all the nooks and crannies of the campus where the buses could not go. At any time of the day, you could simply waive at the driver, who would pull over and give you a ride. A similar service was later created to serve the happy revelers in the bustling nightlife of downtown Austin. It consists of hundreds of pedi-cabs, which look very similar to the Chinese rickshaws of old, except these carts are carts pulled by people on modified bicycles. A few small electric golf-cart type vehicles have also started to make an appearance in the Austin nightlife. For late night partiers, these pedi-cabs and electric carts are a godsend.

Serial entrepreneurs become serial entrepreneurs because they can't stop seeing problems in need of a solution. It is simply something they *can't turn off.*

In 1978, when Richard Branson was still quite young, he went to the British Virgin Islands with his girlfriend. When it came time to leave the island, you had to fly to Puerto Rico in order to get to Great Britain. But on this occasion, the flight to Puerto Rico was cancelled. The airport was full of stranded passengers. There would not be another flight for several days. He hung around with all the other miserable passengers in the waiting area waiting and waiting for the airplane. But after a while Branson decided to take matters into his own hands.

He called around to see if there were any small privately owned planes in the area that he could hire to take him and his girlfriend to Puerto Rico. He found a pilot that would do it for a flat fee of $2,000, an enormous sum back in 1978. But Branson saw an opportunity that was invisible to everyone else. He divided the price by the number of seats on the airplane, and wrote these words on a blackboard in the waiting area. "VIRGIN AIRWAYS: $39.00 ONE WAY FLIGHT TO PUERTO RICO." Then he walked around the waiting area talking to people. Soon every seat on the plane was filled. The money he made from selling those extra seats was enough to pay for the private charter and put a little extra money in his pocket. It was then that one of the passengers on that fight mentioned, "Hey, you could make a real business out of this. Smarten up the service a little and you could be in business."[52] The idea for Virgin Atlantic was born as the solution to a problem.

Fast forward six years to 1984. Branson had no experience, education or training in the airline industry. But he launched his new airline, Virgin Atlantic Airways, with a rented second hand Boeing airplane which he flew out of a rented hangar at Gatwick Airport. But no dream is without obstacles. His long-time business partner told him, "For God's sake. You're crazy. Come off it. You're mad. You're a megalomaniac. We've been friends since we were teenagers, but if you do this I'm not sure that we can carry on working together. What I'm telling you is that you go ahead with this over my dead body."[53]

Branson went forward anyway. He invited news reporters and film crews to witness the maiden flight of his first airplane. It was a grand event. On the virgin flight of Virgin Atlantic, as the plane was circling the airport, it flew into a flock of birds. Some of the birds got sucked into one of the engines, which promptly caught fire and exploded. The plane landed with a long trail of black smoke pouring from the engine. Richard Branson stood there watching in horror, knowing that the whole thing had been captured on film and would be broadcast to the world. If you had seen that explosion on national TV, would you run out and buy a ticket on this unheard of airline? This was day one of his new business!

> *Those who hear not the music think the dancer's mad.*
> —FRIEDRICH NIETZSCHE

But Branson did not give up. He simply replaced the engine and re-launched his airline. "We launched our airline on a wing and a prayer, and when the engine blew up on our test flight it might have been over before it had begun. We were lucky: each time something went wrong, we were the smallest jump ahead of the banks. However tight things are, you still need to have the big picture at the forefront of your mind."[54] British Airlines vigorously opposed the licensing and permitting process and consistently slandered *Virgin Atlantic* and Richard Branson in the press. This resulted in a series of multi-million dollar lawsuits. But in the end, Virgin Atlantic prevailed, Branson won a multimillion dollar verdict in his slander lawsuit, and the airline has experienced explosive growth ever since.

Serial entrepreneurs simply can't turn off their ability to see opportunities and solutions all around them. It is not money they seek. They simply have a heightened awareness of problems in need of a solution. Once they identify that problem, they set out in search of a solution. Because they know there is no such thing as a problem without a solution, they either find a solution, or they make one.

A good 40 years before the "law of attraction" became popular, Estée Lauder asked this question, "Have you ever noticed that when you're concentrating with passion on a project, you start hearing or reading about things germane to that project? Perhaps it's because your antennae are up, but I always considered it fascinating to note how the world around me responds to my particular current interests."[55]

So how do you get your "antennae up?" How do you develop this state of heightened awareness? You have to take charge of three internal choices. Choices you may not even know you are making.

✳

THINGS TO PONDER

+ You open the eye of the brain by putting yourself into a state of heightened awareness.

+ You have the ability to put yourself in a heightened state of awareness anytime you want.

+ You put yourself in a state of heightened awareness by isolating something specific in the world as relevant, and then focusing on it constantly wherever you go.

+ When you decide something is relevant, your brain starts becoming attuned to it. You start seeing it everywhere.

✳

CHAPTER 8

--- ·◄◄◆►► · ---

Three Choices You Don't Realize You're Making

On July 3, 1988, U.S. Navy Captain Will C. Rogers of the U.S.S. *Vincennes,* issued an order to fire Aegis guided missiles at an unidentified Iranian aircraft headed directly toward his vessel. The unidentified aircraft was destroyed, but it turned out to be a commercial passenger jet. This decision cost the lives of 290 civilians. Many speculate that the Iranians later ordered the bombing of Pan Am flight 103 over Lockerbie, Scotland, in retaliation for the *Vincennes* incident.

What factors were shaping the captain's perceptions when he made that decision? The captain had just been in a surface battle with high-speed Iranian attack boats when radar operators reported that an unidentified Iranian aircraft was descending from an altitude of 7,500 feet toward his ship. His emotions were tense. *His most recent experience influenced what he was focusing on.* He was focusing on the possibility of another attack.

Before he fired, he sent three warnings on civilian radio frequencies and four warnings on military frequencies. The aircraft failed to respond to any of these warnings. Based on this information, the captain concluded that the intent of the aircraft was most likely hostile. Captain Rogers had to make a decision quickly. He had to choose between the lives of those in the approaching aircraft and those of his own men and his duty to his country. Captain Rogers shot down the aircraft.

Captain Rogers' perception of the situation was greatly influenced by his most recent experience. His ship had just been attacked. He did everything he could to determine whether the situation was truly as he believed it was. He could not have known the exact identity of the incoming aircraft before it was within range to launch airborne cruise missiles at his ship. He was forced to choose between the lives of his own men (and his ship) and the lives of the people who were aboard what could only be interpreted as a hostile aircraft. He had considered the possibility that the aircraft might be a civilian aircraft, but the jet had failed to respond to all warnings on civilian frequencies. Therefore, he ruled out the likelihood of it being a civilian aircraft. Were the costs of a wrong choice greater than the benefits of a right choice? Hindsight is always 20/20. Had he known the aircraft was a passenger jet, Captain Rogers never would have shot it down. However, if it had been a military jet and he had failed to shoot it down, he would have jeopardized the safety of his men and his vessel.

This story shows that our most recent experience influences what we *focus* on. In fact, the more powerful the external stimulus, the greater its ability to affect our focus. For example, if you were sitting in a quiet restaurant, and you heard a gunshot, every head in the room would turn in the direction of the gunshot. Involuntarily. If you merely heard a horn honking outside, you would simply ignore it. If you live in New York City, you might not even hear it. The more primal the external stimulus, the greater its ability to kidnap our brain.

What we focus on is critical because it determines what we *believe*. What we believe determines what we *expect*. What we expect determines what we *see*. We tend to see what we are *expecting* to see. Captain Rogers saw a civilian aircraft as a hostile military aircraft.

And yet, a better solution to the problem was right in front of him had he *chosen to look* for it and focus on it. The airplane had never made any aggressive moves toward him, and had never engaged its weapons. It had no weapons to engage. Even if the airplane had launched missiles, there are several defensive maneuvers the captain could have made to avoid being hit, including firing at the missiles themselves. It was not like the captain was defenseless. He could have chosen to watch and wait for more evidence.

Your ability to develop a heightened awareness of the solutions that are all around you depends on three critical choices: (1) the choice of what to *focus* on; (2) the choice of what to *believe*; and

(3) the choice of what to *expect*. Most people are not even aware that they are making these choices. But they are—moment by moment and day by day. You are in a constant battle against the external forces that are trying to kidnap your brain. The historical record shows that your ability to see the solutions that are all around you depends on what you *focus* on, what you *believe*, and what you *expect*—day in and day out. These are the most critical decisions you will ever make because they determine what you see or don't see in the world around you.

> *Individuals behave not in accordance with reality,*
> *but in accordance with their perception of reality.*
> —DENIS WAITLEY

You will probably never be the captain of a military ship called upon to make a decision to fire missiles or not, but this story illustrates the principle that *our most recent experience almost always determines what we focus on.*

The Bedouin nomads who live in the desert have a story they tell their children that can teach us a great deal about how we make decisions. According to the story, there was once a man living in the desert with his family. He saw a cloud of dust and sand approaching from the horizon and said to himself, "It is a terrible beast coming to eat me and my family!" Then, as the cloud of dust got closer, he saw that it was actually a man in black on horseback. He then said to himself, "It is my enemy, coming to take over my well!" He went to get his rifle to defend himself. Then as the horseman got closer and the man could see the rider clearly through the sights of his rifle, he recognized the rider and said to himself, "No, it is my brother." The three lessons of this story are that: (1) what we *focus* on determines what we believe; (2) what we *believe* determines what we expect; and (3) we tend to see what we're *expecting* to see.

These principles are also demonstrated by a story told by journalist Peter Godwin in Zimbabwe. In his book, *Mukiwa,* Godwin tells of a critical decision he made while trying to escape the military police of Zimbabwe during his efforts to expose the government's civil rights abuses.[56] He knew the military was looking for him. As he was making his way out of the "prohibited zone," he saw a soldier of the dreaded Fifth Brigade standing in the road, flagging him down. He froze. The hair on the back of his neck stood up. It was a primal experience.

Godwin quickly ran his options through his mind. He could turn around and head back at full speed. He could dump the truck he was in and run for it into the bush. Most of the soldiers weren't terribly fit and it would take them too long to summon air support. Or he could put his foot down on the accelerator and drive straight through. As his options raced through his mind, so did several important questions. Was this a proper stop, with a stronger roadblock fifty yards beyond this lone soldier, or was it a shabby roadblock that he could get away from? How many soldiers were there? What weapons would they have? Did their radio work? (Many troops had faulty radios.) Had this particular group been alerted about his presence in the "prohibited zone"? Images of being captured and tortured flashed through Godwin's head. That's what he was focusing on.

In the remaining seconds, Godwin decided to go for it. But, as he slammed down his foot on the accelerator, he noticed something that prompted him to double-check his perception against reality. The soldier didn't have a weapon. The Fifth Brigade never moved without weapons, especially in the "prohibited zone." Godwin slowed his truck. Then he noticed that the soldier was smiling and that his movements were not "commanding" enough. He brought the truck to a halt in a cloud of dust. The soldier turned out to be a 2nd lieutenant looking for a ride. Godwin offered the officer a ride and told him he was a local farmer. A few miles down the road, they came upon a real roadblock, with spikes, a machine gun, and a proper radio antenna shooting into the air. A sergeant of the Fifth Brigade sharply saluted the lieutenant in the truck as they approached and explained that they were looking for a young white man who was helping the dissidents. They were under strict orders to stop any white man, to check IDs and to question them. It was Code Red. No exceptions were to be made.

The lieutenant got out of the pickup and went to talk to the sergeant. The remaining soldiers had machine guns pointed straight at Godwin, ready to shoot at the blink of an eye, while the lieutenant spoke with the sergeant. After a few minutes, the lieutenant came back and said, "Let's go." Godwin couldn't believe it. The lieutenant told Godwin that the sergeant suspected Godwin of being a journalist spy. But in order to avoid a delay, the lieutenant had convinced the sergeant that the white man he was with was a local farmer that he had known from a long time back. He told him that the two were "old friends." With that, Godwin made it out of the "prohibited zone" safely, and he later wrote a story that eventually helped put a stop to the civil rights abuses.

Godwin almost made a critical mistake. His most recent *experience* determined what he was focusing on. It was primal. It had the ability to kidnap his brain. In heat of that moment, what he was focusing on determined what he believed. Moreover, what he *believed* determined what he expected. His *expectation* was that soldiers would be looking for him. When he saw a soldier, he saw what he *was expecting to see*—a threat. But, *he made a conscious choice* to take back his focus.

Godwin *chose* to truly examine the evidence before him. He *chose* where to put his focus despite what was going on in the world around him. That's when the eye of his brain was opened. That's why he noticed that the soldier was not carrying a weapon. He saw what most people would have missed.

Godwin compared his original perception to the actual evidence. He quickly sniffed out the clues. He made use of all of the available information as well as his quick wit. He didn't panic. He analyzed all the information he had within the amount of time he had. He asked himself all the right questions, and the answers gave him what he needed. *He saw things he hadn't seen at first.* This is what made him a hero. Then, he made a decision that saved his life—several miles down the road. If he had sped past the lone soldier, he would have run into the real roadblock down the road with no ally at his side.

Godwin followed the principles that apply when you are dealing with a serious problem that seems to have no solution. Here the decision *behind his decision* was to stop, and take back his focus. This gave him the ability to check the evidence against what he was expecting to see.

Likewise, you have an internal choice to make before you make your final choice. Will you stop and consider the possibility that what you are seeing may be the result of what you are focusing on? Will you stop and consider that external forces may have kidnapped your brain? Will you choose to stop and double check the evidence? Or will you plunge forward unchecked? Even when there is a true emergency and time is of the essence, you have the option to stop and quickly check your perception against the tangible evidence around you.

In order to open the eye of the brain, you have to make three critical choices: (1) the choice to take back your focus; (2) the choice to take back your beliefs; and (3) the choice to take back your expectations. It is when we let external forces dictate our focus, our beliefs, and our expectations that we become blind to the solutions that are right in front of us.

Don't waste brain cells and energy looking for money. Make a deliberate choice every day to be on the lookout for problems in need of a solution. This is how you choose your focus. You make a conscious choice. When you find a really nasty, hairy problem, you study that problem. Saturate your brain with all the available information about it. Immerse yourself in it. Become so obsessed with finding a solution that you dream about it. But choose your focus carefully. What you choose to focus on, and *how* you choose to focus on it, determines your beliefs.

✳ THINGS TO PONDER

+ Is it possible that what you are seeing in your life right now is a result of what you have been focusing on?

+ Question your beliefs and assumptions. They determine what you can and cannot see.

+ In order to open the eye of the brain, make a conscious choice to: (1) take back your *focus*; (2) take back your *beliefs*; and (3) take back your *expectations*—in the heat of the moment.

+ Then you will begin to see things that were there all along.

CHAPTER 9

How Does Your Focus Affect Your Beliefs?

As I was sitting in the lobby of my allergist's office last week, an adorable 2-year-old girl came up to me and grabbed a Christmas ornament on the table next to me, held it up, and said, "Ish not for play with." A giant grin broke out on my face. This little girl looked just like Cindy-Lou-Who, the tiniest Who, from the *Grinch that Stole Christmas*. Just then, her mom came swooping from around the corner and said, "Suzie, leave this poor man alone. He just wants to read his newspaper." "No, it's alright," I said. "She reminds me of my two daughters when they were her age." Suzie and I then examined each of the shiny, sparkly designs on the Christmas ornament in detail. She told me the colors she saw, and said she wanted a candy cane for Christmas. "What does Santa say?" I asked her. "Ho, Ho, Ho," she said. I have a feeling Suzie got absolutely everything she wanted for Christmas.

It's easy to understand the fishbowl through which Suzie views the world. Her mom had recently been explaining that Christmas ornaments are not toys, and are "not to play with." Our earliest focus comes from those who raised us. But as we grow older, we realize that we have the ability to choose our own focus.

Focus is one of the most powerful tools that humans possess. It is also one of the most dangerous. Focus acts like a magnifying glass. It causes us to overestimate and exaggerate the importance of whatever we happen to be focusing on. We interpret everything else we see, hear, and feel in light of what we are focusing on right now. It warps our vision.

Captain Will C. Rogers of the U.S.S. *Vincennes* experienced this first hand when he shot down a *civilian* aircraft—simply because he had recently been attacked by an Iranian gunboat.

Focus is akin to looking at the world through a fishbowl of our own making. When you look through it, it makes everything a little round and irregular looking. The lens you choose always skews your present perception of reality into the shape of what you've been focusing on lately. Sometimes it blinds us to obvious risks. Sometimes it blinds us to obvious solutions. Most importantly, it *always affects* what you believe about the situation you presently find yourself in.

A few days after I met Suzie, I got pulled over for failing to turn on my blinker before making a lane change. It was a quiet Sunday night and I was driving home from the book store. There was virtually no traffic on the road. I showed the officer my driver's license and proof of insurance and watched as he walked back to his vehicle to run my driver's license through his database. It was all very routine. While I was waiting to see whether I was going to get a ticket or a warning, I took the opportunity to check Facebook to see what my friends were up to. They always tell you not to do that while you're driving right? But I was sitting safely on the side of the road, so it was ok.

After what seemed like an eternity, the officer came back to my car and said, "I'm giving you a warning. By the way, it's not a good idea to get on your cell phone while you're being detained by an officer." I was dumbfounded. "Is that illegal?" I asked. "No, but it makes me really nervous because you might have a trunk full of cocaine, and you might be calling someone with a machine gun to come and kill me so you can get away." I was speechless. This particular officer patrols one of the quietest and most educated zip codes in all of Austin, Texas. We are not known for having an overabundance of drug lords here. All I could think of to say was, "Wow, I never thought about that."

On the drive home, I glanced down at my cell phone and heard Suzie's adorable little voice, "Ish not for play with." This particular officer had spent so much time focusing on worst case scenarios, that he was now terrified when the average citizen gets on his cell phone while being detained. And he thinks his fears are *normal and rational.*

He has no idea that he looks at the world through a fishbowl of his own making. Everything he sees is warped in the shape of that fishbowl. Choose your focus wisely. It not only affects how you see the world. It dramatically affects your beliefs.

For example, if you bet one dollar that the coin will fall on heads, your odds of winning are 50/50. But if we happen to win 7 times in a row, we subconsciously believe that the odds of the coin landing on heads an eighth time are mysteriously in our favor. But they are not. The odds of the coin landing on heads are still only 50/50. But most of us would bet all 7 dollars that we just won on the eighth flip, and that's when we would lose it all. Our perception of the risk has become skewed by our most recent string of success.

Confirmation bias is the human tendency to focus solely on the evidence that supports our beliefs and ignore all evidence to the contrary—even though it may be staring us in the face. It blinds us to the risks.

But it also blinds us to solutions that are right in front of us— because the solution does not fit with our current belief system. History, and this book, are filled with stories of many astronomers, physicists and medical doctors over the last several thousand years who were blinded to the solutions that were right in front of them— solely because their belief systems filtered them right out.

Focus also becomes a problem because it can magnify and exaggerate the importance of minor problems. Imagine how you would have reacted if an engine on your *only airplane* had exploded on its maiden flight on the day you launched your commercial airline. Would you feel defeated? Would you say to yourself, "Why do these things always happen to me?" Would you consider it a bad omen? A sign of things to come? A sign from God that you're not supposed to be doing this?

What you choose to focus on not only determines your mood, it determines your beliefs and your actions going forward. Legendary entrepreneurs like Richard Branson have an undying, almost delusional belief, that somehow, everything will work out. Because of this, they tend to ignore minor problems like an engine blowing up on launch day. They quickly replace the engine and keep right on flying. They know there is no such thing as a problem without a solution. They believe that a solution will eventually present itself, and most of the time, it does. Richard Branson explains it this way. "My interest in life comes from setting myself huge, apparently unachievable challenges and trying to rise above them."[57] People like Richard Branson expect to succeed despite the odds, and it is because of this undying belief that they most often do.[58] Legendary innovators and entrepreneurs recognize the dangers of focusing on the wrong things. They don't get fixated on the problem. Instead, they become obsessed with finding the solution to the problem. But in order to be obsessed with finding a solution, you have start with an undying belief that a solution exists.

THINGS TO PONDER

+ We interpret everything we see, hear, and feel in light of what we are focusing on right now.

+ Hyper-focus on any one thing warps our vision of everything else.

+ What you focus on now determines what you will end up believing about the situation you find yourself in.

CHAPTER 10

How Do Your Beliefs Affect Your Biology?

Twenty people agreed to have their brains scanned using a functional MRI while they tasted five different wines, each with a different price. However, in reality there were only three wines, two of which were given to the subjects twice, once at the highest price and once at the lowest price. The labels on the bottles were decorative, but did not indicate who made the wine or in what country. The subjects gave the cheapest wine the lowest scores and the most expensive wine the highest score. To corroborate the ratings, neurologists hooked the brains of the subjects to brain scanners with electrodes. When the subjects tasted the most expensive wine, the brain scans showed a higher degree of activity in the orbitofrontal cortex, the area of the brain associated with pleasure. The neurologists who conducted the test concluded that our beliefs and expectations significantly affect our taste buds. But the more significant conclusion is that our beliefs actually alter our experience at the neurological level.[59] It is one thing for our beliefs to color how we *subjectively describe* what we are experiencing. But apparently, the power of belief can actually affect the way our neurons fire in our brains. Our beliefs can actually determine whether the neurons in our brain generate pleasure or pain. If you think about it, this is a startling revelation. Something intangible can affect something tangible.

In the 1940s, Louis Cheskin was hired by a margarine company to come up with a way to increase sales of margarine. Cheskin was known for pioneering the philosophy that consumers transfer their feelings about the packaging of a product to the product itself. He taught that people buy the package, not the product. He told the company to call the margarine *Imperial Margarine*, put an impressive blue crown on the package, color the margarine yellow, and wrap the margarine itself in gold foil. Taste testers gave subjects two samples that were the identical product. One sample was plain white and came in a plain white box with opaque wrapping. The other sample was yellow and it was wrapped in shiny gold foil. It came in a box that said *Imperial Margarine* with the blue crown. The subjects were asked to open each package and spread the margarine on a piece of bread and taste it. The sample that came in the *Imperial Margarine* box, and was wrapped in gold foil won every taste test every single time.

The Journal of the American Medical Association issued a report explaining the results of a series of tests conducted on 82 subjects to see if an expensive placebo gives greater pain relief than a common ten cent one.[60] The investigators tested the 82 subjects by asking them to rate the degree of pain they felt from electric shocks applied to their wrists before and after taking a pain pill. One pill was described as a new pain reliever priced at $2.50. The other pill was described as a common pain reliever priced at ten cents. But in fact, both were placebos.

Eighty five percent of those who used the expensive pill reported significant pain relief, compared with only sixty one percent of those who took the cheaper pill. "It's all about expectations" said Dan Ariely, a professor at Duke University and the author of *Predictably Irrational: The Hidden Forces that Shape Our Decisions.* "When you're expecting pain relief, you're secreting your own opioids, and when you get it at a discount, you doubt it, and your body doesn't react as well."[61]

People who believe they have undergone a surgical treatment often feel much better—even though the treatment was a sham. In a study of back pain, 20–40 percent of patients had decreased pain and much improved functioning when treated with a sham transcutaneous electrical stimulation and hot packs.[62] In another back pain study, 346 people received sham surgery for herniated discs (although no disc herniation was present). Out of this group, 37 percent expressed relief of sciatica pain, and 43 percent expressed relief of back pain.[63]

In another experiment, a group of asthmatics was told that they were inhaling irritants or allergens when in fact they were inhaling only a nebulized saline solution. A staggering 47.5 percent experienced substantially increased airway blockage.[64] Twelve of the subjects experienced full-blown asthma attacks. When they were given the exact same nebulized saline solution and told it was medication, they experienced full relief.[65] The power of human expectation and belief on our biology is well documented indeed.

Neurobiologists have recently confirmed that the power of belief actually affects the neurotransmitters in the brain by stimulating opioids, dopamine, and endorphins. These neurotransmitters are released even before the event during the *anticipation* of the benefit. It seems that when we are expecting good things to happen to our body, our body instantly begins to make us feel better, and continues to make us feel better after we take the pill, even though the pill consists of nothing scientifically beneficial.

Dr. Kevin Thompson, head of the sports and exercise department at Northumbrian University in England conducted a series of tests to determine the impact of belief on the physical abilities of athletes. He asked a group of cyclists to pedal as hard as they could on a stationary bicycle for 2.5 miles. The cyclists did this several times to establish their fastest times. Then he asked the cyclists to race against an avatar, a picture of a cyclist on a computer screen. The rider was shown two avatars, one of which was himself in real time, moving at the same speed the cyclist was pedaling at the moment. The second avatar was riding along at the pace of the rider's most recent best time. The cyclists were told to try to match their own best time by keeping up with the second avatar. Each of the cyclists kept up with the second avatar to the very end. However, unbeknown to the cyclists, the second avatar was actually programmed to go two percent faster than the cyclist's best time. They had each ridden faster than they had ever gone before because they believed they were capable of doing it. Two percent may seem small, but in a real race, it is a huge advantage. "It comes back to the belief system within the athlete," says Dr. Thompson. "Within limits, if an athlete thinks a certain pace is possible, he or she can draw on an energy reserve that the brain usually holds in abeyance."[66]

Up until the early 1950s, it was believed that no human being could run faster than a four minute mile. But on May 6, 1954, Roger Banister proved them wrong by running a mile in 3 minutes 59.4 seconds. He was the very first person to run a mile in under four minutes. Without a degree in psychology or neuroscience, Banister declared, "It's the brain, not the heart or lungs that is the critical organ. It's the brain." Just 21 days later, another athlete beat Bannister's record with a time of 3 minutes 57.9 seconds. Bannister later came back and beat that record with a time of 3 minutes 56.8 seconds. Since those days, many athletes have run sub-four minute miles.

On February 4, 1999, four New York City police officers shot to death a 23-year-old legal immigrant from West Africa named Amadou Diallo. They had merely shown up to ask him a few questions. There had been a rape in the area. Diallo fit the description of the alleged rapist. Upon seeing four armed policemen, and thinking they were there to challenge his immigration status, he reached for his wallet to show them his identification. Police fired 41 shots, 19 of which found their mark. The officers were tried for second-degree murder, but the jury believed their testimony when they said they believed he was reaching for a gun. All four policemen were acquitted. This is a tragic story on all levels.

In this situation, the eyes do not inform the brain, the *brain informs the eyes*, and all it takes is a grain of truth (a dark object) to confirm the truth we have already chosen to believe.

It is now well known that police officers (including black officers) often react more aggressively to a black man pulling something black out of his pocket (such as a wallet or a cell phone) than to any other racial group. Many behavioral and psychological tests have been conducted on police officers over the years. Study after study has confirmed that it is the *beliefs* of the officers going into a stressful situation that causes them to see a gun instead of what is actually there. Entrenched, unwavering beliefs, mixed with a high stress, adrenaline filled situation leads to tragedy. We *see what we believe* much more than we believe what we see.

Most people think they are in control of what they believe. But the following stories demonstrate how little control we actually have over what we believe. During the Korean War, the North Korean officers running the POW camps experimented on prisoners by telling those with minor injuries that their injuries were severe and that they were going to die. They also told those with severe injuries that their injuries were minor and they would surely live. Amazingly, many of those with minor injuries died because they *believed* they could not live. Many of those with major injuries lived because they *believed* they would not die. What they believed determined what they expected. What they expected came to pass because they expected it to come to pass.

How did the North Koreans accomplish this? The POWs had no evidence to contradict what their captors were telling them. Therefore, the only thing they had to focus on was the words of their captors. If someone can control what we focus on, they can control what we believe. What we believe determines what we expect. Sometimes what we believe can determine whether we live or die.

Okay, so you're not exactly a prisoner of war right now. I realize that, but let me give you another example. Have you ever wondered how otherwise rational people sitting on a jury can acquit someone who is obviously guilty? Have you ever wondered how jurors could acquit someone who *actually confessed* to the crime? Let me give you an inside look at how trial lawyers control what jurors believe.[67]

On May 30, 1997, a man named Montoun Hart allegedly tortured and murdered an English teacher named Jonathan Levin in order to get the PIN for his ATM card. After he was indicted, a witness testified that it was Hart who had made a withdrawal from the ATM at the relevant time. Hart also confessed to the crime, explaining details that no one could have known unless he had been involved. In the face of this overwhelming evidence, the jury found Hart *not guilty and freed him!* The jurors later explained that in the photo of Hart taken after a six-hour police interrogation, it looked like he was "wasted," meaning he looked drunk, tired or high. Therefore, they discounted his confession. Make no mistake. There was no evidence of torture or physical abuse by the police during the interrogation. The jurors simply didn't believe the confession. Instead, the defense attorneys convinced them to *focus* on the photograph above all else. What they focused on determined what they believed.

How did this happen? How could the defense attorneys have turned black into white? How could they have persuaded the jurors that Hart was innocent?

The best way to explain it is to use a highlight football reel as an example. After a football game, coaches and players review the videotapes of the game to see what went right so they can repeat it and what went wrong so they can avoid it. They also use these films to evaluate a player's performance. Multiple video cameras throughout the stadium capture the players and their actions from all different angles. But you can only watch one film at a time—right? In addition, the editors can choose which clips to show and which not to show.

Let's say you watched a review film of Green Pay Packer quarter back Aaron Rodgers. In the tape, he threw four interceptions. He was tackled behind the line of scrimmage three times. He threw six incomplete passes. What would you believe about Aaron Rodgers?

Now let's say you watched a different review film. But in this clip, you saw Aaron Rodgers throw five touchdown passes, and rush for over one hundred yards and win the game? What would you think? Now what if I told you it was the *same game*? You see, the parts of the film your brain focuses on determines your beliefs.

That's the way trial lawyers work. One lawyer shows you the clips of evidence that he wants you to focus on. The opposing lawyer shows you the clips of evidence *he* wants you to focus on. All good trial lawyers know that if they can get you to focus on only their evidence, they can control what you believe. The best trial lawyers are those who can get the jurors to focus primarily on the evidence that they show.

A standard motion filed in every jury trial is called a *Motion In Limine*. A *Motion In Limine* is a motion asking the court not to allow the other lawyer to talk about or introduce certain testimony and exhibits that could possibly kill the client's case. But wait! I thought the purpose of a jury trial was to let the jurors see all of the evidence so they can determine innocence or guilt. That is the ideal, but it is not the reality. The reality is that lawyers try to keep out all kinds of evidence that you are not aware of. The goal is to get you to focus only on their evidence and completely ignore the other side's evidence. If they can control what you focus on, they can control what you believe.

Of course, an actual trial is much more complicated than this, and many factors, such as how believable a witness is, and how the judge rules on certain motions, contribute to who wins. But, this is the basic strategy that all trial lawyers use. Why? Because trial lawyers understand that *what you focus on determines what you believe.*

In July 2002, 5-year-old Samantha Runnion was kidnapped from outside her apartment complex in Southern California while she was playing with a friend. The next day, her naked body was found along a nearby highway. She had been raped and then asphyxiated. The man who was charged with this crime was Alejandro Avila. This horrendous murder could have been prevented if Avila had been convicted of sexual assault two years earlier. Two years previous, Avila had been accused of child molestation. Two nine-year-old girls each testified in graphic detail about the abuse they said Avila had inflicted on them.

The defendant's argument was that Avila's ex-girlfriend had encouraged the girls to make up those stories. The defense attorney repeated this theme over and over, day in and day out, throughout the trial. This is a classic strategy used by both trial lawyers and professional marketers and advertisers. It is called repetition—and it's very powerful. That's why when a company wants to launch a new product, you suddenly start seeing the product everywhere—on TV, in magazines, in newspapers, on billboards. You even hear about in on the radio. They are controlling your focus *without your consent*. And it works. The evidence shows that the more you see and hear about a product, the more you will tend to *believe* it is a product worth buying. It works the same way in jury trials, and the best trial lawyers are those who do it well. Do you still think you are *always* in control of what you believe?

Despite the two girls' detailed and graphic testimony, the defense attorney used the power of repetition to convince the jury that the girls just could not be believed—and he succeeded. Trial lawyers control what you believe by controlling what you focus on. In jury trials and in life, your beliefs are always being influenced by what you focus on. A favorite trial tactic of experienced trial lawyers is to make a loud and long objection, at the exact moment that the opposing side has just asked your star witness that "gotcha" question that's going to blow your whole case. The objective is to distract the jury from the "deer in the headlights" look on the witnesses' face and the lousy answer he's about to give. The jury ends up wondering what the objection was all about and what the judge just said.

Just like your focus determines your beliefs, your beliefs determine your expectations. What we're expecting in any given situation is critically important because it determines what actions we are likely to take. In their book, *Inattentional Blindness*, Psychologists Arien Mack and Irvin Rock have concluded that "When we are intently awaiting something, we often see and hear things that are not there."[68] The brilliant psychologist William James puts it this way:

> When waiting for the distant clock to strike, our mind is so filled with its image that at every moment we think we hear the longed for or dreaded sound. So of an awaited footstep. Every stir in the wood is for the hunter his game; for the fugitive, his pursuers.[69]

If you think about it for a minute, you may be able to remember times when you saw or heard things that weren't there—solely because you were anticipating them. Psychologists have been keenly aware of this phenomenon for many years. As human beings, we tend to see *life*, not as it is, but as we are expecting it to be. If we can control what we *focus* on, we can control what we *believe*. If we can control what we believe, we can control what we *expect* in any given situation.

I have represented hundreds of people who were defrauded over the years. In my research and analysis, I discovered that some of the most intelligent and sophisticated people on the planet have been deceived over the centuries, including doctors, engineers, professors, high level executives and even lawyers (including yours truly). I have often asked myself how this could be. In most cases, there were huge red flags warning these people not to invest their money and not to sign the proposed contracts. Yet they plunged headlong into these traps as though there was not a brain cell left in their heads (including mine). It wasn't until I did the research for this book that I realized the source of the problem.

I realized that if someone waves a big enough carrot in front of us, most people focus on the carrot, which causes us to miss the obvious warning signs or to significantly discount them. When we focus on the benefits rather than the risks, we are more likely to miss the red flags. Once we have made up our minds to focus on the carrot, it doesn't matter that our friends or families may warn us not to take that course of action. We dismiss their concerns by saying they are "just being negative" or they "just don't get it." Then we defend our position by looking for additional evidence that supports what we have already made up our minds to see, and we discount the evidence that contradicts our position.

Charles Perrow is a Professor of Sociology at Yale University who studies why catastrophic accidents occur. In his book, *Normal Accidents,* Perrow explains one of the causes, "[W]e must, of course, make a judgment, even if only a tentative and temporary one. Making a judgment means we create a 'mental model' of an expected universe.... You are actually creating a world that is congruent with your interpretation, even though it may be the wrong world."[70] Although Perrow is attempting to explain one of the reasons why catastrophic accidents occur, this principle applies to all of life. *We tend to filter out what we're not expecting to see.*

It is precisely because we see what we're expecting to see, and filter out what we're not expecting to see that we fail to see the solutions that are all around us. Sometimes we fail to see a solution because it doesn't look like what it is *supposed to* look like.

Other times we fail to see a solution to a problem because it is not located *where* it is "supposed to be." When I was a young lawyer working for a huge, ivory tower law firm, I had to wear an expensive suit and a silk tie to work every day. At first, it felt very prestigious. But after a while, it just got annoying. Every Monday morning, people started counting the days until "casual Friday."

One particular Friday morning, I was getting ready for work, looking for my casual shoes that I wear with my khaki pants on Fridays. I couldn't find them anywhere. I looked where I always look—in the closet, next to the bed, under the bed, in the living room. I couldn't find them. I looked in all those same places again, thinking I had just overlooked them, but they were nowhere to be found. I thought, maybe I was just a little sleepy. I would look again, slowly and carefully. Not there again. I expanded my search. I looked in the kids' room, in my office, in the bathroom, in the kids' bathroom. Nowhere.

Now I was getting desperate. I was going to be late for work if I didn't find them soon, or—Horror of Horrors! I would have to wear dress shoes (and a suit to match) on a Friday! It was a crisis. But I was strong. I thought I would look in the usual places one more time. And then it hit me. If I kept looking in the same places I had already looked, I would never find the shoes. I was only wasting time, frustrating myself, and making myself late for work. The shoes clearly were not in the places I had been looking. I was in a bit of a dilemma because I had no idea where to look if the shoes were not where they were *supposed* to be. What were my realistic alternatives? The shoes could not possibly be anywhere else.

Something told me that if I wanted to find my shoes, I had to look where I had never looked before, even if it made no sense to look there. When I made the decision to change my pattern to include the out of the ordinary, the first off-the-wall place I could think to look was the garage. I never put my shoes in the garage because I don't take my shoes off before entering the house.

Nevertheless, out of obedience to my inner voice, I opened the garage door and looked around. I was right. My inner voice was wrong. The shoes weren't there. But sitting there as big as day was the car I drove only on weekends. I had driven that car to see my folks the previous weekend. Then I remembered I had taken my casual shoes with me. I opened the car door, and there they were, sitting on the back seat, staring at me as if to say, "I told you so." My inner voice was right after all.

It was then that a light turned on in my head. I stood there staring at my shoes, pondering the lesson that life was trying to teach me. I was overwhelmed with one question. In my life, had I also been looking in the same places over and over for solutions that I already knew weren't there? Was I ignoring the messages life was sending me? Was I going in circles in my life, hoping that the next time I passed that way, what I was looking for would suddenly materialize? I had actually convinced myself that the things I had been dissatisfied with for years would suddenly improve if I just improved my attitude, gritted my teeth, and kept going.

I suddenly realized that if I wanted to change the results I was getting, I had to change not only the decisions I was making, but also *how* I went about making those decisions. I had to change my actions if I wanted different results. I had to change my pattern of behavior to include things I had never tried before. This, of course, would require considering options I had never considered before—even if in my mind they had previously been inconceivable, illogical, or even *forbidden*. I had to get out of my mental and emotional rut, my regular way of making decisions.

I also learned that my expectations of the way the world *ought to be* don't always reflect the way the world really is. The lesson of the missing shoes is that the solution we're looking for in life isn't necessarily where it's *supposed* to be. Our preconceived notions don't always work. They aren't always consistent with reality. Is it possible that what you've been taught all your life about the problem you are facing isn't necessarily correct? We need to adjust our beliefs to factor in what life is trying to teach us. We shouldn't blindly and ignorantly keep repeating the same patterns of behavior over and over, oblivious to the results. We need to listen to life's wake-up calls. One thing is true: *When you start looking in places you've never looked before, you will start seeing things you've never seen before.*

The military has developed "smart bombs" that have internal maps of where they are going and how to get there. But they only succeed by surveying the territory over which they are traveling and constantly giving themselves feedback to correct their movements.

Have we progressed to the point that the weapons we have made to destroy each other are smarter than we are?

Steve Andreas and Charles Faulkner introduced the idea that, "The map is not the territory" in their book called *NLP: The New Technology of Achievement*.[71] The concept is simple, but profound. The map is only a piece of paper. The territory is the actual earth, which you are experiencing as you walk through this life. The map is never 100% accurate because the earth is constantly changing. Also, a map is only a perception of what someone else remembers having seen, which you have adopted and have *chosen* to believe. What mental "map" have you been following all your life? Is what you've been taught working for you? Have you stopped to check the "map" against your actual experience? Are you communicating with yourself like a smart bomb to adjust for what you are actually experiencing?

If the power of belief can change your taste buds, alter your breathing and affect the molecules in your body, can it open your eyes to see the solutions that are right in front of you? Archimedes said, "Give me a big enough lever and a place to stand and I can move the world." The power of belief works the same way. Even a tiny amount of belief, with enough action behind it, can change a life forever.

THINGS TO PONDER

+ Sometimes we fail to see a solution because it doesn't look like what it's *supposed to look like.*

+ Sometimes we fail to see a solution because it isn't where it's *supposed to be.*

+ When you start looking in places you've never looked before, you'll start seeing things you've never seen before.

+ The brain informs the eyes, and not the other way around.

+ We see what we believe much more than we believe what we see.

+ Even a tiny amount of belief can change your whole life forever— if you act as if what you believe is true.

CHAPTER 11

————— ⟨⟨⟨⟨•⟩⟩⟩⟩ —————

How Do Your Beliefs Affect What You See?

When primitive human eyes first looked upward and began to try to make sense of what they saw, they saw that the sun rose in the east, made a big arch, and set in the west. It was clear that the sun was moving in a big circle around the earth. The stars and the moon moved in a similar pattern, rising in the east, moving across the sky, and setting in the west. Even such intellectual giants as Plato and Aristotle taught that the earth was the center of the universe, and that the sun, the moon and planets moved around the earth in perfect circles. Their philosophies dominated astronomy for thousands of years.

Everything in the heavens acted the way it did, held the properties it held, and moved the way it moved because it was following some divine principle or law, and those laws were perfect and immutable. In contrast, the physical, observable, tangible world was less than perfect, and even corrupt for the sole reason that it was not divine. The physical universe was but a poor replica or a shadow of the perfect spiritual universe. The entire premise of Plato's cave metaphor was that the things we can touch, taste, smell, hear and see are mere shadows of a more perfect world that we are only vaguely aware of, but cannot experience as long as we are mortal.[72]

Humans then, and now, crave perfection and stability in an imperfect, arbitrary and unstable world. To all primitive religions and philosophies on all parts of the globe, the circle was a symbol of perfection, stability, eternity, and protection in an otherwise unstable,

91

arbitrary and imperfect world. In many religions today, it still is. To the ancient Greeks, the spiritual world included the stars and the planets, which were perfect and unconnected to earthly things. The stars and planets were spiritual beings whose movements dictated the events on earth. Heavenly bodies were divine and, therefore, obeyed spiritual, not physical laws. Since they were perfect, they had to move in perfect circles and at uniform speeds.

But, there was a problem. There were a handful of rogue stars that did not seem to move in perfect circles. In fact, they did not seem to be following any kind of pattern at all. Sometimes they would move east. Sometimes they would circle back and move west and then east again. Sometimes they moved fast. Sometimes they moved slow. Sometimes they were very bright. Sometimes they were very dim. They certainly did not move in a perfect circle. No divine or spiritual principle could explain their strange behavior.

Faced with this problem, and a good two thousand years before the invention of the telescope, Aristarchus of Samos (310 B.C.– 230 B.C.) wrote *On the Sizes and Distances of the Sun and Moon*. In this book, Aristarchus posited that the sun, not the earth, was the center of the solar system. Even though he was right, and he was looking at the same night sky as all the philosophers and astronomers that came before him and after him, his teachings were summarily ignored for approximately 2,000 more years. But why was Aristarchus able to see things that were invisible to everyone else? He was not super human. Nor did he have extraordinary vision or even a telescope. Visual observations were rejected in favor of spiritual and religious beliefs of the day. Thus, for thousands of years, humans were blind to what their visual observations and mathematical calculations told them.

The solution was literally staring them in the face and they failed to see it. Part of this blindness was due to the prevailing Greek philosophy that "true knowledge" and "pure truth" could only come from that which was divine. It could not possibly come from the physical, observable universe, which was carnal and corrupt. Astronomy was a science based on philosophy, and religion, not on observation. The earliest astronomers were priests and philosophers, not scientists or mathematicians. Astronomy was absolutely divorced from math and physics.

For the next nearly two thousand years, mathematicians, and astronomers struggled with trying to come up with calculations that proved the planets moved in perfect circles and at uniform speeds. Ptolemy himself wrote, "We believe that the object which the astronomer must strive to achieve is this: to demonstrate that all the phenomena in the sky are produced by uniform and circular motions."[73] They didn't know what to do with the fact that the planets differed in size and brightness at various times of the year, and that they seemed to double back on themselves, form loops and then keep going in the original direction they were headed. Nor did they know what to do with the fact that they appeared to speed up as they approached the sun. They were trying to force what they saw into a model of the universe that did not quite fit.

In 1491 (the year before Columbus sailed the ocean blue), Copernicus began studying the ancient astronomical writings of the Chaldeans, the Greeks and the Arabs who lived thousands of years before him. He recorded very few of his own visual observations. He relied heavily on the works of Aristarchus, Ptolemy, Hipparchus and Eratosthenes. Copernicus concluded that the sun is the center of the universe and that the sun and stars only appear to go around the earth because the earth spins on its own axis. Yet, Copernicus himself doubted his own conclusions and *refused to publish* them for forty years. In fact, he actually scratched out of his original manuscript his explanation that the planets moved around the sun, not in perfect circles, but in an irregular pattern, an ellipse. Only near the end of his life, did he make the following observations in a formally published document:

1. That the heavenly bodies do not all move around the same center.

2. That the earth is not the center of the universe, only of the moon's orbit.

3. That the sun is the center of the planetary system.

4. That, compared to the distance of the stars, the earth's distance from the sun is relatively close.

5. That the apparent daily revolution of the sun and the stars is due to the earth's rotation on its own axis.

6. That the apparent annual motion of the sun is due to the fact that the earth, like the other planets, revolves around the sun.

7. That the apparent motions of the planets are due to the same cause.

Thus, Copernicus laid the foundation for everything we know about the solar system today. The amazing thing is that Copernicus did not have a telescope. He was relying on the same mathematical calculations made by the Greeks, Chaldean and Arab astronomers that lived before the time of Christ. He was relying on the visual observations and calculations of Ptolemy and Hipparchus and Eratosthenes. Those ancient Greeks, Chaldeans and Arabs had the same observational data, the same instruments, and the same knowledge of geometry as Copernicus. Why didn't they see what Copernicus saw? Why didn't they see what Aristarchus saw?

Copernicus's book, *Revolutions of the Heavenly Spheres,* was published in 1543, just a few years after Martin Luther nailed his Ninety-Five Theses to the door of the Wittenberg Church. Despite its profound truth and revolutionary discoveries, it was ignored for approximately 100 more years. Thus, even when an expert stands on the mountain of knowledge and shouts the truth, we as humans are capable of ignoring it, disagreeing with it, criticizing it, and even physically threatening or attacking those who preach it. It wasn't until Kepler and Galileo started recording their observations, that Copernicus' conclusions found validity.

In 1621, Johannes Kepler concluded that as a planet travels further away from the sun, it slows down. As it approaches the sun, it speeds up. Although he didn't quite understand why, he conjectured that, "there must be a force emanating from the sun" which drives the planets round their orbits. Because he was not acquainted with the concept of gravity, Kepler concluded that this force must be the Holy Spirit. He was getting close.

The truth is often hidden, not by blatant lies, or falsehoods, but by "near-truths," false starts, accidents, and mistakes. Sometimes the greatest achievements and discoveries come from simply clearing away the rubble of almost-truths, and false expectations of the way the world *ought to be.* When we do this, what has been standing before us all along magically appears and becomes "obvious."

Kepler's description of this invisible force holding the planets in their orbit reveals his religious upbringing. His description was in error, but he was correct in saying that there was an unseen force driving the motions of the planets. Aristotelian physics, which is all Kepler knew at that time, required that for an object to be moved, something physical and tangible had to move it. But there was no physical object connecting or moving the planets. Only space. It was a problem in need of a solution. Although Kepler didn't solve the problem, his "almost truth" provided fertile ground upon which Newton could deduce the law of gravity and the first four laws of physics.[74] When human error is committed in an earnest search for truth, it can yield delightful results, and give birth to the ultimate truth as long as the seekers continue to seek it, and don't get bogged by down by "near-truths."

Before Kepler, the sole job of astronomers was to observe, record, and predict the movements of the stars, the moon, and the planets. No one had dared ask the question "why" they did what they did until Kepler came along. *Why* did the planets speed up as they approached the sun? *Why* did they seem to double back on themselves, go backwards and then proceed in the direction they were first headed? *Why* did their orbits not actually follow a perfect circular pattern? *Why* do eclipses happen? To ask *why* is to suggest causation. Kepler's simple question of *why* was the first step toward attributing a physical cause, rather than a spiritual one, to the movements of the planets. In 1609, Kepler wrote *A New Astronomy Based on Causation, or a Physics of the Sky.* It was the first true marriage of physics with astronomy.

But first, Kepler had to grapple with the commonly accepted "facts" of his day—that the planets moved in perfect circles and at uniform speeds. The biggest breakthrough came when Kepler realized that his meticulously calculated measurements of Mars' movements were eight minutes off of what they should be if Mars moved in at a uniform speed and in a perfect circle around the sun. Kepler was weighing what humans had believed for thousands of years against his own observations and calculations, and he was struggling to reconcile them.[75] How many times in your life has an "inconvenient truth" violently interrupted your tranquil, Eden-like beliefs about the way the world should be?

> *If you would be a real seeker after truth,*
> *it is necessary that at least once in your life*
> *you doubt, as far as possible, all things.*
>
> —RENÉ DESCARTES

Galileo, in challenging the prevailing beliefs of his day (he was a contemporary of Kepler) explained it this way:

> Showing a greater fondness for their own opinions than for truth, they sought to deny and disprove the new things which, if they had cared to look for themselves, their own senses would have demonstrated to them.

Galileo was well aware of how humans tend to filter out solutions that are staring us in the face.[76] In response to Galileo, the Catholic Church argued that it *had to be* the sun that moved, for didn't Joshua command the sun to stand still, and not the earth.[77]

You know you are at a Kepler-like crossroads when you are forced to choose between objectively verifiable data and what you are "supposed to believe." New truths can never change your life unless you let them break through your wall of *near truths*. Frustration is the net result of trying to hold onto your beliefs in the face of concrete evidence to the contrary. If you are frustrated, depressed or ready to give up, it may be time to take inventory of what you have believed your whole life, and like Kepler, take hold of a new truth. The truth that is staring you in the face. The truth of your own experience and personal observations. If you are facing what appears to be an unsolvable problem, it may be because you are not willing to accept the solutions that are right in front of you.

The truth shall set you free.—JOHN 8:32

Kepler finally solved the problem of the eight minute gap by figuring out that the shape of Mars' orbit was not a perfect circle, but was a "squashed circle" called an ellipse. He then immediately criticized his own findings as a "cart full of dung" because no heavenly body could possibly move in a pattern that was an "imperfect circle." Even when he held the truth in his hand, he could not believe it. He had solved the puzzle, but he did not realize he had solved it. He put this solution on the shelf for twenty-five years. It simply could not be. His own belief system blinded him to the truth.

Twenty-five years after first rejecting his own discovery, Kepler finally solved the problem by unceremoniously yanking it from its spiritual context and placing it *illogically* (according to him) into a context that never existed before—the realm of physics. In doing this, Kepler redefined a problem, which had no solution, into one for which there was a solution. Kepler saw a different problem than everyone else because he began to look at it through the eyes of a physicist, not a spiritualist. He began to see that there were physical laws of cause and effect that actually governed the heavens. Everyone else was looking at the problem through the eyes of theologians and philosophers. It must have been incredibly difficult to look at planetary motion through the eyes of a physicist when the laws of physics had not yet been discovered or explained. Nevertheless, when he did this, it all made sense.

If you think you are faced with an unsolvable problem, it may be because you are trying to solve the wrong problem. Or you may be using the wrong set of tools. If the tools you were given early in life are not working, it may be time to create your own set of tools.

The first person to record the shape of an "ellipse" in nature was Apollonius of Perga. He discovered the shape of an ellipse by slicing a cone at an angle.

Kepler looked up and saw this same shape in the sky. Neither of these men "invented" the ellipse. They simply opened their eyes and acknowledged what they saw. This is the true definition of discovery—the act of seeing and accepting something that *was always there*.

In your life, what are the problems that seem to have no solution? You will not start seeing the solutions that are all around you until you start shifting your beliefs. When your life's experience starts coming in direct conflict with what you have believed your whole life, it will cause stress, frustration, depression and maybe even disillusionment. Perhaps these gnawing feelings are life's way of telling you it's time to wake up and start paying attention. Start paying attention to the messages life is trying to send you.

THINGS TO PONDER

+ Is it possible to redefine the problem for which there is no solution into a problem for which there *is* a solution?

+ If you are faced with an unsolvable problem, it could be because you are not willing to accept the solutions that are right in front of you.

+ Don't let near truths blind you to new truths.

+ Start paying attention to the lessons life is trying to teach you.

CHAPTER 12

Are Your Words Limiting
What You Can See?

In 1541, Viceroy Mendoza gave certain Aztec chieftains gifts of horses to better lead their tribesmen in the Mixton War of Central Mexico. This appears to have been the first time that horses were officially given to the Indians. The Indians, not knowing what horses were, referred to them as "big dogs." It was not a perfect solution, but it allowed them to gain a basic understanding of this new creature. To this day, the South American Indian word for horse means "big dog."

Humans have always found it easier to describe things we don't understand in terms of things we do understand. When the automobile was invented, we didn't know what to call it, so we called it a "horseless carriage." We also had no words to describe how much power the engine had. So we compared it to the only thing we were familiar with—"horse power." The British word for flashlight is still—"torch." We say our computer program has a "bug" in it. Describing the unknown in terms of the known is a very primitive skill. Apes can do this too. Upon seeing a swan for the first time, a chimp trained in sign language signed the words "water bird."[78]

All forms of communication are mere weak representations of what we see, feel, hear and smell. Words are not truth. They are an *approximation* of truth. Each form of communication suffers from its own limitations because it causes us to focus on only one aspect of what we are describing at a time. The sound of harmonious music, by itself, cannot convey or explain the mathematical ratios involved. The mathematical ratios cannot convey the sound of your favorite song—or the feeling it gives you inside. When we choose which aspect of a thing to describe, by definition, we are sacrificing all the other aspects of it. When we highlight only one aspect of what we are describing, we are distorting it in the process. Words can be so overly precise that they no longer paint an accurate picture.

> *The forceps of our brain are clumsy things,*
> *and crush the truth a little with the taking hold of it.*
>
> —H.G. WELLS

All forms of communication reflect our feeble attempts to create order out of chaos and find meaning where it would not otherwise exist. They represent our attempts to explain things we don't fully understand to another person who doesn't fully understand them either. Perhaps a million years from now, all of our sophisticated mathematical equations that we think are so accurate and precise will look like primitive cave drawings to some race of people with super human intelligence and a superior form of communication.[79]

> *As far as the laws of mathematics refer to reality,*
> *they are not certain; and as far as they are certain,*
> *they do not refer to reality.*
>
> —ALBERT EINSTEIN

Although analogies are helpful tools when we are trying to understand something new and unfamiliar, we sometimes become so wedded to the analogy that it blocks the truth of what we are actually observing. Our analogies become a veil between the observer and the observed. They blind us to what is actually there.

> *Physics is mathematical not because we know so much about*
> *the physical world, but because we know so little: it is only*
> *its mathematical properties that we can discover.*"[80]
>
> —ARTHUR KOESTLER

For example, Aristotle taught that in order for something to move, it must be moved by something in contact with it. The example he gave was a horse pulling a cart. The cart cannot move by itself. When the horse stops moving, so does the cart. For approximately two thousand years, this philosophy governed all the laws of motion. It caused huge problems when early astronomers tried to explain the movement of the planets because there was nothing visible connecting them and nothing visible causing them to move. And yet they moved. The belief was that they must be divine entities that do not follow the laws of physical motion at all. But early philosophers and astronomers were focusing on the wrong analogy. It was blinding them to the truth. The analogy could not explain what they were actually observing when they looked up at the night sky. If Aristotle had instead focused on the flight of an arrow when shot from a bow, or the motion of a stone when flung with a sling, this would have opened his eyes to the possibility that it was the laws of momentum and gravity that were causing the planets to move in orbital patterns. A flawed analogy can be a huge stumbling block when we start believing the analogy more than the observable truth.

> *Every time you define something, you subtract from it.* [81]
> —HERB KELLEHER
> Founder of Southwest Airlines

For thousands of years, we as humans believed that the atom could not be split. But why? We had no scientific proof confirming or denying this belief. Could it be in part because the word "atom" is a Greek word that literally means "unsplittable?" When such a belief so deeply penetrates our culture that it embodies the literal definition of our words, how can we escape that belief? The very words we use to define the problem could be part of the problem—and we don't even realize it.

The very words you are *choosing to describe* the problem may be steering brains cells and energy off course. For example, in a divorce situation where there is a dispute over custody, you could ask the question one of two ways: (1) Who should be granted custody? or (2) Who should be denied custody? If you ask it the first way, it will prompt the brain to look for positive attributes in both parties. If you ask it the second way, it will prompt the brain to look for negative attributes in both parties. Our words determine what the brain focuses on.[82] What we focus on determines what we see.

Similarly, if you are dealing with the problem of how to make a better can opener, you could ask the question one of two ways. The first is the most obvious because it focuses on the device itself. "How can we make a better can opener? The second is not quite as obvious because it focuses on the thing to be opened. "What are all the ways we can make it easier for a can to be opened?" If you ask the second question, it will prompt the brain to come up with such innovative solutions as pressurized cans that have "pull tabs" that break the seal in order to open the can. This particular solution would make the can opener obsolete. But then again, the goal is not to sell can openers, but to help people open cans more smoothly and efficiently. Every day, you should be asking, "How can I make my product or service obsolete?" If you don't, someone else, like Steve Jobs, will come along and do it for you.

How you ask the question determines the direction in which you are sending your brain cells and your energy. The key is not to seek the right answers, but to ask the right questions. How you ask the question determines what the brain focuses on . . . and ultimately sees. Are you looking for better ways to make a product, or better ways to solve a problem?

Can you really find the right answers when you don't even know if you're asking the right questions? Try asking the question in a different way. Try describing the problem in light of the ultimate goal. Is the main objective really to make a better can opener or to make it easier for consumers to open cans?

In the 1800s the railroad industry was having trouble with trains falling off the tracks. The question they asked was, "How do we make tracks that trains won't fall off of?" But this led only to unsatisfactory solutions, such as re-engineering thousands of miles of already laid train tracks. Finally, someone changed the question to, "How do we make train wheels that will stay on the tracks?" The answer was easy. They started making wheels with flanges.[83]

In 1764, when the smallpox epidemic was killing millions of people, everyone was asking "Why do people get smallpox?" But Edward Jenner stopped and asked, "Why do dairy workers *not* get smallpox?"[84] The answer was that milkmaids were exposed to cow pox through blisters on their hands, and built up immunities to cow pox, which was similar enough to small pox to also protect them from that disease. He developed the first vaccination against cow pox.[85]

Leonardo da Vinci used to break down the problem he was struggling with into each of its essential piece parts and then study them individually. Most people are aware that he actually dissected human bodies in order to get a better look at the muscles, bones and sinew that would ultimately find expression in his incredible paintings. But they are not aware that he did the same thing when he was sorting out other problems in need of a solution. He dissected on paper all of the bridges, tanks, flying machines, machine guns, and exploding bombs that he invented. He drew them in order to see visually how they might work, what additional problems might have to be worked out, and whether he could replace one part with a different part to make it work better.

Following this method, Professor Tony McCaffrey of the University of Massachusetts Amherst asked his students to describe objects generically by their shape, size, and materials—rather than by their common name.[86] For example, one of his students might describe a candle as a wax tube, and a wick as a string. The only rule was to avoid describing the object in a way that implied a particular use. Students who were able to break down common objects into their generic piece parts showed a 67 percent increase in their problem solving skills.

For example, when given a set of metal rings, and a candle, and asked to connect the rings, those who had previously broken down the candle into a "wax tube" and a "string" were much quicker to pull out the string and connect the rings with it.[87]

In another problem solving test, students were asked to build a simple circuit board with a terminal, wires and a screwdriver, but the wires were too short. The students who had previously broken down the screwdriver into two piece parts consisting of a four inch metal bar mounted into a plastic tube, were much more likely to see that the metal bar could be used to bridge the gap and conduct the electricity that was required to solve the problem.[88]

In the 1890s the horse and carriage trade still dominated the personal transportation industry. This means of personal transportation had not really evolved beyond where it was since the time of the Romans. Only the method of manufacturing these ancient carriages had evolved. Through the process of mechanization and the assembly line, the industrial revolution had made it possible to manufacture one complete carriage every six minutes.[89] But while the carriage industry was still focusing on the product, someone else was focusing on a better way to solve the real problem. The question they asked was, "what if it were possible for the carriage to propel itself?" Only someone outside the carriage industry would dare ask this question, and only someone outside the industry could answer it.

It was someone outside the carriage trade who invented the combustible engine.[90] The largest manufacturers of the traditional carriage stood in the best position to take advantage of the combustible engine.[91] The internal combustion engine was invented in 1857. By 1879, the two-stroke engine had been invented. By the 1890s the biggest carriage makers already had the huge manufacturing plants, the capital, and the technology to quickly and efficiently make wheels, the seats, and the body of the vehicle itself.[92] All they had to do was add the engine and the drive train—right? But every one of the major carriage makers went out of business soon after the first cars began to appear on the road. Why? It was because they were focusing on the question "How can we manufacture the carriage better, faster, and more efficiently?" rather than "How can we make it easier for people to travel?" They were focused more *on their product* than on the needs of their customers.[93] They thought they were in the carriage business when they were really in the personal transportation business.

The photographic film industry nearly suffered the exact same downfall when the digital camera was born. The reason? Film producers were asking "How can we make better film?" instead of asking

"How can we make it easier for people to capture and store memories?"[94] The manufacturers of cassette tapes and CDs suffered the same crisis when digital music and the iPod were born. Instead of focusing on their own product lines, they should have been asking, "How can we make it easier for people to purchase, to store, and to share music?"[95]

Remember Elisha Gray? Even though he was the first to invent the telephone, he set it aside because it did not look like the result he was expecting. Gray was focused more on the device he was tinkering with—the telegraph. While Gray was asking "How can I create a better telegraph?" while Alexander Graham Bell was asking, "How can I make it easier for people to communicate?"

Ask yourself, "What is the ultimate goal of my service or product?" Try describing your products and services not so much in terms of their features and functions, but in terms of what problems you solve. Try describing them in terms of the difference they make in people's lives. Legendary innovators and entrepreneurs know they cannot make a profit unless they first make a difference.

The association newspaper for the carriage industry actually called the horseless carriage a "rich man's toy" and described it as a fad that would soon pass.[96] As humans, we often dismiss novel information because it challenges our truth. We often dismiss it as heresy because it is inconsistent with our own mental model of the world. We have come to believe our model of truth (our analogy) more than the actual truth.

We don't like information that is inconsistent with our belief system. It is uncomfortable. It disrupts our model of how the world works. We have more reasons to *not believe* it than we have to believe it because we have so much invested in our model, mentally, emotionally and financially. We don't want to change our behavior or our language so late in the game. Keep in mind—that uncomfortable feeling in your gut doesn't mean the new information is false. It just means you are experiencing growing pains.

You can tell your model of the universe is outdated when you start ignoring or suppressing troubling facts. When new information challenges our old belief system, we are at a crossroads. We can either ignore the new information or we can abandon our old beliefs and adopt new ones based on the new input.[97]

Like Kepler, you know your mental model of the world is flawed when your old metaphors and analogies can no longer *accurately* explain what you are truly observing and experiencing. This question is—are you going to keep believing what you are *supposed to believe* or believe in what your own life's experience and observations are telling you.

Words are very powerful. They help us communicate our thoughts. They help us describe problems. They help us *solve* problems. But words can be so overly precise that they no longer paint an accurate picture. The words you are using may be steering brain cells off course. If you become too wedded to your ordinary way of describing things; if you start to believe that your metaphors and analogies are the actual truth, rather than a weak approximation of truth, you may be missing the *real* opportunities and *true* solutions that are all around you.

In order to peel back the layers of the onion, you have to start asking yourself *how* and *why*.

1. Why do I keep describing the problem the way I do?

2. Does my description of the problem contain assumptions that I've never bothered to challenge?

3. How are the words I'm using limiting my range of options?

4. Do I describe my business in terms of what I sell instead of the difference I make in people's lives?

5. How are the words I'm using directing brain cells and energy off course?

Successful marketing is not singing the song in your own heart loudly. It is singing the song in someone else's heart softly. Change the song and you change your focus. Change your focus and you change what you can and can't see.

THINGS TO PONDER

+ Words are not truth. They are an approximation of truth.

+ Our words steer our brain cells.

+ Opening the eye of the brain involves abandoning old analogies and metaphors and adopting new ones.

+ The key is not to seek the right answers, but to ask the right questions.

+ Take inventory of the words you are using to describe the problem.

+ Are you describing your business in terms of the products and services you generate or in terms of the difference you make in people's lives?

+ Redefine the business you are in. Are you in the carriage business or in the personal transportation business?

+ Is the goal to make a better music player, or to make it easier for people to listen to music?

+ Successful marketing does not consist of singing the song in your own heart loudly. It consists of singing the song in someone else's heart softly.

CHAPTER 13

Why Do We Create Our Own Truth?

Sometimes, when my dog is on a leash, he accidentally wraps himself around a tree, a pole, or a fire hydrant. I sit there and watch to see if he can figure out that all he needs to do is reverse his direction and go the other way. But all he does is sit there and look up at me with those sad puppy dog eyes. He knows he's in trouble, but he can't figure out how he got there, or how to get out. The reason—he doesn't have the ability to ask the question *why* or to find the answers.

To be fair, my dog does recognize that when he pees on the carpet, he gets swatted. So, he modifies this behavior by tapping on the jingle bell I have hanging from the back door whenever he needs to pee. To the casual observer, it looks like he has recognized a pattern and has adjusted his behavior accordingly. But in reality, he is only responding to pleasure and pain. He does not understand *why* it's not a good idea to pee on the carpet. Humans are the only creatures on the planet that have the ability to ask the question *why*. We are also the only creatures that have the ability to then seek out and find the answer to that question.

Even a four-year-old child will pester you with the constant question *why* until you are ready to pull your hair out. But why are human beings constantly seeking the answer to *why*? There are at least two reasons: (1) humans have an insatiable curiosity; and (2) humans cannot tolerate arbitrariness and randomness. It causes stress and anxiety. We always seek the answer to the question *why* when confronted with a new and puzzling situation. We instinctively know that every effect has a cause, and we simply *have to know* what it is. When no answers are readily apparent, we invent our own, and these reasons give us comfort, and make us feel better about our world. But our made-up answers often become our reality and blind us to the truth even when we later stumble upon the real facts.

When the world becomes unbearable, we must withdraw from it, and create a world of artificial perfection.

—ARTHUR KOESTLER

For example, if we were living thousands of years ago, a solar eclipse might mean the gods are angry and are demanding a virgin sacrifice. When the eclipse goes away, we would conclude that the virgin sacrifice worked, and repeat this behavior at the next eclipse.[98] It would give us a certain false confidence that we were in control. If we saw a falling star, and an important leader died that month, we might conclude that every time we see a falling star an important leader is going to die.[99]

But the tendency to invent our own answers is not relegated to the dark ages or cave men. For thousands of years, healers, shamans, and all gastrointestinal doctors believed that peptic ulcers were caused by worry and stress. The inside of the stomach is bathed daily with digestive enzymes and hydrochloric acid, and it was believed that undue stress caused an excess secretion of these acids, which in turn ate away at the stomach lining.

In 1950, Fran Alexander, an expert on peptic ulcers wrote a book called *Psychosomatic Medicine.* In it, he declared triumphantly that ulcers were caused by internal conflict caused by a regressive dependence on others as though they are idealized parents. But when those we love disappoint us or reject us, it causes stress which causes an ulcer. In a similar vein, in 1968 the brilliant psychiatrist Harold G. Wolff wrote a book called *Stress and Disease.* In it he claimed that excess gastric secretion was the result of "competitive striving" and the day to day stress of living in a complex society. These two treatises were the gospels on peptic ulcers.

All of the medication throughout the ages was designed to make the patient feel better, but nothing could actually cure the ulcer itself. All doctors could do was suggest a change in diet and prescribe acid inhibitors. People who suffered from ulcers found themselves eating nothing but creamy soups and drinks mixed with magnesia powder or sodium bicarbonate powder.

The pharmaceutical industry responded to the books by Alexander and Wolff with medications designed to reduce the normal acidic reaction of the stomach to every day foods. In the 1970s, acid inhibitors such as cimetidine (Tagamet) and ranitidine (Zantac) were the world's best-selling prescription drugs. By 1992, the market for acid inhibitors was $6 billion per year. No one ever considered a bacterial cause for ulcers because it was well known that bacteria could never survive in the harsh and hostile acidic gastric juices of the stomach. In fact, a tooth immersed in a jar of gastric juices overnight would be stripped of all its enamel.

Upon this backdrop entered Barry Marshall, a 20-something-year-old resident of internal medicine at the Royal Perth Hospital in Western Australia. It was considered the remotest outback of internal medicine. In September 1981, this inexperienced doctor, still in his residency, treated a patient with severe abdominal discomfort with an antibiotic called tetracycline. After 14 days, the gastritis cleared up. An antibiotic would normally have no effect on the gastritis unless … it was caused by something other than stress … something like bacteria. This was his first clue that the gastritis might be caused by something other than stress.

Marshall took samples of the stomach lining and tried to get the bacteria to grow in a petri dish and colonize so he could study it. After many months of trying to grow the bacteria, nothing happened. It was unclear whether any bacteria had really been involved at all.

But one day Marshall accidentally left his samples in a dark, humid incubator for the long Easter weekend. They were there for five days. Under normal circumstances, a bacteria cell only needs 48 hours to grow. Therefore, researchers routinely cleaned out the petri dishes after 48 hours. No one had ever thought bacteria would need five days to grow. However, upon returning from the Easter weekend, Marshall was surprised to see the bacteria thriving in colonies in the petri dish. When he examined the bacteria under an electron microscope, he saw dozens of cork-screw shaped organisms he had never seen before. It was an entirely new genus of bacteria unknown to science.

This new type of bacteria protected itself from the harsh stomach acids by using its whip-like tail to quickly swim through the gastric juices and then used its corkscrew shape to burrow through the thick mucus lining of the stomach where it cocooned itself. This same mucus is what protects the lining of the stomach itself from the acids and enzymes. It was therefore sufficient to protect the bacteria. When this particular bacteria secrets its own toxic waste products, this causes damage to the stomach lining. The result is a peptic ulcer.

In 1983, Marshall published his first paper declaring that he had found the true cause of peptic ulcers. All the noted experts in the field publicly declared him to be *out of his mind.* After all, he was young and inexperienced, and knew nothing about peptic ulcers. To prove them all wrong, Marshall did something absurd. He made a putrid-tasting cocktail filled with this mysterious new bacteria and drank it. After a week he started vomiting, and for weeks had severe headaches and foul breath. Then he took a biopsy of his own stomach lining and confirmed that the spiral shaped bacteria had indeed taken up residence in his stomach lining. Then he treated himself with an antibiotic. His symptoms quickly disappeared and a second biopsy confirmed that the bacteria was gone. Only then did the experts start paying attention. In 1995, Marshall received the coveted Albert Lasker Clinical Medical Research Award. He had finally been vindicated.

The bacteria was given the name *H. pylori.* It turns out this wily bacteria has another survival strategy. In unfavorable environments, such as one with a lack of nutrients, it will actually roll itself up into a ball like a pill bug and survive for years in a dormant state. The *H. pylori* bacterium has been found in the stomach lining of dried up mummies thousands of years old—still alive in a dormant state.

The irony is that several years earlier, a pathologist named J. Robin Sarren, had been studying the biopsies of several deceased patients who had suffered from gastritis and had noticed a large number of curved and spiral shaped bacteria beneath the mucus layer of the stomach lining. He also saw that the stomach cells surrounding this bacteria had been damaged. But he failed to connect the dots. He was staring right at the solution to the cause of ulcers, but he failed to see it because he was not looking for it. Moreover, it was set in stone that no bacterium could survive long enough in the stomach to cause any harm. His beliefs blinded him to what he had seen.

It is now obvious that the so called experts were doing the same thing primitive humans did thousands of years ago when they asked the question *why* and there was no apparent answer. They simply made up an answer. The experts declared that ulcers were caused by stress. It made them feel better and it gave them the illusion of control. Perhaps it shrouded the shamans, the gurus, and even the modern day gastrointestinal experts with the illusion of intelligence and credibility in front of those who expected it of them.[100] The problem is—this made-up answer had so deeply penetrated the belief systems of the medical industry that they were blind *and even hostile* to the actual truth when Marshall presented it to them.

But our willingness to believe in our own truth in the face of overriding evidence is not limited to matters of science or religion. In 1940, the whole world knew that Hitler was going to invade France. He had already invaded Austria, Czechoslovakia, and Poland. In his book *Mein Kamf*, he had publicly declared his goal to conquer France. The only question was *where* he would attack. France had heavily prepared its defenses in every spot except one—the Ardennes forest, which it had declared *impénétrable*. That location had no permanently installed fortifications or heavy artillery designed to stop tanks. It was only lightly defended by infantrymen carrying small arms. So stubborn was France's belief that its borders were safe that it did not even regularly fly reconnaissance airplanes over its borders to watch the movements of the German army, which had been building up for years.

A few days before the Germans invaded, one French pilot whose mission was to drop leaflets in Germany urging the people to overthrow Hitler happened to look down and see a sixty-mile line of tanks and trucks headed straight for the Ardennes forest. He reported this to the highest officials. They rejected the warning as not credible.[101]

This report was a visual confirmation of an earlier report when a German airplane flew off course and was forced to land in Belgium, a French ally. The officers were carrying secret documents detailing the plan to invade France through the Ardennes forest.[102] The French authorities concluded that the documents were a plant and the whole mission was a ruse meant to deceive the enemy. After all, the Ardennes forest was *impénétrable*.

The Germans penetrated the forest in two days. So swift and deadly was the German invasion that when the Nazi juggernaut emerged on the French side of the Ardennes, 200,000 French soldiers, and their officers, simply dropped their weapons and ran.[103] They traded their military uniforms for civilian clothes and disappeared into the French countryside. There was now nothing between the German army and Paris except 125 miles of farmland. Upon hearing that the entire Ninth Army had disappeared overnight, Churchill admonished the French to call up the reserve troops. He was dumb-founded to hear that they had no reserve troops.[104] When the French tanks finally did show up, the drivers had no radios with which to communicate with each other.[105] They could not mount an organized attack, and were easily wiped out by the German tanks.

This unwillingness to believe the truth when it was screaming at them in the face resulted in the loss of an entire nation, the loss of freedom, the loss of sovereignty, the loss of millions of lives. Have you counted the cost of clinging too dearly to your own truths?

Here are two simple rules for avoiding these kinds of errors:

> "First, there are no sacred truths; all assumptions must be critically examined; arguments from authority are worthless. Second, whatever is inconsistent with the facts must be discarded or revised. We must understand the cosmos as it is and not confuse how it is with how we wish it to be. The obvious is sometimes false; the unexpected is sometimes true."[106]

Truth does not discriminate. She reveals herself to all who search for her in earnest. But only those who are willing to abandon their own dearly held truths will ever see it.

✳

THINGS TO PONDER

+ When we can't find the answer to why, we make up our own answers and this becomes our truth.

+ Truths that have never been seen before will always look strange, stupid, and laughable—at first.

+ Is it possible that your beliefs might be blinding you to truths that are right in front of you?

+ Even if you are absolutely right, and you know it, and everyone around you knows it, always ask yourself:

  1. What are the consequences to myself if I am wrong?

  2. What are the consequences *to others* if I am wrong?

  3. Can I live with those consequences?

  4. What will my legacy be if I am wrong?

+ Always have a backup plan.

✳

-≪‹•›≫-

CHAPTER 14

How Do We Turn Background Noise into Information?

Imagine, if you will, that you are living in ancient Greece between 580 and 500 B.C. People are walking around in togas. A donkey is pulling a cart full of wheat. A herd of sheep is walking down the middle of a dirt road being tended by a shepherd. A busy open-air market is buzzing with the sounds of people selling freshly butchered meat, dates, spices and fish.

As you are walking, you hear the familiar clanging and banging of iron against iron coming from a blacksmith's shop. The sounds of heavy steel hammers pounding horse shoes, wheels, axes and swords. The sound of a roaring fire. These are sounds you've heard your whole life. It's just background noise, right? Not if your name is Pythagoras. On this day, he heard *harmony*. He immediately ran into the black-smith's shop to investigate the source of the harmony. He noticed that some of the hammers could be struck simultaneously to generate a harmonious sound, but many could not. Upon testing the hammers, he realized that those that were harmonious with each other had a simple mathematical relationship. Their masses were simple ratios or fractions of each other. Pythagoras discovered that the pitch of a note depends on the length of the pipe that produces it, and the har-monious intervals in any musical scale, are produced by numerical ratios. Pythagoras has discovered musical intervals, and in so doing, had merged mathematics with music.

How do we turn background noise into information? The entire uni-verse, as we know it, can be reduced to stimuli and receptors. Without receptors, all stimuli are just sound waves, light waves, and scents wafting through the air. They are various forms of energy, vibrating, pulsating in the universe for no apparent reason. It is only because we have receptors that we can receive that energy and transform it into information. For thousands of years, the Hindus have tried to teach us that we never really experience our environment as it truly is. We are always and only ever experiencing our five senses. The way a dog experiences a rose is dramatically different from how you experience it. Dogs are almost color blind so they can't see the beautiful red color as you do. But their sense of smell is much more powerful than ours, so they get to enjoy the sweet fragrance in a way we never will.

The energy pulsating through the air in the form of light, color, scent, flavor, sound waves and texture only reaches our brain if it is able to penetrate one of our five senses. If you block all five senses, the external stimuli would still exist, but you would not be experiencing it as you do now. You would only be experiencing it the way a rock does. The heat and cold would have the normal effects of contraction and expansion upon you. The wind might blow tiny grains of sand against you and soften you and wear you down over the millennia. But you would not be conscious of it. Nor would you feel it. Therefore, we never truly experience nature the way it is. Indeed, we are *always and only* experiencing our own five senses.

Keep in mind, even though a completely healthy person has five senses, those five senses only have a limited ability to pick up information from our environment. We can't see things an eagle can see. We can't hear things a bat can hear. We can't smell things a dog can smell. On top of those inherent limitations, the external environment is filtered a second time through our beliefs, biases and expectations.

When that external stimuli penetrates our five senses, it only *becomes information* because we isolate certain rhythms and patterns and assign meaning to them. But do these rhythms and patterns really convey information to us, or is it we who are assigning meaning to them?

What does Picasso see when he looks at an apple? Is it any different from what the grocery boy sees? When a Hindu looks at a Brahma bull, does he see anything different from what a rancher from Texas sees? What we see depends on a variety of factors—only one of which is the position from which we are standing.

Imagine if you will a sidewalk café in Paris across the street from the Eiffel Tower. It is sunset and the waiter is lighting each of the candles placed elegantly on the white table cloths of each table. Pigeons are pecking at crumbs at the feet of the guests. A group of kids are kicking around a soccer ball nearby. The lights of the Eiffel Tower begin to twinkle. At one table is a young couple holding hands and staring dreamily into each other's eyes. At another table are two lawyers trying to hammer out the details of a billion dollar corporate merger. As chance may have it, the people at both tables happen to order the same type of wine, and the exact same entrées.

Are their experiences any different? Does the wine and food taste different in each of their mouths? Do the lawyers notice the pigeons pecking at their feet? Do they hear the laughter and shouts of the kids playing soccer? Do they take time to savor and enjoy the twinkling lights of the Eiffel Tower? Do they actually let each sip of wine swirl around in their mouths before they swallow? How can two groups of people be having an almost identical experience and yet see, feel, taste and hear something entirely different?

Their experiences are different primarily because of what they are focusing on, what they believe and what they are expecting to see—in that moment.

Writer Joel Achenbach of the *Washington Post* tells of a true story that happened on the morning of September 11, 2001 in Washington, D.C. Two airplanes had just crashed into the Twin Towers of the World Trade Center in New York City. A third aircraft had just crashed into the Pentagon. Smoke was pouring out of the building and could be seen for miles. Washington, D.C. was in a state of emergency. Rumors were flying all around that the city was under attack. But less than two miles away from the Pentagon, there was a man sitting on a park bench, quietly reading the newspaper. Achenbach saw him sitting there and asked him if he knew what was happening. The man said yes, but that he had no interest in joining any evacuation or even listening to the latest news bulletin. He figured he was in no danger and everything would return to normal soon.

Why didn't the man flee? Why didn't he panic? The only answer is what he chose to *focus* on, what he chose to *believe*, and what he chose to *expect*—in the heat of that moment. These three critical choices affect our life's experience every moment of every day, whether we like it or not. They act as filters to keep out sights, sounds, scents, tastes, and feelings that are not relevant to the task at hand. They are also like magnets drawing in those that are.

All things are meaningless accidents, works of chance, unless your marveling gaze, as it probes, connects and orders, makes them divine . . .[107]

WILHELM WILLMS

We are constantly faced with an unconscious choice of what meaning to give that random, arbitrary stimuli. Only when we isolate certain patterns, rhythms, and frequencies, can we put it into some kind of order that is useful to us. But we can only isolate those patterns, rhythms, and frequencies if we first choose to focus on them, and then isolate what is relevant.

Think about it. The act of listening means filtering out what is not important. Otherwise all we would hear is chaos. Have you ever wondered how you can both hear and understand the person you are talking to at a crowded cocktail party over the loud music and all the conversations going on around you? You are using the same tools a momma bat uses to identify the unique squeaks of her babies in a cave filled with millions of squeaking bats. You are not listening with your ears. You are listening with your brain. Your ears are simply conduits for raw external data to enter the brain. Your brain is actively filtering out what is not relevant.

Focus is like a narrow, highly intense beam of light that illuminates one corner of a very large and cluttered room. The other things in the room are still there, but you just can't see them in that moment because they are not important.

When reading a page, you focus only on a few words at a time. The rest of the page is a blur. In fact, the room you are sitting in is a blur while you are reading this page. You are vaguely aware of its existence, but in the moment of reading, it fades into the background. The sights and sounds in the room are not relevant to the task of reading *this sentence*. In contrast, try looking at the four corners of the page you are now reading and take a guess at what the dimensions of this page are. While you are in the act of looking at the four corners of this page, you cannot simultaneously read any specific sentence because the words are no longer relevant to the task.

Legendary innovators and entrepreneurs have a heightened ability to see solutions that are invisible to others, not because of what they see, but because of what they *choose to ignore*. They ignore most of the chaotic background noise that is so distracting to the rest of us. They focus on and isolate only those things that are relevant to solving the problem they are facing. They are like momma bats listening for the squeaks of their babies. As a result, they recognize patterns, rhythms, and frequencies where the rest of us see and hear only chaos.

Like Rosie Gutierrez, whom you met in chapter two, they see the riches in the rubble. Like Pythagoras, they hear harmony where others hear only noise. They don't necessarily believe that the rubble has any inherent value. They simply find a way to turn it into something of value. They simply believe in themselves and their ability to bring value and order to the chaos. Without them, the chaos and garbage would still be there, and within the rubble would lie a hidden pattern, a rhythm, a frequency waiting to be discovered.

> *Before reaching awareness, the input is filtered, processed, distorted, interpreted, and reorganized in a series of relay stations at various levels of the nervous system.*
>
> —WILLIAM JAMES

But how do people like Pythagoras walk by a blacksmith shop and come away with something as profound as the law of musical intervals that governs that favorite song of yours?

✳

THINGS TO PONDER

+ You are always *only* experiencing your five senses.

+ What you see only becomes information when you assign meaning to it.

+ The brain filters out things that are not relevant to the task.

+ Your ability to connect the dots and see hidden patterns depends on what you determine to be relevant.

+ There is order in the disorder if you know what to look for.

+ There is harmony in the cacophony if you know what to listen for.

✳

CHAPTER 15

Can You See the Hidden Connection?

Archimedes of Syracuse was a Greek mathematician, physicist, engineer, inventor, and astronomer who lived from 287 B.C. to 212 B.C. According to Vitruvius, a crown had been made for King Hiero II, who had supplied the pure gold to be used. Hiero II asked Archimedes to determine whether some silver had been substituted by the goldsmith. Archimedes had to solve the problem without damaging the crown. He could not melt it down into a cube in order to calculate its volume and density.

He had been obsessing with this problem for months. One day as he was getting into a bathtub, he noticed that the level of the water in the tub rose as he got in. He realized that the amount of water that was displaced by his body was equal in volume to the volume of his body. Likewise, the volume of the crown could be determined by the volume of water it displaced. By dividing the mass of the crown by the volume of water displaced, the density of the crown could be accurately calculated. He could then compare this density to the density of a block of pure gold of the same volume. If the density of the crown was less than the density of a block of pure gold of the same volume, he could determine if cheaper and less dense metals had been used in making the crown. Archimedes was so excited at his discovery that he ran out into the streets naked shouting, "Eureka!" ("I have found it!"). Archimedes applied his test to the crown and discovered that, in fact, silver had indeed been added to the gold to make the crown.

This is a well-known story, but few have seen the hidden lesson in it. How many times did Archimedes get in and out of the tub without seeing the law of displacement? Moreover, how many millions of people in history up to that point had gotten in and out of the tub without discovering the law of displacement? Nobody before Archimedes had ever seen the relationship between the volume of the object dipped into water and an equal volume of water spilling out over the sides of the tub. The only reason Archimedes saw it on this particular occasion is because he had a particular problem on his mind which he had been contemplating for quite some time. The act of getting into the tub was not an attempt to solve the problem. It was to take a bath. It just so happened that the solution presented itself to him at that moment because he had been contemplating the problem for so long and it was still on his mind at the exact right moment. His brain was so saturated with the problem that when the solution presented itself, the hidden connection leaped out at him.

Creativity is not the act of creating something that has never existed. It is the act of seeing hidden connections that were always there. It is the act of connecting two familiar objects in new and different ways. It requires an almost brutal yanking of an object or concept from its original context and placing it in a context where it does not belong—just as Pythagoras yanked harmonious sounds out of the realm of music and put them smack dab in the middle of mathematics.

Brilliant mathematician Alan Turing did the same thing when he helped crack the secret code used by the Nazis to transmit messages during World War II. The encryption device the Nazis created was called *Enigma*. It was one of history's earliest analog computers. For years, the Allied Powers could not crack it, and the German's use of it was causing devastating losses to the United States and Great Britain. After getting nowhere by using other analog computers to crack the code of the *Enigma*, Turing did something illogical. He created a *digital* computer to solve an *analog* problem. It was like trying to mix oil and water. It was a crude, homemade digital computer, but it worked.[108] Had Turing not decoded the *Enigma*, Great Britain might have become a German colony. With the cracking of the code, the

Allied Powers could now listen in to German communications and know in advance what they were going to do. The tide of the war began to turn.

The essence of innovation, invention, and entrepreneurship lies not in the discovery of new facts, but in the discovery of new ways to think about them. Legendary entrepreneurs walk around constantly connecting unrelated objects, seeing hidden analogies, connecting the dots in ways no one else has before.

> *A problem cannot be solved with the*
> *same level of thinking that created it.*
>
> —ALBERT EINSTEIN

So how do innovators and entrepreneurs see these hidden connections? This vision occurs behind the eyes—in the brain. The eyes are just a conduit for raw data. It comes from the ability to imagine seemingly irrational things that do not exist as though they do exist. It comes from fusing two unrelated things into one with the eyes of the brain.

Wolfgang Koehler is one of the first psychologists to study the minds of apes. In his seminal work *The Mentality of Apes*, he describes how apes find solutions to problems. He recorded his observations and findings in 1914.[109]

A young female chimpanzee named Nueva is the subject of an experiment. The caretaker puts a stick in her cage. She plays with it. Scrapes the ground with it. Pushes old banana skins together in a pile. Then drops the stick on the ground.

Ten minutes later, a cluster of bananas is placed outside her cage just beyond her reach. She grasps at it in vain. She presses her face against the cage and stretches her lips towards it. She shrieks and whimpers. She gives big puppy dog sad eyes to the caretaker. She throws herself back and writhes around in frustration.

Approximately seven minutes later, her eyes happen to fall on the stick. She stops moaning, picks up the stick, stretches it outside the cage, puts it strategically behind the bananas and pulls the prize close enough for her outstretched hand to grab them.

After an hour, more bananas are placed outside her cage just beyond her reach again. This time, she picks up the stick sooner.

After another hour, the caretaker repeats the test. This time, she picks up the stick immediately.

We have known for a long time that apes have the ability to use tools. The question here, however, is how they reach that "aha" moment. Here, the moment of epiphany came when Nueva's eyes happened upon the stick while in the process of thinking about ways to reach the bananas.

When the instrument already looks like a tool in the exact shape and size needed to solve the problem, the "aha" moment comes easily. Apparently, even a monkey can do it. But what about when the solution doesn't look like what it's supposed to look like?

A young male chimpanzee named Sultan has already been through the same experiment as Nueva. He already knows that a stick makes a good tool for reaching bananas. But this time there is no stick in his cage. Lying on the ground inside the cage is a large bush with various branches and leaves growing from it. It is impossible to stick the bush through the bars of the cage because of all the branches sticking out of it. Sultan goes through the same routine Nueva went through. Reaching his outstretched hand in vain toward the prize, pressing his face against the cage and stretching his lips towards it, throwing himself on the ground and shrieking and whimpering, and making faces to play upon the sympathies of the caretaker. Nothing works. After approximately twenty-three minutes, Sultan's eyes happen upon the bush.

He drags it around and whacks it against the bars of the cage, expressing his frustration. Leaves and twigs break off and fall to the ground. He begins to play with the bush and discovers that he can easily break off twigs and branches.

After fifty-six minutes, he breaks off a long branch and begins to play with it, poking and prodding things, but the twigs and leaves sticking out of the branch still make it impossible to stick it through the bars of the cage. More twigs and leaves fall off in the process of play. After another fourteen minutes, Sultan deliberately breaks off the remaining twigs and leaves from the branch to make a long, slender stick. Now he has his tool. He uses the tool to pull the bananas close enough for him to grasp them with his outstretched hand.

The experiment is repeated three times. Each time, Sultan sees the tool in the bush faster, and breaks a branch off the bush, fashions it into a stick and retrieves the bananas.

After this experience, Sultan's view of the world has been permanently shifted. He can never look at a bush without seeing the tool again. His *world-processor* has been changed. In his mind, branches have suddenly been transformed into tools.

Archimedes' moment of epiphany also occurred when he was able to connect two totally unrelated objects. It was when he got into the tub that it finally hit him that his body displaced the exact volume of water as the volume of his body. Then it hit him that the volume of gold could also be measured by the volume of water it displaced. He saw that "this" was like "that." His ability to see a hidden connection was his brilliance. Could it be that Archimedes, like the apes Nueva and Sultan, only arrived at his "aha" moment because his eyes happened upon a common, everyday occurrence while his mind was in the act of contemplating a difficult problem?

It turns out that this is *one of* the big secrets of entrepreneurs throughout the ages. Entrepreneurs don't focus primarily on money. They look for a problem that needs a solution. They study that problem. They saturate their minds with it. They walk around with the shape of that problem constantly in their heads like a keyhole in need of a key. Their brains are simultaneously performing two functions. In one part of the brain, they hold the problem like a locked door with a big brass keyhole in it. In the other part of the brain, they are constantly scanning the environment for a key that fits that keyhole. The moment of epiphany comes when they stumble upon a key that fits. The mind of the entrepreneur is always prepared for that "chance" opportunity. They stumble across the right key, not because they know what the key looks like, but because in their minds, they always carry the shape of the keyhole.

They pass up many keys along the way, but the shape of the keyhole is always with them, floating around in their heads. Then one day, when they happen upon a key that fits the problem, they latch onto it with all their might and grab that key and stick it in the keyhole and unlock the door. If they don't find the right key, they fashion one out of something that at first doesn't look like the right tool. Like Sultan, they can see the tool in the bush.

> *We will either find a way or make one.*
>
> —HANNIBAL
> Carthaginian General

In 1974, Art Fry was singing in his church choir at the North Presbyterian Church in North St. Paul, Minnesota. He had been using scraps of paper to mark certain pages in his choir book, but the pieces of paper kept falling out. This was a problem because he needed to be able to quickly find the right page of the next song the choir was about to sing. It just so happened that Fry was also employed by the 3M company at the time. He worked in the product development department. It was while grappling with this problem during a church service that his mind wandered back to a failed product that had been created by another 3M employee, Dr. Spencer Silver. A few years earlier, Dr. Silver had created an adhesive that was not quite sticky enough to be of any use. The next day, Fry went to work and sought out Dr. Silver who had to dig around in his old dusty pile of discarded experiments to find that bottle of failed adhesive. Fry applied some of it to a scrap piece of paper, and sure enough, it was sticky enough to temporarily attach the scrap to another piece of paper, and could be easily be pulled off. It was then that he had his *eureka* moment. He had found the solution to his choir book problem. Then he began to visualize other uses for the adhesive—such as for note pads and reminders. Fry had seen the *tool in the bush*. The Post-it Note was born.

After the fact, everyone says "Wow! That's brilliant!" and "How did you come up with that idea?" As billionaire Red McCombs says, "After an entrepreneur solves the problem, the solution always looks obvious."

The art of seeing a hidden connection which no one has seen before is the essence of entrepreneurship and innovation. The moment of epiphany comes when we realize that "this" is like "that." Once you see the hidden connection, you can never see the two objects in the same way again. From that moment on, your *world processor* is changed forever.

Before Kepler, there was a huge disconnect between what astronomers actually observed and what they believed was *supposed to be there*. The actual calculations were not consistent with the entrenched belief that the planets moved in perfect circles and at uniform speeds. Kepler solved this problem by combining two unrelated concepts. The moment of epiphany came when Kepler realized that the planets moved like a stone in a sling being swung by a warrior. A stone in a sling does not move in a perfect circle or at a uniform speed. The light bulb came on when he realized that "this" was like "that."

How many people throughout history have seen an apple, or a pecan, or an acorn fall from tree? When Isaac Newton saw an apple fall from a tree, he had a sudden moment of enlightenment. He realized that the earth must be drawing the apple to itself. And if the force drawing the apple to itself were strong enough, it might also draw other objects in the sky to itself—such as the moon. He concluded that the moon kept circling the earth because of the same gravitational force. The earth was constantly drawing the moon to itself, but the centrifugal force which drove the moon forward kept it from actually colliding with the earth.

It is similar to a man throwing a baseball. If there is enough force behind it, the ball will travel a great distance in a straight line before slowly falling to the earth in a descending arch. If you shoot a .50 caliber bullet out of a Barrett M82 sniper rifle, it will travel almost one mile before it begins to fall to the earth in a descending arch. Why? Because the force behind it is much greater, and it takes much longer for gravity to take its effect. If that same bullet were shot out of a cannon or something with enough force to keep it suspended in the air long enough, it would actually circle the whole earth and come back to where it started. This is how the moon circles the earth continuously. Centrifugal force keeps pulling the moon away from the earth. Gravity keeps pulling the moon toward the earth. The result is a perfectly balanced orbit around the earth. Newton saw the hidden analogy between two very different objects, an apple and the moon. He saw that "this" was like "that."

Before Louis Pasteur, it was common knowledge that humans who had been exposed to cow pox were somehow immune to smallpox. But no one understood exactly why. Pasteur had been growing cholera cultures in petri dishes and injecting them into chickens as an experiment. But one day he went on an extended vacation. When he returned, he discovered that the cholera bacteria in the petri dishes had become spoiled and therefore weaker. When he injected the spoiled bacteria into the chickens, he noticed that those chickens did not die. They just became slightly ill. Then he injected those same chickens with a full strength cholera bacteria from a different petri dish, and they showed no sign of illness at all. Pasteur immediately saw the significance of this event. He discovered a hidden analogy between the surviving chickens who were inoculated by the weakened cholera culture and the humans who were protected from smallpox once they had survived cow pox. Pasteur concluded that it was possible to make this immunity happen on purpose by vaccinating people with a weakened form of small pox.[110] He saw that "this" was like "that."

Benjamin Franklin was trying to capture electricity with a lightning rod, but he couldn't figure out how to get a lightning rod high enough in the sky to attract the lightning. There were no buildings tall enough to elevate his lighting rod close enough to the storm clouds. He remembered how, as a boy, he used to tie the string of a kite to his toe while he was swimming, and while-away the day as the kite soared high above him. In a flash, Franklin combined two unrelated objects. He saw that flying a kite was like climbing to the top of a tall building. You could reach the same height either way. This is how he came up with his idea of tying a lightning rod to the tip of a kite to attract the lightning. It was the act of combining two dissimilar objects that allowed him to solve an unsolvable problem.

Before Kekule, scientists believed molecules were linear structures opened at each end. But in a dream, Friedrich August von Kekule saw that the benzene molecule was like a snake eating its own tail.

This revolutionized organic chemistry. He single-handedly created an analogy no one had ever seen before. Organic compounds are not like "this." They are like "that." After Kekule, scientists could not look at any molecule the same way again.

Gutenberg combined what he knew about the wine press with what he knew about the coin punch to invent the printing press. Instead of punching a governmental seal on a coin, he would use ink (i.e. the wine stains) to "punch" letters and words onto paper. By combining two unrelated concepts, he created an entirely new industry, the industry that allows you to read this book.

In World War I, *staph* infections from unclean wounds killed at least half of the ten million soldiers who died. Scientists around the world were desperately looking for a way to cure the dreaded *staphylococcus* bacteria.

In 1922, Alexander Fleming was busy trying to find a cure for this disease, plus a variety of other diseases caused by bacteria. He kept a collection of different petri dishes each of which contained a different type of bacteria for testing. One day he caught a cold. A drip from his nose fell into a petri dish in his lab. He noticed the nasal slime killed some of the bacteria in the petri dish. Fleming isolated the active ingredient in the mucus and called it "Lysozyme." He discovered that this active ingredient was also present in human tears, and was part of the body's natural immunity system. But it was only strong enough to kill off less dangerous types of bacteria.

After seven more long years of searching for a cure for *staphylococcus,* one day a mold spore happened to blow in from an open window and land in one of Fleming's petri dishes which contained the deadly *staphylococcus* culture. Fleming noticed that whatever this mold spore was, it was strong enough to kill the bacteria in the petri dish. The mold spore was called *"penicillium notatum."* Suddenly, Fleming saw that the mold spore was like the drip from his nose. He saw that "this" was like "that" and with this he created the antibiotic penicillin.

What does the moment of epiphany feel like when you finally see a hidden likeness that was always there? Helen Keller was born deaf and blind. She could neither hear, nor speak, nor see. The only experience she had with the outside world was through the sense of touch and smell. One day, her instructor poured cool water over her hands and taught her how to spell the word "w-a-t-e-r" with her fingers. Many years later she said, "Suddenly, I felt a misty consciousness as if something forgotten—a thrill of returning thought."[111]

The power of combining two unrelated objects in our brains allows us to solve previously unsolvable problems with solutions that were always there. In fact, it is fair to say that all significant advances in the business world have been the result of cross-fertilization between different disciplines.

Michael Dell, a college student at the time, saw that computers were like pizzas. They could be made to order (and only when ordered), and the manufacturer didn't have to prebuild lots of computers and put them in store windows in hopes that someone would want them.

Bob Fabbio of Austin, Texas started a new business called White-Glove Health, which provides health care to patients at home or at work. Fabbio calls it "the Costco of Medical Care." The description is fitting, but the more compelling question is how Fabbio was *able to see* the hidden connection between the Costco business model and the medical industry. This analogy always existed, but no one ever saw it before. Why not?

Fabbio conceived of the idea after going through a five hour process of seeking medical care, and growing frustrated. He decided there had to be a better way to provide medical care. But how would he bring doctors into the homes of patients in an affordable manner?

Fabbio borrowed from the Costco model to come up with a low monthly membership that members pay whether they are sick or not. Then when they need a doctor, they make a simple phone call (or schedule online) and a nurse practitioner, or other appropriate medical provider is dispatched to the patient's home or place of work. If after the initial evaluation, the medical problem requires a specialist, the visiting medical professional simply refers the patient to a specialist.

WhiteGlove has found great success with large corporations who seek to provide low cost medical care to their employees and dependents. At last count, WhiteGlove has over 150 employers signed up and takes care of over 500,000 patients.

How many times have you waited and waited in your doctor's lobby only to receive a cursory fifteen minute evaluation and a large bill—but walked out without seeing a solution to the problem? Bob Fabbio saw that the medical care business model could be like Costco.

Red McCombs bought the highly unprofitable Minnesota Vikings franchise in 1998. The team had losing seasons in eight out of ten years before he bought it. He paid $240 million for the team. He had never owned a football franchise in his life. He had no experience, education or training in the professional football industry. I said to him, "Red, what on earth made you think you could turn around a pro football team that had lost money eight out of ten years in a row? You had no experience, education or training in that industry." He just looked at me blankly and said, "Well, anyone could see they weren't doing a very good job of it. So I figured I could do it better." Red proceeded to sell out every game, including the preseason games, in every season during the seven years he owned the team. The Vikings had winning seasons every year that Red owned the team. He finally sold the team in 2005 for $625 million making a sweet $385 million profit.

Given Red's lack of experience, education, and training in the professional football industry, his confidence in his ability to turn the team around borders on the delusional. Delusional, unless you know one additional fact. Many years before, while he was still an unknown used car salesman in Corpus Christi, Texas, he had bought a bankrupt minor league baseball team and turned it into a profitable one. Then he sold it for a $100,000 profit. It was more money that he had ever seen in his life. He had no education, experience, or training in owning a baseball team at that time either. Now, many years later, when he was considering buying the Minnesota Vikings, Red could see that "this" was like "that."

If Red had asked anyone's advice, any logical person would have told him that owning a minor league baseball team that no one has ever heard of was drastically different than owning the Minnesota Vikings. The neocortex has a hard time combining two unrelated concepts because it is the "gatekeeper" that only allows things that make sense to enter. But the ability to see hidden connections comes from the ability to imagine things that do not exist as though they do exist. It comes from fusing two dissimilar things into one with the eye of the brain.

The power of hidden connections is very liberating once you grasp the magnitude of it. The beauty of this concept is that you don't have to singularly create something that never existed before. Remember, Einstein didn't discover the concepts of energy, mass or the speed of light. Rockefeller didn't discover oil or the oil refining process. Vanderbilt did not invent the steam engine or railroads. J.P. Morgan did not invent investment banking. Carnegie didn't discover how to turn iron ore into steel. Henry Ford didn't invent the combustible engine, the automobile, or the assembly line. Neither IBM, Bill Gates, nor Michael Dell invented the computer. Ray Kroc did not invent hamburgers or french fries. Colonel Sanders did not invent fried chicken. Howard Schultz did not invent espresso or the warm cozy coffee shop. Sam Walton did not invent the concept of discount retail stores. Red McCombs did not invent the used car industry, or the professional football industry. Neither Google, nor Yahoo, nor AOL, invented the internet. Mark Zuckerberg didn't invent social networking. Orrin Woodward didn't invent the concept of multi-level marketing. Steve Jobs did not invent the cell phone, digital music, or pocket-held music players.

These people only added to the base of available knowledge and found creative ways to connect previously known technologies and concepts in a new and different way. If they can do it, so can you. Remember, there are ideas all around you—waiting to be plucked out of the air. Everything you need to create something new already exists somewhere near you, and it's closer than you think. Discovery is the sudden conscious awareness of a hidden connection that was always there.

✳

THINGS TO PONDER

+ The more you can see that "this" is like "that," the more creative solutions you will see. But you must consciously, deliberately create those analogies.

+ Once you see the "tool in the bush," you will never look at the world in the same way again. Your *world-processor* has been permanently shifted.

+ Keep the shape of the problem in your head until you stumble across a key that fits.

+ The art of seeing hidden connections is the essence of entrepreneurship and innovation.

+ Creativity is not the act of creating something that never existed. It is the act of connecting the dots in new and different ways.

✳

CHAPTER 16

Is It Okay to Wander
While You Wonder?

Albert Einstein's obsessive dedication to his work is well known. He would often work for days on end without sleep until he collapsed. On one particular occasion, Einstein had been conducting intense mathematical exercises for months with very little rest, and he was exhausted. He finally gave himself a break and let his imagination wander. Various images began to float into his mind. Then it occurred to him—if two bolts of lightning struck the front and back of a moving train at the same time, would an observer standing next to the train and an observer standing on the moving train see the strikes as though they were simultaneous? The answer was—no. In an instant, Einstein's mind exploded with ideas and he quickly wrote down the ingenious theory of relativity. With that single idea, Einstein turned our perceptions of space and time inside out.

Einstein says of this moment, "After seven years of reflection in vain the solution came to me suddenly with the thought that our concepts and laws of space and time can only claim validity insofar as they stand in a clear relation to our experience, and that experience could very well lead to the alteration of these concepts and laws."[112]

Some of history's greatest discoveries and inventions were the result of intense periods of obsessive concentration on work followed by a period of exhaustion and then rest. The historical record is filled with many examples of how, during periods of rest, scientists were guided by spontaneous intuitions, unconscious flashes of light and sudden leaps of imagination which they themselves were at a loss to explain.

Before Otto Loewi, the scientific community believed that our ability to control our muscle movements was due to an electrical impulse from the nerve endings to the muscles. But there were inconsistencies and problems with this theory. After studying this problem for seventeen years, one night Loewi was awakened in the middle of the night with a new hypothesis suggesting that muscle movement was actually caused by organically created chemicals, not electrical impulses. He had dreamed of an experiment involving the hearts of two frogs. He quickly sat up and scribbled down some notes and fell back asleep. But the next day he couldn't read his notes. He struggled all day to try to recall what his dream had been during the night, but to no avail. The next night, he had the same dream and woke up again. This time, he stayed awake and went immediately to his lab to conduct the experiment in the middle of the night. The experiment worked and proved that the nerves actually emit biologically generated chemicals through the *vagus* nerve that has a stimulating effect on the muscles.[113]

Loewi concluded that neurons communicate with each other by the transmission of chemicals across a small gap called the *synapse*. He called these chemicals called *neurotransmitters*. These neurotransmitters float across the synapse where they are accepted by the next neuron at a specialized site called a *receptor*. Twenty five years after his discovery, Loewi later published a report in which he stated, "If carefully considered in the daytime, I would undoubtedly have rejected the kind of experiment I performed."[114] For this discovery, Lowei was awarded the Nobel Prize in medicine.

The irony is that while we exalt the neocortex as the part of our brain that separates us from the animals and gives us the ability to reason, to form words, and to solve problems, it is while the neocortex is in a state of rest that we come up with our best ideas. It is during this period that raw facts and data incubate and merge in an almost irrational way to form the final solution.

Arthur Koestler put it this way:

A branch of knowledge which operates predominantly with abstract symbols, whose entire rationale and credo are objectivity, verifiability, logically, turns out to be dependent on mental processes which are subjective, irrational, and verifiable only after the fact.[115]

The truth is often hidden in paradoxes that cannot be solved by logical reasoning.

The manner in which Samuel Taylor Coleridge came up with his most famous poem about Kubla Khan is well known. One day while he was under the influence of opium, which he took to cure dysentery, he was reading a very plain vanilla passage from a book called *Purcha's Pilgrimage*. He kept slipping in and out of a deep sleep in which he actually saw an incredible palace with colors and details so vivid he felt like he was there. Coleridge says he did not so much compose the poem as merely describe what he saw. I would be remiss if I did not offer you a taste of this delicious poem for your own enjoyment:

> In Xanadu did Kubla Khan
> A stately pleasure-dome decree:
> Where Alph, the sacred river, ran
> Through caverns measureless to man
> Down to a sunless sea.
>
> So twice five miles of fertile ground
> With walls and towers were girdled round:
> And there were gardens bright with sinuous rills,
> Where blossomed many an incense-bearing tree;
> And here were forests ancient as the hills,
> Enfolding sunny spots of greenery.

The poem continues on for 54 lines, and has found its place in history as one of the most beautiful poems ever composed. Whether Coleridge could have composed this same poem in a fully awake and rational state, the world will never know. But the fact remains that he wrote it in a half-asleep state while under the influence of opium.

"The intuitive mind is a sacred gift and the rational mind is a faithful servant. We have created a society that honors the servant and has forgotten the gift."

—Albert Einstein

You read in the previous chapter how German chemist Friedrich August Kekule, discovered the round shape of the benzene ring because he was able to see that "this" was like "that." But now you get to hear the rest of the story. This awakening happened while he was taking a nap after working in the lab for hours on end. Benzene is a natural constituent of crude oil, but it is usually synthesized from other compounds present in petroleum. For many years, the formula of benzene (C_6H_6) mystified scientists who could not figure out its structure. After many years of studying the nature of carbon-carbon bonds, Kekule fell asleep and had a dream. In his dream, Kekule saw an image of a snake swallowing its own tail. This was the break he needed. He had seen the ring-like shape, which enabled him to finally solve the problem of how carbon atoms could bond to up to four other atoms at the same time. This break allowed for the development of a process for commercially producing benzene.

```
                          H                        H
                          |                        |
  H   H   H   H   H      H H-C-H H   H        H  H-C-H  H
  |   |   |   |   |      |   |   |   |        |    |    |
H-C—C—C—C—C-H    H-C—C—C—C-H  H-C—C—C-H
  |   |   |   |   |      |   |   |   |        |    |    |
  H   H   H   H   H      H   H   H   H        H  H-C-H  H
                                                    |
                                                    H
```

By unfolding the mysteries of the benzene molecule, Kekule made it possible for humans to create plastics, high octane gasoline, synthetic rubber, textile fabrics such as Dacron, synthetic detergents, aspirin, and many dyes used to make the colorful clothes you wear.[116]

Genius often appeared in the twilight peripheries of awareness.

—Arthur Koestler[117]

While Professor Don Newman was teaching at the Massachusetts Institute of Technology, he was struggling with a particular math problem, which he could not solve. "I was . . . trying to get somewhere with it, and I couldn't, and I couldn't, and I couldn't," he says. One night while he went to bed thinking about the problem, Nobel Laureate John Nash (who was still living) appeared to him in a dream. In his dream, Newman asked Nash to help him solve the problem. To his complete surprise, Nash helped him solve it. When he awoke, he had the answer. He published his findings in a mathematics journal, and included a footnote thanking Nash. A year later, Nash recalled that Newman was forever gracious and thankful to Nash every time he saw him at conferences—as though the real Nash had actually helped him solve the problem.

Dmitri Mendeleev came up with his form of the periodic table while dreaming. Engineer Paul Horowitz came up with his design for laser telescope controls while dreaming. Alan Huang also came up with his design for laser computing while dreaming. Mary Shelly dreamed up the storyline and the characters for *Frankenstein* while sound asleep. Robert Louis Stevenson came up with *Dr. Jekyll and Mr. Hyde* the same way. Some of Ludwig van Beethoven greatest sonatas came to him while dreaming. Incredibly, he was hearing music that did not exist being played on instruments that did not exist. The piano had not yet been invented. His incredibly vivid dreams are what gave him the ability to compose his Ninth Symphony after he went completely deaf.

Paul McCartney dreamed the entire melody and words to the song "Yesterday" and quickly woke up and wrote them down word for word just as he had heard them. The song was so real to him that he diligently asked everyone he knew in the music business if they had heard it before. He did not want to be accused of plagiarism. Mahatma Gandhi came up with the idea of peaceful resistance to protest British rule in India while dreaming. Architect Solange Faiao's design for the Museum of Ocean and Surf in France came to him in a dream.

During World War II, German V-1 "buzz bombs" were obliterating England. The British only had manual and mechanical anti-aircraft guns, which were slow and highly inaccurate. In 1944, an engineer named David B. Parkinson was working for Bell Labs. He was developing a device that would electronically control the high speed variations of rapidly moving pens with great accuracy for the purpose of recording voltages on a strip of paper. He called it a potentiometer.

One night, he had a dream in which he saw himself in England standing near an anti-aircraft gun, which was being operated by some British soldiers. He watched as they shot down German planes. Every shot they fired nailed a German plane with 100% accuracy. "After three or four shots, one of the men in the crew smiled at me and beckoned me to come closer to the gun. When I drew near he pointed to the exposed end of the left trunnion. Mounted there was the control potentiometer of my level recorder. There was no mistaking it. It was the identical item."[118]

The next day, Parkinson pondered whether his device, which was successfully controlling the high speed gyrations of a rapidly moving pen with great accuracy, could do the same thing for an anti-aircraft gun. He proposed to Bell Labs the idea of installing his device into anti-aircraft guns to increase their accuracy. Bell Labs agreed to give it a try. The experiment was a success. They called the device an Electrical Director. The device used electrical circuits to make its calculations with great accuracy. All the operator has to do is point the telescope at the target. The device then uses ballistic tables to find the direction, speed, and elevation of the target, and calculates the exact speed and trajectory the missile needs to fly in order to hit the target. The device aims the missile, not at the plane, but where the plane is going to be. It then fires a missile that travels on a path that will converge with the path of the plane. The anti-aircraft gun was called the M9. But for the M9, the good people of London would be eating sauerkraut and drinking Riesling.

Even King David, the hero of the Old Testament, explained how ideas came to him at night: "I will praise the Lord who counsels me; even at night my heart instructs me."[119]

Leo Szilard was the Hungarian physicist who came up with the method and the means to use the neutrons released from one splitting atom to split other atoms in order to form a chain reaction. He said the idea occurred to him not while laboriously conducting experiments in his lab, but while crossing the street in London. He had been struggling with this problem for several weeks after having read a report by another noted physicist Ernest Rutherford explaining that this was not possible. Szilard's discovery is what led to nuclear fission, nuclear bombs, and nuclear reactors.

Biochemist Kary Mullis came up with a way to amplify a single copy of a piece of DNA across several orders of magnitude, generating thousands to millions of copies of a particular DNA sequence. The method he came up with is called the polymerase chain reaction (PCR) and is used in molecular biology for cloning and all kinds of genetic research into the causes of various diseases. Mullis said the idea came to him while driving on California Highway 128 from Berkeley to Mendocino where he had a weekend cabin in the woods. In an interview, he said, "That's when I did most of my thinking . . . because my day-to-day life at the lab doesn't allow a lot of time."

Nobel Laureate Orhan Pamuk credits daydreaming for giving birth to one of his greatest novels—*Snow*. In his acceptance speech, he explained his writing process as follows:

> I long for inspiration to come to me in dramatic ways, preferable in scenes and situations that might sit well in a novel. If I wait patiently and attentively, my dream comes true. To write a novel is to be open to these desires, winds and inspirations, and also to the dark recesses of our minds and their moment of mist and stillness. For what is a novel but a story that fills its sails with these winds, that answers and builds upon inspirations that blow in from unknown quarters, and seizes upon all the daydreams we've invented for our diversion, bringing them together into a meaningful whole?

A more poetic description of the creative process has not been written.

Melvin Calvin was awarded the Nobel Prize in Chemistry in 1961 for discovering photosynthesis. He arrived at the puzzling solution to how plants generate oxygen while sitting in his car waiting for his wife. He had conducted years of study when the solution suddenly came to him. He explains as follows:

> I was waiting, sitting at the wheel, probably parked in the red zone, when the recognition of the missing compound occurred. It occurred just like that—quite suddenly—and suddenly, also in the matter of seconds, the cycle character of the path of carbon became apparent to me . . . in a matter of 30 seconds. So there is such a thing as inspiration, I suppose, but one has to be ready for it.[120]

Sir Walter Scott said, "The half hour between waking and rising has all my life proved propitious to any task which was exercising my invention . . . It was always when I first opened my eyes that the desired ideas thronged upon me."

James Brindly, the famous canal engineer from the 17th century, reports that when faced with a difficult engineering problem, he would go to bed for several days until he solved the problem. The famous mathematician and philosopher René Descartes reports that those times when he was sick and was forced to stay in bed were the primary source of his philosophy and mathematics. Famous French mathematician Jules Henri Poincaré reported that he often had flashes of insight in the middle of the night that helped him solve various math problems. Walter B. Cannon, who discovered adrenalin and coined the phrase "fight or flight," admits that he often woke up in the middle of the night with insights that led to brilliant solutions.

> *I am accustomed to sleep and in my dreams to imagine*
> *the same things that lunatics imagine when awake.*
> —RENÉ DESCARTES

Leonardo da Vinci said, "I have the advantage of experience, when you are in bed in the darkness, in going over in the imagination the outlines of forms already studied or other noteworthy objects conceived by ingenious thought; this is a recommendable practice and useful in fixing things in the memory."[121]

Leonardo da Vinci was often criticized for sometimes taking too long, sometimes years, to finish a painting. On one occasion, he responded as follows: "It is at the moment that they are working the least that higher minds achieve the most; they are then mentally in search of the unprecedented and find the perfect form for the ideas, which they afterward express by tracing with their hands what they have conceived in their minds."[122] Only Leonardo da Vinci could have said this and gotten away with it. Geniuses are working most when they appear to be working least.

Arthur Koestler describes sudden flashes of insight this way:

> Such intuitions give the appearance of miraculous flashes, or short-circuits of reasoning. In fact, they may be likened to an immersed chain, of which only the beginning and the end are visible above the surface of consciousness. The diver vanishes at one end of the chain and comes up at the other end, guided by invisible links.[123]

Neuroendochronoligist Ullrich Wagner of the University of Luebeck in Germany conducted studies to see how a short nap affected people's problem-solving skills. He gave the subjects several challenges that consisted of figuring out a series of number sequences. Then he gave them two rules of logic for solving the problem. But there was also a "hidden rule" for solving the problem that would work quickly if the subjects found it. The subjects worked at solving the problem and then were told to take a break. Some slept during the break, others did not. The people that slept during the break found the hidden rule much more quickly and more consistently than those who did not. Wagner concluded that sudden insights and improved problem solving skills happen during sleep because it is during these resting states that new information is consolidated with knowledge that is already in the memory.

> *Saturate yourself through and through*
> *with your subject . . . and wait.*
>
> —LLOYD MORGAN

Neurologist Jeffrey Ellenbogen conducted research to determine why some people can see patterns better than others. The ability to recognize patterns is tied to what is called "relational memory." A group of behavioral scientists from Harvard University and McGill University presented students with several groups of random design patterns and asked to match those that were similar and then to rank them according to a hierarchy of which ones were the most distinct. The students were given a certain period of time. Then there was a waiting period after which they were tested. Students who were tested only twenty minutes after the observation period performed no better than if they had randomly guessed. Students who were tested after at least 12 hours were much more successful. Students who had slept during an even more extended rest period outperformed the other students by far. Neurologist Jeffrey Ellenbogen, who led the study, concluded that the process of binding memories together improves over time.

The further away we get from the problem, and the more we "sleep on it," the better our minds become at seeing the "big picture" and seeing the problems, the patterns and the solutions. That's why "cramming for an exam" never really worked in college.

It's almost like baking a cake. You must spend a certain amount of time gathering the ingredients, then mixing them, then pouring them into the pan. However, even after doing all that work, what you have is not a cake, but the raw ingredients for a cake sitting in an unrefined state. It looks like a soupy mess. Putting the cake pan full of ingredients into the oven and letting them bake causes the ingredients to merge together, to change composition, and change form until what magically appears is a mouth-watering, melt-in-your-mouth, cake. Without this incubation period, you only have raw ingredients.

Neurologists believe that during sleep, the neurons in your brain are actually generating new proteins and creating new neuropathways to allow the newly learned information to connect with things you already know.[124] When someone says, "let me sleep on it," it turns out that something very real is actually occurring at the neurological level. Neurologists call this process "consolidation of knowledge."

The metaphor most people use is "connecting the dots." Many people who have all the right ingredients for a solution never see the solution because they never put the cake in the oven and let it bake. Geniuses do.

Every now and then go away, have a little relaxation, for when you come back to your work your judgment will be surer; since to remain constantly at work will cause you to lose power of judgment . . . go some distance away because the work appears smaller and more of it can be taken in at a glance, and a lack of harmony or proportion is more readily seen.
—LEONARDO DA VINCI

Thus, it appears that the best way to solve a difficult problem is by engaging in intense periods of research (i.e. gathering the ingredients) and concentration followed by rest, then another period of intense research and concentration followed by rest, and so on.

Everything in the universe breathes. Everything expands and contracts according to its own cycle. There is a natural rise and fall in the expulsion of all energy. A burst of energy followed by rest. A period of abundance and prosperity is typically followed by a period of scarcity. We must exhale that which is bad for us so that we can inhale that which is good for us. Just as the universe breathes, we must allow our brain to breathe. Good things happen when we rest.

Neuroscientists have begun using positron-emission tomography (PET) scans to see which areas of the brain are the most active in dreaming. The part of the brain associated with visual imagery becomes much more active when we are dreaming than when we are awake. Moreover, the neocortex, which compels us to think rationally and logically, is much less active while we are dreaming.[125] This means that our thoughts are free to wander, liberated from the constraints of our rational brain at night and during periods of extended rest. There is less censorship during this time. There is less critiquing and judging going on. There is much less filtering of thoughts and ideas. Images that are illogical, irrational and nonsensical during the day time are now free to roam around unleashed. The vivid imagination of innovators, inventors, and entrepreneurs allows them to wander into the darkness with a small candle . . . of their own making.

So, now you have a good excuse. Take a power nap. Take a long drive for no reason. Get outside and see the sun for a change. Go for a long walk to nowhere. Go get an ice-cream cone or watch a funny movie. Go shoot some hoops. Go bounce on a trampoline. Shoot your buddy down the hall with a Nerf gun.[126] You deserve it, and the break you take might just allow the irrational part of your brain to see a hidden connection your rational brain could never see or accept. Purposeful wandering by people with obsessive drive is what changed the world.

THINGS TO PONDER

+ Saturate your brain fully with all the available knowledge of the problem and all possible solutions.

+ Then take a nap, or go for a long walk in the woods.

+ Your brain will do the rest.

+ Trust the process.

+ Purposeful wandering by people with obsessive drive is what changed the world.

CHAPTER 17

------------------------- ⫷⫸ -------------------------

Can You Think in 3-D?

I was recently in an all day workshop. It was the kind of workshop where each student sits in front of a laptop computer and clicks along with the instructor as he demonstrates what to do on a projector. Assistants were walking around making sure we were clicking on just the right spot. When we came back from lunch, the screen on my laptop was completely black. I clicked here and there and poked and prodded various keys. Nothing. I flagged down one of the assistants. She came over and clicked my mouse. Then she wiggled my mouse. She poked various keys individually. She held down the "ctrl" key in combination with various other keys. Nothing. Then she held down the "shift" key in combination with other keys. Still nothing. She stared at my blank screen completely baffled.

About that time, another assistant happened to walk by on the other side of my laptop and said, "Hey, did you know your power cord came unplugged?" Sure enough, the power cord was lying helplessly there on the floor. The only way the other assistant could have seen that my power cord was unplugged was if she were standing on the opposite side of my computer. She plugged it in and my computer came back to life. Problem solved.

In life, one of the reasons we get stuck is because we can only see one side of the problem at a time. We can stare at that side of the problem, and poke and prod it for days and still not see the solution. We find it difficult to walk around to the other side of the problem because it never occurs to us that there might be a different side to it. It never occurs to us that someone else's vantage point might actually be better than ours. We are like the proverbial blind man trying to describe an entire elephant based solely on the part of the elephant he is experiencing at that moment. We think the part represents the whole. It's all we *can know* because it's all we are experiencing in that moment. It consumes us.

Our limited point of view actually creates a preliminary problem that must be solved before the actual problem can be solved. But few of us ever recognize that this preliminary problem is a problem at all. Instead, we plunge headlong into the problem *as we see it*, and blindly poke and prod and waste precious time and brain cells, hoping a solution will present itself. It never occurs to us to walk around the problem. It never occurs to us to flip it over, to turn it on its side, to turn it on its head. It never occurs to us to dissect the problem and lay out the piece parts on the table. Why should we? We didn't ask for this problem? Here we were happily going about our business, when "plop"—this messy problem landed in our lap. We don't have time for this! We just want it to go away.

But legendary entrepreneurs are different. They instinctively look at all sides of the problem. They have the ability to hold opposite sides of the problem in their head at the same time. Even if the problem is intangible and purely conceptual, they paint a picture of it in their minds. They create a three dimensional object in their heads that represents the problem.

The greatest thinkers in history were visual thinkers. They always found a way to visualize even the most abstract of concepts and problems. Einstein's legendary theory of relativity came to him in the form of a simple picture of a man standing on a train traveling at the speed of light. A child could have drawn it. It was simple, elegant, brilliant, and it fundamentally shifted the way we look at time and space.

Most people are two dimensional thinkers. Their thoughts progress only in linear fashion. East and West. Left and right. Up and down. They see the world in terms of "in here" and "out there." The divide people between "us" and "them." They see only the "right way" and the "wrong way." Even people who claim to be very tolerant of divergent views, tend to see those views on a sliding scale—along the same linear path of "right" and "wrong."

When they discover new knowledge, they call it a "paradigm shift." But most often it is merely a slight modification or expansion of what they already knew. In reality, they have simply progressed a little further down the linear path they were already on.

Legendary entrepreneurs and innovators are different. Their thoughts are not linear. They are three dimensional. Their thoughts have shape and form. There are not just fifty shades of gray. There are trillions of possible shapes and sizes, and those shapes have color and light. Instead of seeing the world in black and white with shades of gray in between, they see the world in brilliant technicolor, constantly mixing, sometimes clashing, sometimes complimentary—similar to the Northern Lights. The colors and the shapes of their thoughts are always shifting, dancing, shimmering, illuminating the darkness.

In fact, quantum physics teaches us that time and space do not exist in a straight line or sequentially, but all together and in all directions at the same time. There is no "before" or "after." There is no "in here" and "out there."[127]

Norman Vincent Peale, who wrote the *Power of Positive Thinking*, and founded *Guideposts* magazine, was first and foremost a counselor. When someone came to him with a catastrophic problem, he had them visualize the problem as though it were a box made of cold, hard steel. At first, the box seemed impenetrable. But then he would ask his clients to touch the box, to feel the sides, the corners and the seams, to try to find a soft spot, a weakness in the joints. He taught his clients that somewhere in the impenetrable box, there was a soft spot.

He had them find that soft spot with their fingers. Then he would ask them to pry it open with their hands and some basic tools. Only when they were able to open the three dimensional box in their head would Peale allow them to start describing to him the details of the problem they were facing.

The greatest thinkers in history gave shape to their thoughts. Einstein only came up with the theory of relativity because he was willing to escape the dimensions of time and space as we know them.

Leonardo da Vinci, who is known as much for his futuristic inventions as for his art said, "You will never succeed if you do not have the universal power to represent by your art all the varieties of form present in nature—and indeed you will find this impossible unless you can first see them and hold them in your mind."[128] He was a visual thinker.

Leonardo da Vinci reduced his thoughts to pictures every chance he got. He always carried around with him a little notebook, and when he got an idea, he drew a picture of what he was thinking. Only rarely did he add a few words as commentary to his pictures. Then he flipped the objects he had drawn over so he could see the underside. Then he drew what he saw in his mind. He turned them on their sides. Then he drew it from that angle. He looked at them from *all* angles. He explains that it is important to visualize things "as if you were holding it in your hand and turning it over and over."[129] Then he dissected the object on paper and took it apart piece by piece to see what was on the inside. This is how brilliant innovators and entrepreneurs think. From his pictures, we can see that he was visualizing absurd three dimensional objects that did not yet exist. He drew flying machines, bicycles, machine guns, tanks, dams, exploding cannon balls, canals from Florence to the sea, solar energy, robotics, helicopters, parachutes, a scuba diving suit, a submarine, and many more futuristic inventions that were still a good five to six hundred years away from becoming a reality.

Leonardo da Vinci explained that the best way to understand a problem is to separate the parts from the whole and understand each part separately before moving to the whole. He says, "if you wish to gain knowledge of the forms of things, begin with the detail and only move from one detail to another when you have fixed the first firmly in your memory and become well acquainted with it." [130]

Nobel Prize winner Paul Ehrlich came up with the world's first diphtheria antitoxin when he visualized the toxins and anti-toxins fitting together like a lock and key. Ehrlich explained the power of visual thinking:

> Mine is a kind of visual three dimensional chemistry. Ben-
> zene rings and structural formulae disport themselves
> in space before my eyes. It is this faculty that has been of
> supreme value to me . . . Sometimes I am able to see things

recognized only much later by the disciples of systematic chemistry.[131]

Visual thinking allows us to escape the shores of verbal thought. When neuroscientists measured the brain wave activity of people in the act of creating something new, they found that the neocortex, the part of the brain that requires that things be logical and make sense, was much less active. They also found that the most active part of the brain during the creative process was the posterior brain region, which is responsible for visuospatial skills.[132]

Visual thinking comes from a much older and more primitive part of the brain. The human brain was thinking in pictures long before it was thinking in words. In fact, our earliest form of communication consisted entirely of pictures and symbols. This is how we communicated for thousands of years. These pictures and symbols, only turned into letters and words in the very recent past.

Evangelina G. Chrysikou, a professor who teaches cognitive neuroscience at the University of Kansas, explains that "Innovative ideas can arise from paying attention to the visual properties of things, such as their shape, size and material makeup."[133]

When the now famous entrepreneur Orrin Woodward was still an employee of General Motors in Flint, Michigan, he was handed a problem that no engineer at GM had been able to solve. They had been working on it for five years. The problem involved a tiny pump that moves gas from your gas tank to the engine where it can be used. It's a part of the car you never see. But when you turn your car at a sharp angle, the gas sloshes over to one side of the tank, and robs the pump of the ability to transfer gasoline to the engine. The engine chugs and stalls. The surface level solution was easy. Create a bucket within the gas tank that would always contain enough gas to feed the engine even during a turn. But this required the use of three separate pumps, which was cost prohibitive.

Woodward studied the problem night and day, informing himself of every aspect of the problem. He became so obsessed with it that he even dreamed about it. One morning, in the twilight moments between sleep and awake, he had a dream in which he saw a "pump within a pump." When I asked him for a further explanation, he said "I saw a three dimensional pump, and inside it was another pump. It was like I was hovering around it, and was able to move below and around the thing. I could see it from every angle. I could even see inside of it." Upon waking, he drew it out on a sheet of paper and refined it. Then he presented it to GM. They loved it, and it solved the problem no other engineer at GM had been able to solve.

I once asked serial entrepreneur Bob Fabbio a test question. I asked him to visualize a business problem he was facing in the form of a huge box. A box the size of Mount Everest. "Tell me how many sides of the problem you can see *at one time?*" I asked him. He paused at first and then said, "It depends. Do I have access to an airplane? Do I have remote access video cameras on the other side of the box? Do I have giant mirrors that I can strategically place on the other side of the box?" I laughed out loud and said "Bravo!" In my five years of research into the lives of brilliant entrepreneurs, I had discovered entrepreneurs and innovators who make history don't just look at one side of the problem. They look at *all sides* of the problem—at the same time. They instinctively know that the part does not represent the whole. They find a way to elevate themselves to see the problem from 30,000 feet up. They find a way to crawl underneath it and look at its roots. They find a way to get around to the other side of it, or at least to hire consultants from other industries, who are already on the other side of the problem. They know that it is almost impossible for the average human being to think outside of their own box, so they hire experts *from other industries* who are already outside the box.[134]

They find a way to dissect the problem. Then they describe the problem from every angle and give proper respect to each. They have the ability to hold, in one thought, opposing views of the same problem and have them both make sense.

On October 19, 1899, 17-year-old Robert H. Goddard had a vision while he was sitting in a cherry tree. The automobile was in its early stages of being conceived. The airplane had not yet been invented. It was at this point in history that he saw a rocket ship transporting humans into outer space. From that moment on, he devoted himself to the task of making it happen. He explains that moment as follows:

On this day I climbed a tall cherry tree at the back of the barn . . . and as I looked toward the fields at the east, I imagined how wonderful it would be to make some device which had even the *possibility* of ascending to Mars, and how it would look on a small scale, if sent up from the meadow at my feet. I have several photographs of the tree, taken since, with the little ladder I made to climb it, leaning against it.

It seemed to me then that a weight whirling around a horizontal shaft, moving more rapidly above than below, could furnish lift by virtue of the greater centrifugal force at the top of the path.

I was a different boy when I descended the tree from when I ascended. Existence at last seemed very purposive.[135]

Goddard had found a way to create an absurd three dimensional object that did not exist to represent the conceptual problem with which he was dealing. For many years, the press ridiculed him for his ideas promoting space flight. But, years later, he built the world's first liquid fueled rocket, which he launched on March 16, 1926. Every year for the rest of his life, on October 19th, he climbed that same tree and relived that moment.

Do you have the ability to give shape to your thoughts? Can you concoct a totally absurd three dimensional object to represent the problem you are facing and then pry it open, dissect it, turn it on its side, turn it upside down, and look at it from all angles? If you do, you just might be able to see the solution that was right in front of you the whole time.

✳
THINGS TO PONDER

+ The part of the problem you are experiencing right now is never the whole problem. The part does not represent the whole.

+ Learn to think in 3-D.

+ When you learn to give shape to the problem, you will find yourself giving shape to the solution.

✳

CHAPTER 18

—«««◆»»»—

Are You Blinded By Logic?

From the very beginning of our education, we are taught that all things must be consistent in order to make sense. The famous federal court judge Oliver Wendell Holmes put it this way: "People who honestly mean to be true contradict themselves much less than those who try to be consistent."

However, it turns out that nature itself is not consistent at all. It is well known among quantum physicists that light is both a particle and a wave—at the same time. Moreover, it turns out that everything has within it the seeds of its opposite. Every atom has within it both a positive and a negative charge. Every man has within his body a very small bit of estrogen. Every woman has within her being a tiny bit of testosterone. That's the natural state of our being. It's the way we are. Water has oxygen in it. Air has moisture in it.

A foolish consistency is the hobgoblin of little minds.

—RALPH WALDO EMERSON

Greek philosopher Heraclitus was the first to publicly declare that all pairs of opposites formed a unity. Even Isaac Newton recognized the unity of opposites in his Third Law of Physics, which states, "For every force, there is an equal and opposite force." Even at the quantum level, physicists discovered that every particle inside an atom has an equal and opposite anti-particle.[136]

Moreover, as early as the 1800s scientists discovered that electricity and magnetism are different forms of the same energy.[137] If you run electricity through a wire, the wire becomes a magnet. If you spin a magnet near a loop of wire, it will send electricity through the wire.

According to the laws of electromagnetism, like forces repel each other. Opposite forces attract each other. That's the only reason your flashlight works. The electrons from the negative end of the battery are always seeking the positive end.[138] They seek completeness. They seek to become one.

In fact, for every atom in the universe, the negatively charged electron is always seeking the positively charged nucleus. The more you try to separate them the stronger the bond becomes.[139] Without this bond, without this balance, there would be nothing holding the universe together. The Daoists call it *yin* and *yang*. Quantum physics confirms that each part contains the whole and the whole contains each part.[140] We can easily see this in nature. Every seed of a pine tree contains a whole forest, and every forest contains trillions of seeds. That's what allows entrepreneurs like Ray Kroc to see a trillion cheese burgers in one hamburger patty, and Howard Schultz to see an entire chain of Starbucks coffee shops in a single coffee bean.

> *I ask you to look both ways. For the road to a knowledge of the stars leads through the atom; and important knowledge of the atom has been reached through the stars.*
>
> —SIR ARTHUR EDDINGTON

Poets, philosophers and spiritual gurus have known this for a very long time, and have been trying to share it with anyone who would listen.

> *To see a world in a grain of sand,*
> *and a heaven in a wild flower,*
> *hold infinity in the palm of your hand,*
> *and eternity in an hour.*
>
> —WILLIAM BLAKE

In molecular biology, Louis Pasteur discovered that many living organisms are made up of right and left handed molecules. They look like mirror images of each other. This phenomenon is known as *chirality.* Amino acids and sugars are made up of chiral molecules. Spearmint leaves and caraway seeds also have chiral molecules. Our olfactory receptors in the brain also have chiral molecules. This is *yin* and *yang* at the molecular level.

The greatest thinkers in history were those who were able to hold inconsistent thoughts, feelings, and ideas in their head at one time and have them both make sense. Leonardo da Vinci's writings reveal that he believed that science is an art and art is a science.

Leonardo da Vinci once sketched a picture of two men facing away from each other, but joined at the chest. One of the men is old and is holding the branch of an oak in one hand and flames in the other. The other is young and handsome and is holding a reed in one hand and some gold coins in the other, which he is letting fall carelessly to the ground. They represent Pain and Pleasure. We know this because Leonardo provided the following caption:

> Pleasure and Pain are shown as if they were twins, joined together, for one never comes without the other; and they are turning their backs on each other because they are opposed to each other. If you choose Pleasure, know that behind him is someone who will bring you nothing but tribulation and repentance. Such are Pleasure and Pain ... They are represented back to back, as if opposed to each other, but springing forth from a common trunk because they have one and the same foundation, for fatigue and pain are the foundation of pleasure, and lascivious pleasure the foundation of pain.[141]

With this commentary, and the drawing he created, Leonardo exquisitely captured the unity of opposites that philosophers and spiritual leaders have been aware of thousands of years.

But philosophers like Leonardo da Vinci were not alone. One of Einstein's biographers once said of him,

Einstein has such a faculty for embracing both sides of a contradiction that one would have to be of the same frame of mind to follow his thought, it is so peculiarly his own. The whole Relativity theory is as easy to follow as the path of a bat in the air at night.

—Jeremiah Joseph

Consider what the following great thinkers had to say about conflict and contradiction and opposites.

Do I contradict myself? Very well, then I contradict myself,
I am large, I contain multitudes.

—Walt Whitman

Contradiction is not a sign of falsity,
nor the lack of contradiction a sign of truth.

—Blaise Pascal

The well-bred contradict other people.
The wise contradict themselves.

—Oscar Wilde

I happen to feel that the degree of a person's intelligence is
directly reflected by the number of conflicting attitudes
she can bring to bear on the same topic.

—Lisa Alther

I believe that truth has only one face:
that of a violent contradiction.

—Georges Bataille

What an antithetical mind!—tenderness, roughness—
delicacy, coarseness—sentiment, sensuality—
soaring and groveling, dirt and deity—
all mixed up in that one compound of inspired clay!
—LORD BYRON

Let me never fall into the vulgar mistake of dreaming
that I am persecuted whenever I am contradicted.
—RALPH WALDO EMERSON

A warrior does not try to be coherent;
he has learned to live with his contradictions.
—PAULO COELHO

I would rather be right than consistent.
—WINSTON CHURCHILL

If you think about it, how many proverbs, maxims and guiding principles that you follow are self-contradictory. In his now famous book, *Maybe, Maybe Not*, Robert Fulghum gives the following examples:

- **Actions speak louder than words. | The pen is mightier than the sword.**
- **Look before you leap. | He who hesitates is lost.**
- **Many hands make light work. | Too many cooks spoil the broth.**
- **A silent man is a wise one. | A man without words is a man without thoughts.**
- **Beware of Greeks bearing gifts. | Don't look a gift horse in the mouth.**
- **Clothes make the man. | Don't judge a book by its cover. (or) All that glitters is not gold.**

- Nothing ventured, nothing gained. | Better safe than sorry.

- The bigger, the better. | The best things come in small packages.

- Absence makes the heart grow fonder. | Out of sight, out of mind.

- What will be, will be. | Life is what you make it.

- Cross your bridges when you come to them. | Forewarned is forearmed.

- What's good for the goose is good for the gander. | One man's meat is another man's poison.

- With age comes wisdom. | Out of the mouths of babes and sucklings come all wise sayings.

- The more, the merrier. | Two's company; three's a crowd.

- The best things in life are free. | You get what you pay for.

- It never rains, then it pours. | Lightning never strikes twice in the same place.

- Better to ask the way than to go astray. | Ask no questions and hear no lies.

- Never do evil, that good may come of it. | The end justifies the means.

- Variety is the spice of life. | Don't change horses in the middle of a stream.

- There is nothing permanent except change. | There is nothing new under the sun.

- Never too old to learn. | You can't teach an old dog new tricks.

- Everything comes to him who waits. | He who hesitates is lost.

If you think about it, such contradictions must exist in order for there to be balance in the universe. Even in the Bible, we see the unity of opposites. God is depicted as both a lion and a lamb. The "Alpha and the Omega." The "Beginning and the End." Jesus referred to himself as both the "Son of God" and the "Son of Man." He also said, "The first shall be last, and the last shall be first," and "If you would find life, you must lose it." He taught us to bless those who curse us and love those who hate us.

Some of the greatest accomplishments in history were born of conflicting thoughts and feelings both of which were driving the person at the same time. Leonardo da Vinci captures this type of moment perfectly when he describes how he came upon a rocky cave one day while walking in the country side:

> I shaded my frowning eyes to peer in. I leaned this way and that, trying to see if there was anything inside, despite the darkness that reigned there; after I had remained thus for a moment, two emotions suddenly awoke in me: fear and desire—fear of the dark, threatening cave, and desire to see if it contained some miraculous thing.[142]

Fear and desire. Desire and fear. These two raw and primal emotions seem inconsistent. Yet how many times have you felt them at the same time? Indeed, these two powerful emotions are what drove almost every great accomplishment in history.

Leaping Beyond the Reach of Logic Will Take You to New Shores You Have Not Yet Seen

Recently, while sitting on the beach in Costa Rica watching the sun go down, all at once I was taken back in time. I was a young man living in Italy in the 1400s, staring out at the vast expanse of ocean, wondering what lay beyond what I could not see. While I was sitting there, I was overwhelmed by those same two emotions—fear and desire. Fear because of the great sea creatures that lived in the ocean and what they would do to anyone who ventured out there. Fear that if I ventured out there, I might not ever return. Yet, desire to find out "what if?" Desire to see for myself if there was anything worthwhile out there. As I sat there wondering, the giant waves kept crashing with foamy rage against my desire. It seemed the ocean itself and the contrary winds were pushing against me, telling me to stay home. Besides,

I had no money and no ship to sail out there anyway. Even the seagulls, hovering around close to the wharf, seemed to be telling me to stay close to home where there was food.

And yet I knew that if I did not set sail, my entire world, my entire existence up to that point would forever remain as it has always been. Safe, secure, and boring. Indeed, all that I had is all that I ever *would have.* I refused to be satisfied.

And then it hit me. What kind of passion, what kind of desire, must have driven Christopher Columbus to beg King Ferdinand and Queen Isabella for fifteen years to invest millions of dollars in ships, weapons and manpower to fuel his unverified vision? His preposterous belief that he could find India by traveling in the opposite direction? What kind of burning desire did it take for one man to invest his time, his reputation, what little money he had, and indeed his very life just to see what lay beyond what he could see? Beyond the limits of logic and reason?

Yet this is what all great innovators, entrepreneurs, inventors, artists and scientists throughout the ages have done. They reach with their hearts and minds beyond that which they can see, touch, feel, hear and smell. Beyond what is logical and rational. Beyond what makes sense. Indeed it is because of this willingness to sail off beyond the bounds of reason that their vision often exceeds their sight, and their reach exceeds their grasp. That is the kind of person I long to be. That is the kind of person I mold myself after. In the end, you are going to lose your life anyway. Why not lose it in pursuit of a great cause that is greater than yourself?

Throughout history, geniuses, entrepreneurs, heroes and legends were able to see solutions that were invisible to others because they were willing to look beyond the bounds of logic and reason. They refused to be derailed by things that at first made no sense, and in fact, seemed contradictory and inconsistent.

It turns out that logic, common sense, consistency and order are all based on a model of the universe that is entirely too limited. We think everything has to make sense. But it doesn't. When we limit our model of the universe to only what makes sense, we become blinded to truths that are just beyond the ocean's horizon. When our old model runs into conflicting facts and observations, we become frustrated, confused, and sometimes disillusioned. We have too much invested in our old way to thinking to be told it was incorrect after all these years. Sometimes we become angry at, or even hostile to, the messenger. We have seen this error committed over and over throughout history, from the Catholic Church's hostility to Galileo to the medical community's hostility to Barry Marshall when he discovered that ulcers were caused by bacteria, not by stress.

These are what I call growing pains. We are being invited by the universe to adopt new models. Invited to grow. In order to get to the next level, we must acknowledge that our old models are merely approximations of reality, not reality itself. Do you have the ability to see beyond the bounds of logic and reason? Do you have the ability to hold in one thought two opposite concepts and have them both make sense?

> *When I thought I was learning to live, I was learning to die.*
>
> —LEONARDO DA VINCI

✳

THINGS TO PONDER

+ Logic, common sense, and consistency are all built on a model of the universe that is entirely too limiting.

+ Become a student of the impossible.

+ Can you hold two opposing concepts in your head at the same time and have them both make sense?

+ Do you have the ability to see beyond the limits of logic and reason?

+ Embrace contradiction.

+ Don't be encumbered by reality.

+ Always ask "What if?" and "Why not?"

✳

CHAPTER 19

Why Do Outsiders See More Solutions?

The historical record reveals that many of the biggest breakthroughs in technology and entrepreneurship came from people outside the industry. They weren't blinded by a set of rigid, industry-accepted beliefs and expectations that artificially defined what was possible and impossible.

Indeed, in the history of mankind, many of the most innovative ideas came from people with little or no education or training in the industry. As Dr. Morton A. Meyers, accurately points out, "A curved line viewed from one side is convex but viewed from the other side is concave."[143] The accuracy of one person's description of the curved line does not make the other person's description wrong.

But how do you get out of your own brain and see the problem from a totally different point of view? The phrase "think outside the box" has been so over-used, it has now lost all meaning. What we describe as "outside the box" thinking usually only amounts to getting outside of one corner of our box and moving to another corner of the same box. We call that a "paradigm shift" and pat ourselves on the back.

It is very difficult to get out of your own box—because the box is everything you know and believe about the world. Your "box" consists of a lifetime of experiences, education, beliefs, expectations, and training. How can you escape that?

Israeli scientific philosophers, Aharon Kantorovich and Yuval Ne'eman, have described the problem with "outside the box" thinking this way:

Since the scientist is in general imprisoned within the prevailing paradigm or world picture, he would not intentionally try to go beyond the boundaries of what is considered true or plausible. And even if he is aware of the limitations of the scientific world picture and desires to transcend it, he does not have a clue how to do it.[144]

In researching the role of serendipity in medical discoveries, Dr. Morton A. Meyers, explains that, "The overthrow of long-held but false concepts is initiated not by those at the top of their fields but rather by those at the fringes."[145]

Medical historian W.I.B. Beveridge, writes that, "[W]here knowledge is no longer growing and the field has been worked out, a revolutionary new approach is required and is more likely to come from the outsider. The skepticism with which the experts nearly always greet these revolutionary ideas confirms that the available knowledge has been a handicap."[146]

That is, in part, why so many revolutionary ideas, solutions, discoveries, inventions come from people who have very little, if any, experience, education, or training in the field which they ended up turning on its head. They don't have to try to "think outside the box." They are already "outside the box." They don't have to escape the limits of their own experiences, beliefs, education and training. In fact, this phenomenon is happening today with so much frequency that it is becoming almost passé.

Johannes Kepler was a theology student, not an astronomer. Yet he discovered the laws of planetary motion that govern all astronomy today.

Louis Pasteur was a chemist, not a doctor. Yet he discovered the connection between germs and disease.

George Eastman was a bank clerk who invented a small portable camera in his mother's kitchen, which became the Kodak empire.

Einstein was a clerk in the Swiss Patent Office when he came up with the theory of relativity at his kitchen table.

Alexander Graham Bell was a school teacher when he invented the telephone.

Mark Zuckerberg was a college student when he came up with Facebook.

Michael Dell was a college student when he revolutionized the computer industry by coming up with a new way to assemble and sell computers.

Michael Faraday was a chemist when he invented the world's first electric motor.

Nicolaus Copernicus was a priest when he concluded that the earth rotates around the sun, and not the other way around.

Galileo was trained in medicine. Yet he opened our eyes to the universe.

Antoine Lavoisier, the father of modern chemistry, was an accountant working for the *Feme General*, the French version of the IRS in pre-revolutionary France.

Gregor Mendel was a clergyman whose gardening experiments set the foundations of modern genetics.

Hans Christian Oersted was a schoolteacher when he discovered electromagnetism.

Samuel Morse was a painter when he invented Morse Code.

John Wesley Hyatt was a printer when he came up with the world's first recipe for making products from plastic.

The Wright Brothers were making bikes for a living when they invented the world's first successful motor powered flying aircraft.

Konstantin Tsiolkovsky was a Russian schoolteacher when he came up with a workable prototype for a rocket that would eventually take humans to the moon.

It was a mathematician named *Charles Babbage*, not an engineer, who invented the world's first working computer.

James Ritty was a tavern keeper when he invented the world's first mechanical cash register.

Louis Waterman was an insurance salesman when he invented the first leak-proof fountain pen.

Johan Vaaler was a patent clerk when he invented the paper clip.

John Pemperton was a pharmacist when he invented the formula for Coca Cola.

Jeff Bezos was working for a hedge fund management company when he came up with the idea for Amazon.com on a long road trip with his wife, and started the company in his garage.

Herb Kelleher was a business litigation attorney with absolutely no experience, education or training in the airline industry when he decided to start an airline called Southwest Airlines.

Chester Carlson invented the Xerox machine because he got tired of redrawing patent documents and drawings by hand.

Sara Blakely was selling fax machines door to door when she came up with a better pair of women's underwear called Spanx.

Coco Chanel was a part time hat decorator when she created her fashion and perfume empire.

Mary Kay Ash sold Stanley home appliances door to door when she came up with her own line of cosmetics.

Bette Claire McMurry was a secretary with a GED when she created Liquid Paper.

Thomas Edison was a teenage boy working as a transcriber of Morse code by hand when he invented the essential elements of what would become the phonograph.

Barry Marshall discovered that the cause of peptic ulcers was a bacteria previously unknown to science precisely because he was an outsider and was not constrained by the beliefs of the experts in the field. As Dr. Morton A. Meyers, explains, "Marshall was a youthful maverick, not bound by traditional theory and not professionally invested in a widely held set of beliefs. There is such a thing as being too much of an insider. Marshall viewed the problem with fresh eyes and was not constrained by the requirement to obtain approval or funding for his pursuits."[147] You can always tell if you're still thinking "inside the box" if no one is calling you crazy, or dismissing you as nuts.

> *You're only given one little spark of madness.*
> *You mustn't lose it.*
>
> —ROBIN WILLIAMS

Film producer Robert Rodriguez made his very first film with a borrowed video camera that he didn't know how to use. He raised $7,000 by volunteering for various clinical drug trials in Austin, Texas. He was only 23 years old. He was a one man film crew. The movie, *El Mariachi*, later won an award at the Sundance Film Festival. When he recently spoke to an audience of entrepreneurs at RISE in Austin, Texas, he said, "When you don't know anything about the industry, you don't know what *can't be* done." He also said, "Be careful when you make your to-do list. If you write down too many items, you will come to believe the obstacles are insurmountable and you'll never get started. When I started, I never knew what I was up against. I never knew what the obstacles were, and that was a huge advantage. The way I operate is—I simply go forward until I hit a wall. Then I back up and start over and hit it again, and again, until I get bloody. Then maybe I go around it, or under it, or over it."

When you don't know enough to know what *can't be done,* you also don't know the difference between what's "normal" and what's "absurd." It turns out this is a huge advantage.

> *There are no bad ideas. Just the ones that really really suck.*
>
> —ROY SPENCE
> Co-founder of GSD&M Ad Agency

THINGS TO PONDER

+ It is impossible to think outside of your own box. Go to someone who already lives outside of your box.

+ Don't be blinded by your own expertise.

+ Embrace absurdity.

———— ·⟪⟨◆⟩⟫· ————

CHAPTER 20

Can You See What You're Not Looking For?

One of the secrets of innovators and entrepreneurs throughout the ages is that they go out of their way to pay attention to their mistakes, random events, and things they weren't looking for. They themselves will tell you—*it is not a matter of intelligence*. It is a matter of being observant. While most people tend to ignore their mistakes and accidents, legendary innovators and entrepreneurs are different. They are fascinated by the ridiculous and the absurd because that's the stuff they find most interesting. That's usually where the biggest secrets are hidden.

Isaac Asimov once said, "The most exciting phrase to hear in science, the one that heralds new discoveries, is not 'Eureka'—but 'that's funny' . . . " Some of the greatest discoveries in history came from the aggressive pursuit of idle curiosity.

Charles Robert Richet received the Nobel Prize in Physiology in 1913 for his discoveries related to allergies and anaphylaxis. He had this to say about the importance of simply being observant.

> Let me tell you under what circumstances I observed this phenomenon for the first time. I may be permitted to enter into some details on its origin. You will see, as a matter of fact, that it is not at all the result of deep thinking, but of a simple observation, almost accidental; so that I have had no other merit than that of not refusing to see the facts which presented themselves before me, completely evident.[148]

Nobel Prize winner Alexander Fleming explained that if it had not been for his previous experience where a drip from his nose had fallen by accident into a petri dish where he was growing bacteria and killed it, he would not have made the connection seven years later with the random floating of a mold spore that fell into another petri dish and killed the much more dangerous *staphylococcus* bacteria. Fleming explains:

> But for the previous experience, I would have thrown the plate away, as many bacteriologists must have done before... It is also probable that some bacteriologists have noticed similar things ... but in the absence of any interest in naturally occurring antibacterial substances, the cultures have simply been discarded.[149]

Fleming's colleagues often teased him for having a clutter of so many petri dishes lying around. His workbench was often overcrowded with 40–50 petri dishes. While most researches would clean them out and throw them away after use, Fleming kept them around for weeks after his initial experiment was over. Then before cleaning them out, he would examine each one to see if anything interesting or unusual had happened. *Had Fleming been as tidy as his colleagues he might have never discovered penicillin.* Fleming saw what no one else saw primarily because he was messy, observant and he connected the dots.

Scientific historian Dr. Morton A. Meyers explains that "Opportunities for discovery present themselves every day, but not everyone is able to take advantage of them. Failure to follow puzzling observations and unexpected results of experiments has resulted in many missed opportunities."[150] In his research, Meyers discovered that many researchers before Alexander Fleming had observed the phenomenon of mold preventing bacteria from growing. Why was it that only Fleming recognized the *penicillium* mold could be turned into one of the most powerful antibiotics in the world? Meyers also found that several experts had observed bacterial colonies in the lining of the stomach before Barry Marshall, but had shrugged off their findings as inconclusive because it was well-known that it was stress, not bacteria, that caused ulcers.

> *One often finds what one is not looking for.*
>
> —ALEXANDER FLEMING

Hepatitis B kills more than 1.5 million people per year. It is more infectious than the virus that causes AIDS because it can live outside the body on a dry surface for a week. But for hundreds of years, scientists didn't know what it was or how it was transmitted. Throughout history and up through the beginning of World War II, it was simply known as "infectious jaundice." It attacks the liver. It causes a loss of appetite, vomiting, fatigue, and a vivid yellow color in the skin, and the whites of the eyes. Scientists had never actually seen the virus itself and weren't sure exactly where to look for it.

Baruch Blumberg was not an expert in hepatitis. Nor was he even looking for the hepatitis virus. He was conducting a simple study to determine whether people of different ethnic backgrounds show more susceptibility or resistance to various diseases. Blumberg stumbled upon a strange new antibody while studying a blood sample from a hemophiliac. Hemophiliacs often receive blood transfusions from various strangers from all over the globe. The blood of the hemophiliac had developed this strange antibody when it came in contact with the infected blood of an Australian aborigine.

It was in the process of conducting hundreds of more tests to determine the source of the infection that Blumberg stumbled upon the Hepatitis B virus and isolated it. But when Blumberg tried to publish his paper explaining the identity and source of the virus, the established "experts" in the industry rejected it and were hostile to it. Blumberg explained that "We found the hepatitis virus while we were looking at quite different things. We were outsiders not known to the main body of hepatitis investigators, some of whom had been pursuing their field of interest for decades."[151] Blumberg found what he was not looking for because he was observant. Many years after the "experts" acknowledged that his discovery was legitimate, Blumberg responded to the naysayers as follows, "In research, it is often essential to spot the exceptions to the rule—those cases that do not fit what you perceive as the emerging picture . . . Frequently the most interesting findings grow out of the chance or unanticipated results."[152]

Legendary innovators and entrepreneurs don't focus solely on evidence that supports their beliefs and theories. They look for the exceptions, and then ask *why*. The most interesting results are often the ones we're *not looking for*. It is then that we find the answers to questions we *did not ask*.

> *The history of thought knows many barren truths*
> *and fertile errors.*[153]
>
> —ARTHUR KOESTLER

Harvard University awarded Norbert Wiener a Ph.D. in 1912, when he was merely 17 years old, for a dissertation on mathematical logic. Many years later, Weiner went on to explain, "Every scientist must occasionally turn around and ask not merely, 'How can I solve this problem?' but 'Now that I have come to a result, what problem have I solved?' This use of reverse questions is of tremendous value precisely at the deepest parts of science."[154]

In 1916, John Hopkins Medical School assigned one of its young students, Jay McLean, the task of finding a natural bodily substance that would clot blood. Instead, he found the opposite—a blood thinner. He decided to call it *heparin*. It was the world's first effective clot buster. Forty-three years later, McLean wrote, "I had in mind, of course, no thought of an anticoagulant, but the experimental fact was before me."[155] His discovery has saved hundreds of thousands of lives over the last ninety-plus years.

> *Mistakes are the portal of discovery.*
>
> —JAMES JOYCE

In the late 1940s, Lawrence Craven was working as an ear, nose and throat doctor. He would often tell his patients to chew Aspergum to relieve their sore throats. After several years, he noticed a pattern. Those who chewed the most Aspergum tended to bleed more profusely. This led Craven to investigate what properties might be in Aspergum that might be preventing blood from clotting. In the course of his investigation, he discovered the aspirin in Aspergum caused a thinning of the blood. Today cardiologists world-wide agree that chewing one baby aspirin a day (81 mg) helps prevent heart attacks and strokes. It was not Craven's genius that led him to this discovery. It was the act of being observant. Nobel Prize winner Salvador Luria calls it "the chance observation falling on the receptive eye."[156]

J. H. Humphrey, a distinguished immunologist at the National Institute for Medical Research stated, "Most of [my experiments] that led to anything novel or interesting arose because of some unexpected or chance observation that I was fortunate in being able to follow up."[157]

> *Discovery consists of seeing what everybody has seen*
> *and thinking what nobody has thought.*[158]
>
> —ALBERT SZENT-GYORGYI

Several thousand years ago, Greek philosopher Heraclitus said, "Unless you expect the unexpected, you will never find truth." Winston Churchill observed that, "Men occasionally stumble across the truth, but most of them pick themselves up and hurry off as if nothing happened."

Richard Branson said, "I have always lived my life by thriving on opportunity and adventure. Some of the best ideas come out of the blue, and you just have to keep an open mind to see their virtue."[159]

In researching the role of serendipity in scientific discoveries, Dr. A. Morton Meyers said, "So the great secret of science is how much of what is sought is not actually found, and how much of what has been found was not specifically sought."[160]

In 1938, Walter Frederick Morrison and his girlfriend Lucile were having a picnic on the beach in Santa Monica, California. After they finished eating their pie, they began tossing the pie tin back and forth to each other. They noticed that they could toss it for long distances and that it would fly smoothly and perfectly without wobbling. Someone else on the beach saw them having fun and offered Morrison twenty-five cents for the pie tin. Morrison later recalled, "That got the wheels turning, because you could buy a pie pan for five cents, and if people on the beach were willing to pay a quarter for it, well there was a business." But Morrison was not destined to become an *instant* millionaire. World War II soon started and Morrison found himself in the Army. He was captured as a prisoner until the end of the war. During his imprisonment, Morrison kept visualizing the business that he would start with the pie tins if he survived the POW camp and came home. After the war ended, Morrison sketched a design for a flying disc which he called the Whirlo-Way. In 1948, Morrison and his business partner began producing the first plastic flying discs and selling them at fairs. Sales were brisk and he eventually sold the rights to the disc to Wham-O in 1957. Wham-O soon renamed the product the Frisbee after the Frisbie Pie Company that made the original pie pans.

Morrison developed one of the world's most beloved toys and became a millionaire because he was observant. Upon selling a pie tin for twenty five cents, he could have simply said "Wow, I just made five times my money! Cool!" and left it at that. But legendary innovators and entrepreneurs are different. He was very *observant* to what had just happened. He saw a tremendous business opportunity if he could simply duplicate that one sale millions of times over. But he had to be patient until the time was right.

René Antoine Ferchault de Reaumur was the entomologist who discovered that paper could be made from wood pulp by using chemicals—the same way that wasps built their nests. How many other people throughout history have seen and kicked around or peeled back the layers of an old abandoned wasps nest but never made the connection between what they held in their hand and paper? De Reaumur changed the history of paper by being observant and connecting the dots.

Natural rubber comes from a tree in the Amazon rain forest called the *Hevea Brasiliensis. Hevea* is the sap that bleeds from the tree when you cut it. Europeans could find no use for it for two hundred years because it becomes soft and sticky in the heat, and hard and brittle in the cold. Eventually, innovators found a way to make it useful by coating fabric with it to make rain coats and rubber boots. But the products still got soft and sticky in the heat and hard and brittle in the cold. Few people bought these products. In the early 1800s, Charles Goodyear was bound and determined to find a way to make rubber more durable and useful. He spent twenty years conducting experiments to make the rubber more resistant to heat and cold. His obsession with this mission would lead him to financial ruin and eventually to debtor's prison. He was ready to give up.

But one day, while he was experimenting with a mixture of sulfur and rubber, he accidentally allowed it to come in contact with a hot stove in his kitchen. To his utter amazement, the rubber did not melt! Instead, it kept its consistency, but only changed color. That night, he nailed a piece of the mixture outside the kitchen door in the intense cold. The next morning, he brought it in and discovered that it was still just as soft and supple as when he had put it out there the night before. By conducting further tests, Goodyear determined the perfect temperature for stabilizing the rubber mixture. He later applied for and was awarded a patent for the process he called *vulcanization* after the Roman god of fire Vulcan. By 1858, sales of rubber products from his vulcanization process reached five million dollars, and the automobile with its rubber tires had not yet been invented! Goodyear later admitted that he did not intentionally heat up the mixture to test it. It was purely an accident. Goodyear had solved the problem merely by being observant and receptive to the results of this accident.

In 1943, Richard James was a naval mechanical engineer stationed at the William Cramp and Sons shipyards in Philadelphia. He was assigned the task of developing springs that could support and stabilize sensitive instruments aboard ships in rough seas. One day, he accidentally knocked one of the springs from a shelf. Out of the corner of his eye he saw the spring "walk down" a stack of books to a tabletop and finally to the floor where it re-coiled itself and stood upright in a neat stack.

After experimenting with various types of metals to make sure the coil would "walk" every time, James brought the coil home where it was a big hit with his children and their friends. James' wife called the toy a *Slinky*.

James borrowed some money and had 400 Slinky units made by a local machine shop. He hand-wrapped each Slinky in yellow paper. In November 1945, James got permission to set up a board at a forty-five degree angle in the toy section of Gimbels department store in Philadelphia. Then he began "walking" the Slinky down the board. He sold all 400 units within ninety minutes.

To an ordinary person, the Slinky would have been a mistake, a failed attempt to create a spring that could support and stabilize sensitive instruments aboard ships. But what James saw out of the corner of his eye *awakened his inner eye* to the potential of this unique product. If you have ever played with a Slinky, you owe the pleasure of your experience to James' observant eye.

In 1951, Bette Claire McMurry was a single mother working as an executive secretary for W.W. Overton, the Chairman of the Board of the Texas Bank and Trust. Because she had dropped out of high school, she was going to night school to get her GED. She had just started using the brand new IBM electric typewriter. She noticed that whenever she made a mistake in her typing, the only way to correct the mistake was to use an eraser at the end of a pencil. But the eraser too often smeared her work and turned it into a mess.

One day while she was sitting at her desk, she saw some painters decorating a window for the Christmas holidays. She noticed that every time they made a mistake, they would take a white substance and smear it on the mistake and wipe it away. She wondered why this same thing could not be done with her typing mistakes. She went home and poured white tempera paint into a small bottle and took a watercolor brush along with the bottle to work to paint over her mistakes. Her boss never noticed. It was the perfect solution. Soon other secretaries began noticing what she was doing and asked if they could have some of the stuff. She began making big batches of the fluid in her kitchen with a simple blender, adding a tint to match the color of her office stationary. She began taping homemade labels on the bottles and called the stuff *Mistake Out.*

In 1956, she started the Mistake Out Company and kept mixing the fluid in her kitchen. She hired her son Michael and his friends to fill bottles for customers. Her business eventually grew to the point that it was distracting her from her daily tasks at work. Her boss fired her. It was the best thing that ever happened. Now she could devote all her time to her fledgling business.

She kept experimenting with the mixture until she achieved the perfect combination of paint and several other chemicals. The final product was renamed Liquid Paper in 1958. She also obtained a patent and a trademark that year. She offered to sell her business to IBM, but the company turned her down flat.

The Liquid Paper Company experienced explosive growth over the next ten years. By 1967, sales were in excess of one million units per year. In 1975, she opened a 35,000-square-foot manufacturing plant for Liquid Paper in Dallas. A year later, the company's net earnings were $1.5 million and product was being sold in 31 countries around the world. By 1979, the company had 200 employees and was making 25 million bottles of Liquid Paper per year. She ultimately sold the company to the Gillette Corporation for $47.5 million.

How did McMurry go from a single mother working on her GED to become a multimillionaire? By being observant and applying what she saw to a very simple but persistent problem that was universal among all secretaries worldwide.

Patsy Sherman was hired by 3M in 1952. Her team had been assigned the task of developing a new kind of rubber for jet aircraft fuel lines. One day, a lab assistant accidentally dropped a glass bottle that contained a batch of synthetic latex that Sherman had concocted. Some of the latex mixture spilled on the assistant's white canvas tennis shoe. The next day Sherman noticed that the area on the white tennis shoe was not dirty as the rest of the tennis shoe. She also noticed that she could not wash off the stuff that had fallen on the shoe. She immediately recognized the potential application of this synthetic latex to fabric in general. She coined the term *Scotchgard* and 3M began selling the product in 1956. Sherman wasn't trying to invent Scotchgard. She was trying to create fuel lines. Today, you owe your clean carpets, your clean running shoes, and the tents that keep you dry when it's raining to Patsy Sherman's power of observation.

French physiologist Claude Bernard said, "Experimental ideas are often born by chance, with the help of some casual observation. Nothing is more common, and this is really the simplest way of beginning a piece of scientific work."[161]

How many people throughout history have come from a hike in the woods with cockle burs in their socks and didn't think twice about it? In 1941, Swiss engineer, Georges de Mestral went hunting one day in the Alps. When he got home, he noticed that his socks were covered with cockle burs. Curious to know why, he examined one of the cockle burs under a microscope to discover that they had tiny hooks on the ends that allowed them to grab onto any sort of material that formed a loop. Typical clothing made from woven fabric made the perfect field of loops.

De Mestral spent the next fifteen years trying to figure out the perfect material from which he could create a synthetic version of what he experienced in nature. He settled on the recently invented Nylon as the best material because it does not rot, break down, or attract mold. He eventually discovered that when Nylon is heated on one end, it forms a natural hook. Then he found a way to weave Nylon thread into a series of loops in a separate piece of fabric. When the fabric with the hooks was pressed against the fabric with the loops, the two pieces naturally stuck together just like the cockle burs stuck to De Mestral's socks. In 1960, Velek, Ltd., acquired the exclusive right to market the product in North and South America under the name Velcro.

This revolutionary new fabric eventually changed how Marines put on their flak jackets, and how astronauts, scuba divers, and firemen put on their suits, and even how you put on your children's shoes. All because De Mestral paid close attention to what most people ignored.

Medical historian, Dr. Morton A. Meyers explains that, "Discovery requires serendipity. But serendipity is not a chance event alone. It is a process in which a chance event is seized upon by a creative person who chooses to pay attention to the event, unravel its mystery, and find a proper application for it."[162]

> *Be willing to stumble. When you stumble,*
> *you just might stumble upon something great.*
> —ROBERT RODRIGUEZ

Our institutions of higher learning teach our students that the way to make good grades is to memorize facts, charts, graphs, dates, formulas, business plans, and complex procedures. They teach us what to think, but not *how* to think. But no amount of rote knowledge can substitute for the simple of act of *being observant* to the results of unintentional discoveries, accidents, mishaps, and outright failures. Information does not equal inspiration. Knowledge does not equal intuition.

Serial entrepreneur Gary Hoover explains, "There's all these basic human needs and people are ignoring them because they're not sexy. You have to look at the mundane through new eyes. You have to look at the little stuff. You have to be obsessed with the mundane." Often when Hoover's students came to his office at the University of Texas, he would ask them, "Why are you here?" The typical answer was, "I want to be rich." "Wrong office. You need to speak to someone down the hall," was always Hoover's reply.

Large corporations put people on teams and assign them projects, appoint certified project managers and then dictate what they are *supposed to find*. However, in accepting the Nobel Prize in medicine, Alexander Fleming explained, "I was working on a subject having no relation to molds or antiseptics, and if I had been a member of a team engaged on this subject, it is likely that I would have had to neglect the accidental happening and work for the team with the result that penicillin would not then have been described and I would not be here today as a Nobel Laureate."[163] Fleming won the Nobel Prize precisely because he did not "stay on task." He was not a team player. He did not "play well with others." Instead, he allowed himself the luxury of following an irrelevant rabbit trail to its ultimate conclusion. It takes a special eye to see order in the disorder, to see the magic in the trash heap of discarded experiments and failed attempts.

Psychiatrist Nathan Kline once said, "If we were to eliminate from science all the great discoveries that had come about as the result of mistaken hypotheses or fluky experimental data, we would be lacking half of what we now know (or think we know)."

In order to open the eye of the brain to start seeing solutions that are invisible to others, we have to teach ourselves not to reject that which is absurd and outrageous. As the famous geneticist J.B.S. Haldane put it, "The world is not only stranger than we imagine, it is stranger than we can imagine."[164] The universe is as infinitely big as it is infinitely small. The inside of an atom is a mirror of what we see when we look to the heavens. Indeed, the universe of possibilities is so big and ever expanding that what is not possible is guaranteed to happen every now and then.

If history is any indication, the biggest innovations, inventions and discoveries in technology, medicine, genetics, business, and outer space of tomorrow will not come from the hallowed halls of our greatest universities or the "think tanks" of our wealthiest mega-corporations. They will come from the garages, kitchens, basements, and backyards of the renegades among us, those mavericks who defy convention, those who can look at the problem with a fresh pair of eyes precisely because they are unrestrained by tradition, and are free from the accepted beliefs of the industry. The reason? Entrepreneurs are willing to make all the mistakes necessary to get to the right answer. Some of those mistakes will yield solutions they weren't even looking for.

If you are in upper level management at a large corporation, or any corporation, and you come in contact with a renegade who is very good at what he or she does, but has difficulty following direction, take note. Bill Gates first boss, Dr. Edward Roberts, says Bill was "a very bright kid, but he was a constant headache at MITS. You couldn't reason with him. He did things his way or not at all."[165] Dr. Roberts invented the MITS Altair computer, the first personal computer, which appeared on the cover of Popular Electronics in January 1975. Bill Gates dropped out of Harvard to write the programming language that actually ran the machine. The product Gates created, Microsoft Basic, was the foundation of the entire Microsoft empire.

Ernst B. Chain, who won the Nobel Prize in Medicine for helping to turn the mold *penicillium* into the antibiotic penicillin, had this to say about those kind of people. "When they do appear, it is our job to recognize them and give them the opportunities to develop their talents, which is not an easy task, for they are bound to be lone wolves, awkward individualists, non-conformists, and they will not very well fit into any established organization."[166] What will you do when you encounter such a renegade on your team?

Some of science's greatest discoveries were the result of an intentional accident. Scientists solved one problem while trying to find a solution to another. Likewise, history's ancient astronomers stumbled upon nuggets of truth while trying to explain flawed theories. What's going on here? It seems that as long as we keep searching, keep turning over stones, keep looking behind bushes, we will keep discovering things we are not looking for.

The worst thing you can do is nothing. Do something. Anything. Even if it is wrong. Just take action designed to take you in the direction of your dreams. You will stumble and fall many times along the way. You will get lost. You will accidentally take the wrong path a time or two. It doesn't matter.

Start over. Keep searching.

You will turn over many stones before you find the diamond you are looking for. In fact, you may never find the diamond, but you may discover something you weren't looking for at all—and that something may change your life forever.

✳ THINGS TO PONDER

+ Some of the greatest discoveries in history came from the aggressive pursuit of idle curiosity.

+ Intentional Accident: The process of finding the solution to one problem while trying to fix another.

+ Can you see what you're *not* looking for?

+ Can you hear the answers to the questions you *did not ask*?

+ Pay attention to your mistakes and accidents.

+ Pay attention to other people's mistakes and accidents.

+ Unless you are open to the unexpected and the impossible, you will never find the whole truth.

+ The world is not only stranger than we think, it is stranger than we can imagine.

+ Pay attention to people that don't seem to fit in. Buy them a cup of coffee. When they leave to start a billion dollar company, they just might invite you to go with them.

✳

------------◆------------

CHAPTER 21

When Is it Okay to Be Addicted?

Harold Varmus won the Nobel Prize in medicine for his research in the genetic origins of cancer. In describing how obsessed he was with discovering the source and origins of cancer he actually described a sort of chemical dependency to the feeling he got at the moment of discovery. He said, "It's an addiction. It's a drug. It's a craving. I have to have it."[167]

The nuclear physicists who discovered a way to split the atom reported that it was their love for the research and the moment of discovery itself that compelled them forward for so many years. They never really thought of the practical applications or effects of their research.[168] The idea of nuclear power plants and bombs never really occurred to them. They were purists searching for a solution solely for the sake of discovery.

Ernst Chain and Howard Florey were the two biochemists who helped Alexander Fleming bring the all-powerful healing drug, penicillin, into the world. Chain was the first to admit, "That penicillin could have a practical use in medicine did not enter our minds when we started work on it." Florey added, "I don't think it ever crossed our minds about suffering humanity; this was simply an interesting scientific exercise."[169] They were in it for the joy of discovery.

We instinctively want more of that good feeling we get at the moment of discovery. Over the years, our knowledge has advanced to the point that we even know the exact chemical in our bodies that is responsible for that good feeling. It's called dopamine.

Dopamine is a chemical just like any other chemical, and it can become addicting. We not only want more, we want it *all the time*. Perhaps this is what drove early man out of their caves, even when they had all the food, water and shelter they needed. Early man began to explore solely for the sake of exploration, solely for that moment of discovery. We wanted better shelter, better clothes, better food, and better mating opportunities. Humans are the only species that will keep looking for more, for new, and for improved versions of what he already has even though what he has is perfectly satisfying his needs. Why? Because the quest itself is the reward.

This craving for new problems to solve, and new patterns to discover became a huge advantage. Perhaps the animals who followed their instinct to explore were rewarded with more food, a greater variety of nutrients, better sources of shelter, and therefore, a better chance for them and their descendants to survive.

Over the course of human development, we became like "Pavlov's dogs." The exploration of novelty became a self-rewarding activity. It is not so much the new "thing" itself that excites us. It is the *moment* of discovery, and even the *anticipation* of that moment that excites us. Scientists tell us that whether you are actually boarding the plane leaving for Maui, or just thinking about boarding the plane leaving for Maui, your body is flooding your system with dopamine. We also get a shot of dopamine at the moment we get a text message, an email or a letter from someone special—even before we open it to read the contents.[170]

Over several million years, discovery, adventure and raw curiosity were consistently rewarded and are now instinctive in us. In researching the role of curiosity in human evolution, scientists discovered that lab rats will cross an electrical grid and suffer the pain just to see what's on the other side even if no visible reward (like food or sex) is being offered.[171] If you give a mammal something to be curious about, it will pursue it even if the pursuit is dangerous—just to get that shot of dopamine.

Svanbte Paabo, Director of the Max Planck Institute for Evolutionary Anthropology in Leipzig, Germany puts it this way:

No other mammal moves around like we do. We jump borders. We push into new territory even when we have resources where we are. Other animals don't do this. Other humans either. Neanderthals were around hundreds of thousands of years, but they never spread around the world. In just 50,000 years we covered everything. There's a kind of madness to it. Sailing out into the ocean, you have no idea what's on the other side. And now we go to Mars. We never stop. Why?[172]

The answer is dopamine.

That shot of dopamine is also why we read novels and go to movies. We hate it when someone tells us the ending because it spoils the fun. The "fun" we don't want to spoil is that moment of discovery when you finally "get it." It's when the mystery is solved. It's when we figure out "who done it." It's when all the loose ends are finally tied down. When we finally know if the guy gets the girl. When we finally know whether the hero wins, and more importantly *how* he managed to snatch victory from defeat at the last possible moment. This moment of discovery is somehow comforting and satisfying to us. We beg our friends, "Tell me what the movie is about, but *please* don't tell me the ending."

That shot of dopamine which we get at the moment of resolution is also the reason why novels far outsell books that provide us primarily with factual information. Best-selling novelists excel at giving us puzzles that need to be worked out. They excel at "hiding the ball." They excel at keeping us guessing. They create an intense level of anticipation that makes us want to know what comes next. That's what keeps us turning pages.

That shot of dopamine is what made hundreds of millions of people all over the world sign up for Facebook. The number of Facebook subscribers is now greater than the population of some countries. Do you remember when you first created your Facebook account? Remember how addicted you were to it? Our natural curious nature drives us to want to know what our friends, neighbors, and relatives are doing. That curiosity is rewarded when we find out some juicy tidbit of information that we didn't know. Sometimes it's funny. Sometimes it's sad. Sometimes it's exciting. Sometimes it's just plain silly. It satisfies a craving. But it's not the information we seek. Most of the information is absolutely useless. It's that daily shot of dopamine. Some days we log on just to find out how many people "liked" our status, or to see how many "followers" we have.

Innovators and entrepreneurs are merely the next step in the process. Like the earliest *homo sapiens,* they are never satisfied with the way things are—even when they have everything they need. It is not a matter of greed. They are simply always asking the question *why,* and more importantly, they are constantly scanning the environment for something new. Anything, as long as it's new, and it presents a challenge. It is a matter of getting their dopamine fix by finding new problems to solve, by finding better ways to accomplish mundane tasks, and by creating ever more efficient tools.

> *I do not know what I may appear to the world; but to myself*
> *I seem to have been only like a boy, playing on the seashore,*
> *and diverting myself, now and then finding a smoother*
> *pebble or a prettier shell than ordinary, while the great*
> *ocean of truth lay all undiscovered before me.*
>
> —ISAAC NEWTON

The serial entrepreneurs I've interviewed all said the same thing. They don't start new businesses because they need the money or the fame. They do it because they love the thrill of creating something new, the thrill of achieving something no one else has achieved before, defying the odds just for the fun of it. They love finding new solutions to old problems. They love combining unrelated concepts in new and unique ways to create things no one has seen before. They love looking ahead and solving problems before anyone even knows it's a problem. They tell me that's what gets them up in the morning. This is their daily shot of dopamine.

Richard Branson, founder of Virgin Records and Virgin Airlines, has started over 300 businesses under the name The Virgin Group.

Red McCombs has owned approximately 250 businesses. He is now in his mid-eighties. He's already a billionaire. He doesn't need any more money. When I was wrapping up my third interview with him, I finally said, "Red, what are you most excited about these days. What gets you up in the morning?" For the first time during the interview, he sat up in his chair and his eyes lit up. "Formula One!" he said. "What? You mean you like to watch car racing on TV?" I asked. He shook his head. "No, Dan. I'm bringing the Formula One race to Texas. It will be the first time anyone has successfully created a *permanent home* for Formula One in the United States. Everyone else who's ever tried it has failed. There have been a few races here and there, but they all lost money and failed miserably. This is an exclusively European sport, and I want it here!" "Are you serious? But you don't have any experience, education or training in the racing industry," I said. "Why? Why now?" He leaned back in his chair, locked his hands behind his head, smiled a smile as big as Texas, and said, "Because it's never been done before."

I was blown away.[173] Why would a guy in his mid-eighties who has more money than most people dream of having in one lifetime decide to start this kind of herculean project? He should be laying on a beach in Fiji drinking Mai Tais. But that's not what entrepreneurs do. They live for that next challenge. That's what makes them most excited about life. That's what gets their dopamine flowing. When I left, I gave him a big hug, hoping some of his *mojo* would rub off on me.

Sir Richard Branson said, "I have always thrived on havoc and adrenaline;" and "I give free rein to my own instincts. First and foremost, any business proposal has to sound fun. My interest in life comes from setting myself huge, apparently unachievable, challenges and trying to rise above them. But 'fun' is a particularly loaded word for me—it's one of my prime business criteria."[174]

The planet Mercury does not follow a fixed elliptical orbit around the sun. The path it follows wobbles. In 1859, the French mathematician and astronomer Urbain Le Verrier reported that Mercury's strange behavior as it orbits around the Sun could not be completely explained by Newtonian mechanics. Astronomers suspected that there was another planet near Mercury whose gravity was causing the irregular movements. But no such planet could be found. Einstein studied this problem for years. When he came up with the general theory of relativity, he concluded that time and space are both stretched and warped by the size and density of nearby matter. This theory provided a new definition of gravity which created a fourth dimension called "space-time," which is not flat, it is curved. When Einstein applied the curvature of space-time to the orbit of Mercury, the calculations explained the orbit perfectly. Mercury's orbit wobbles because it is very close to the sun—in an area where space-time extremely curved. When he realized that he had solved the problem, he was so excited it gave him heart palpitations.[175] The moment of discovery is what he lived for.

When you find something you really love and you get good at it, it becomes addictive. Serial entrepreneurs happen to be good at starting new businesses solely for the purpose of solving new problems. When they do, they want to do it again. Just for the fun of it. That's the power of newness.

Humans crave newness more than the thing itself. How many toys and stuffed animals do your kids have that they no longer play with? More importantly, how many video games do you have that you no longer play with? Yet you will rush out to buy the latest greatest video game once it's released. The shot of dopamine we get from newness is also what compels people to become addicted to shopping. Jay Leno has approximately 120 sports cars and 33 motorcycles. Imelda Marcos owned 15 mink coats, 508 gowns, 1,000 handbags, and 2,700 pairs of shoes, many of which were still in the box and never opened.[176] It's all chemically driven. We are never really addicted to the tangible thing itself. We are only addicted to the chemical shift it creates in our brains. We are always and only addicted to our own chemicals.

One of the reasons legendary innovators and entrepreneurs can see things that most people cannot is because they look for things that others do not. They do not believe in working simply to pay their bills. They are looking for that next thrill, that next moment of discovery, that next moment of achieving something that's never been done before. They crave that next problem to solve. When they finally solve it, people dump truckloads of gold onto their front yards just to get a taste of that solution. But hard core innovators and entrepreneurs are never satisfied. They quickly move on, leaving the comfort and security of their gilded caves just to find a new problem to solve. They need their fix.

What about you? Are you looking for your next paycheck or that next shot of dopamine? Does solving problems excite you? Or do you dread dealing with problems? If solving problems does excite you, you just might be in a very exclusive club of innovators and entrepreneurs.

THINGS TO PONDER

* The thrill of discovery is its own reward.
* It's okay to become a dopamine addict.

CHAPTER 22

How Do You Get Off the Hamster Wheel?

O ver the course of twenty-five years as an attorney, I have found myself not just giving legal advice, but actually mentoring and coaching hundreds of young entrepreneurs who were starting businesses of every variety. They come to me to create the corporate structure, for licensing agreements, all kinds of compliance issues, and the like. They also ask me to help them resolve crises and restructure deals that were doomed to fail. After a while, I realized that I was no longer just giving legal advice. I was giving *business* advice. The reason? I could often see problems in their business models that they could not see. I could see the land mines hidden just beneath the surface, which they would not discover for several years. They were too close to the project to be objective. They couldn't see the "spinach" in their own teeth. I would go out of my way to make suggestions about marketing strategies, website content, how to improve their products and services, how to better brand their business, how to increase sales, how to improve color schemes, and logos, and how to stay out of trouble in the process.

Eventually, I came to see myself as more of a problem solver than an attorney. People I did not know began calling me and asking me to help them find solutions to their *business* problems. When it seemed like my clients had hit an impenetrable obstacle, I found myself taking a Zen approach. "In order to solve this problem, you have to become like water." After seeing that baffled look on their faces, I would add, "Water doesn't just seek *the* path of least resistance. It seeks *all* paths of least resistance—and at the same time. Plus, water doesn't always flow downhill. Sometimes it evaporates into thin air and rises above the problem and then descends safely on the other side of it. Sometimes, it will change form into a giant glacier and literally bulldoze the problem out of the way, moving giant boulders as though they were pea-gravel. It can level an entire mountain range and create a nice fertile valley where there was once only solid rock. Sometimes it slowly washes away the problem by pounding at its granite-like defenses with millions of gallons of water a day until it cuts a huge canyon right through the heart of it. So yes, if you want to overcome this obstacle and every obstacle you will ever face, you must become like water."

> *Empty your mind, be formless. Shapeless, like water. If you put water into a cup, it becomes the cup. You put water into a bottle and it becomes the bottle. You put it in a teapot it becomes the teapot. Now, water can flow or it can crash. Be water my friend.*
>
> —BRUCE LEE

Einstein once explained the difference between the way he solves problems and the way most people solve them. "When asked to find a needle in a haystack, most people simply look for the needle. I look for all possible needles."[177] Leonardo da Vinci had the same practice. Before focusing on any one possible solution, he would visualize all possible solutions.[178]

If you are looking for "the" solution to the problem you are facing, this may be part of the problem in and of itself. Without knowing it, you have *chosen to believe* that there is only one best solution to the problem. In so doing, you have already cut off hundreds, if not thousands, of other possible solutions. In addition, you have created in your mind a picture of what the perfect solution should look like—and that's the only solution you are actually looking for. Perhaps you've unwittingly chosen to believe that the solution can only come from a certain source or from a person with a certain set of credentials. This makes you blind to all other possible solutions and all other sources.

In truth, the solution you seek may not look at all like it's "supposed to look like." It may not even be where it is "supposed to be."

It is very difficult to rid yourself of all preconceived notions of what the solution is supposed to look like and where it is supposed to come from. But you can start by making a deliberate choice not to reject any possible solution no matter how absurd or ridiculous it may sound, and no matter how unlikely the source. Sometimes, the most creative and innovative thing you can do—is to stop. Stop everything you are doing and take inventory of your life. Is what you are doing truly taking you in the direction of your dreams, or just keeping you occupied as you make your way through this life? Are you focusing more on the arrow than on the target?

> *I thought I was like fire; I was wrong.*
> *I am like water.*
> *Water is powerful.*
> *It can wash away earth,*
> *put out fire,*
> *and even destroy iron.*
> *Water can carve through stone.*
> *And when trapped, water makes a new path.*
>
> —*Memoirs of a Geisha*

Unless you get off the hamster wheel, your brain cannot rest long enough to see what other possibilities are out there. Fueled by the expenditure of your own precious energy and time, your hamster wheel will keep turning and turning and taking you with it—on a path to nowhere—until your time, energy, and money run out. If your ship is sinking, or taking you nowhere, it may be time to abandon ship.

In the War of 1812, the United States was losing badly to the British. At the Battle of Lake Erie, Captain Oliver Hazard Perry was a 27-year-old young man whose assignment was to break the British stronghold in the Northwest. As he sailed his ship called the *Lawrence* into battle, the fellow American captain who was supposed to be at his side captaining the *Niagara* backed off. The British pounded the *Lawrence* mercilessly until it was badly crippled and had nothing left to give. Eighty-five percent of the sailors on the *Lawrence* were dead. But, the *Lawrence* bore a flag with the famous words "Don't give up the ship!" that had been uttered a few months earlier by Captain James Lawrence with his dying breath during a battle in the Boston Harbor.

The little known truth behind the story is that when Captain Perry's ship was of no more use to him, *he did abandon that ship.* He jumped aboard a small open boat and made his way under intense enemy fire to the *Niagara*, which was still unharmed. He persuaded the captain of the *Niagara* to give him control of the ship. The British ships had already been pounded in the battle with the *Lawrence*, and now they were facing the fresh and fully armed *Niagara*. It took only fifteen minutes of pounding by the *Niagara* for the British to surrender. Perry had defeated the British fleet and was now in control of all of Lake Erie. The hidden lesson behind the story: *sometimes the best way to reach your goal is, in fact, by giving up the ship you're on.* The very ship you spent most of your life building. The ship of which you are most proud. Sometimes, the best thing you can do is walk away from it and start over.

But wait. All your life you've heard people say "Don't quit! Keep going! Don't give up. Persistence pays off." In fact, in my first book,[179] I quoted Winston Churchill who said, "Never give up. Never. Never. Never!" But over the years, I have come to realize that persistence simply for the sake of being persistent is really a bad idea. You see, blind persistence is lunacy. Creative persistence is genius.

In fact, some of the most famous people and some of the best known companies in the world started out doing something totally different from what made them famous.

3M—Started out as a failed mining company. Then started selling sand paper; then wet sand paper, then masking tape; scotch tape, scotch guard, post it notes, etc.

IBM—Started out selling coffee grinders and scales for butcher shops.

Motorola—Started out repairing batteries.

Hewlett Packard—Started out making foul line indicators for bowling alleys.

Sony—Started out making an electric rice cooker that did not work.

Marriott—Started out as an A&W Root Beer Stand.

American Express—Started out as a parcel shipping company; then it sold money orders; then travelers checks; then finally credit cards.

DuPont—Started out making black powder for muskets and cannons.

Orville and Wilbur Wright—Started out printing a small weekly newspaper; then started manufacturing bicycles.

Andrew Carnegie—Started out as a "bobbin boy" and then became a messenger at a telegraph office.

Oprah Winfrey—Started out as a TV reporter.

Richard Branson—Founder of Virgin Records and Virgin Airlines—started out selling bootleg records.

Benjamin Franklin—Started out as a printer.

Why would these people and these companies stray so far from what they started out doing? They, like Captain Perry, saw that in order to best achieve their goals, they had to abandon the ship they were on and jump on a totally different ship.

These people succeeded because they became like water. They didn't just change careers. Anyone can do that. They changed their *way of being.* They realized that in order to solve an unsolvable problem, in order to finally find what they were looking for in life, they had to stop using the same old tools, strategies, and belief systems they had been using their entire lives. In short, they became a different person. They became the person they *had to become* in order to fulfill their wildest dreams. This requires more than just changing jobs, changing churches, or changing your daily affirmations. Don't get me wrong.

All of these things may be helpful. But standing alone, they are not enough because they are only surface level changes that never really change who you are on the inside. No, these people experienced a total and complete rebirth by making cataclysmic, life altering decisions designed to "shake the globe" of their life. Like water, they changed form in order to accomplish their goals. In doing so, they didn't just level the playing field. They created a whole new playing field . . . of their own design.

Like water, they did not merely seek *the path* of least resistance. They sought and followed *all paths* of least resistance—until they found the one that was the most efficient. There were many false starts and dead ends along the way. But each of them started with an undying, almost delusional, belief that they could not fail.

Stop for a moment and take stock of your life. Where have you been? Where are you now? If you continue doing what you are doing right now for the next ten years, where will you end up mentally, emotionally, financially?

Make a list of the things you are doing daily that are actually taking you in the direction of your dreams. Make a list of the things you are doing that are taking you off course. Then draw a line in the sand. Make a firm, undying commitment to do more of what's working, and less of what's not. Don't change what you are doing for a living. Change who you *are being* for a living.

THINGS TO PONDER

+ Blind persistence is lunacy. Creative persistence is genius.

+ Water doesn't seek "the" path of least resistance. It seeks "all" paths of least resistance—and at the same time.

+ Become like water.

+ The quickest distance between two points isn't always a straight line.

+ If the hamster wheel you are on is not taking you where you want to go, why are you still on it?

+ Are you focusing more on the arrow than on the target?

+ Sometimes the best way to win the battle is to abandon the ship you're on.

+ In a world that is constantly changing, the worst thing you can is stay where you are.

+ Don't just change what you are doing for a living. Change *who you are being* for a living.

CHAPTER 23

Can You Find the Seam in the Armor?

Many people are reluctant to try their hand at starting their own business because they think there's already too much competition in their field, or because they *believe* they don't have any ideas that are sufficiently unique or innovative to get anyone's attention. But you don't have to completely revolutionize an industry in order to make a comfortable living at it. All you have to do is find the seam in the armor. Can you see the hidden gems the corporate giants have overlooked, and then scoop them up? You don't really need to "stand on the shoulders of giants." All you need to do is walk between their legs.

You can't succeed in defeating a corporate giant by launching a full-scale frontal attack on the front door of the castle. You find the cracks between the bricks. You find the soft spots in the earth and tunnel underground. You chip away slowly at the edges. You start by picking up the leftovers. You start by serving the under-served, the people the corporate giants ignore. That's how Roy and Bert Sosa got started. That's how Sam Walton got started. His first stores were in the rural markets which had been ignored for years by the big corporate retailers.

All you need is a toehold in the market, out of which you can eventually grow your own mini-empire. Then, who knows how big it can grow.

Multi-Level Marketing

How many times have you been invited to a networking event or a luncheon only to find out it's really a pitch to join a multi-level marketing group? If you are like most people, you have been approached more times than you can count. Before you laugh at multi-level marketing, be aware that the historical record shows that this business model is not only legal, *it works*. Amway started in 1959 by Jan Van Andel and Richard DeVos and quickly became a multi-billion dollar company. Van Andel and DeVos did not invent the concept of multi-level marketing. They learned it from a company called Nutrilite. Imagine if you had been the first person to come up with the concept of multi-level marketing? How would your life be different today? Most people believe that there is no money to be made in multi-level marketing unless you were one of the founding partners at the top of the organization with a million people in your down-line. But the evidence shows otherwise.

Orrin Woodward was raised in the tiny town of Columbiaville, Michigan (population—785). He went to a local college and went to work for General Motors just like his father before him. By 1992 he was on the fast track at GM while getting his MBA for University of Michigan. He had hit many home runs with his designs as an engineer for General Motors and was promoted to Senior Engineer at 25 years old. But then one day, he was told that despite his success, he would not be promoted again for many years because the division of GM he worked for was downsizing and had to many staff engineers already. Orrin realized that he had hit a ceiling.

Around that same time, he had sold some of his baseball cards to a guy who happened to be with Amway. The guy told him he would give him his cards back if he came to one Amway meeting. Orrin went simply to get his cards back. He was much too smart to consider joining a multi-level-marketing program of any kind. But something he heard at the meeting stuck in his head. He went home and started listening to some CDs the guy had given him. Then he talked to his wife Laurie about possibly joining. Laurie rolled her eyes and protested. She was pregnant with her first child and was working a full time job. She had heard Amway was a cult, and an illegal pyramid scheme. Plus, she didn't really want her husband going around selling soap.

But Orrin somehow convinced her that it would be okay to join as an experiment. For the next five years, Orrin worked diligently to recruit people into the Amway system to increase his down-line. But after five years of struggling, all he had to show for it was 200 people. It was then that he realized that over the last forty years since its inception, Amway had become stagnant in the market and that negative perception had hobbled it like a ball and chain. He began to think of things he could do different. It was then that he saw a solution to the problem that Amway never saw.

In 1999, Amway announced that it was changing its name to Quixtar. Orrin seized this moment as a great opportunity to increase his recruiting efforts. But Orrin also did something no one at Amway had ever done before. He developed a true team approach by which he committed to help each person who joined grow his/her down-line to ten people before (suggesting) that person start a second down-line. He would focus on building deep instead of building wide. He had found a seam in the armor. His motto was, "You're in business for yourself, but not by yourself. No one gets left behind." The team concept worked. Within twelve months, he grew his organization from 200 to 1,200.

Within five years, he had grown his organization to 15,000 people and he called his group TEAM. The small town boy had become a multimillionaire. But in 2005, Orrin wrote a letter to Doug DeVoss, the son of Rich DeVoss, who founded Amway. In that letter, Orrin essentially dared to tell the emperor that he "wears no clothes." Orrin explained to DeVoss that he had moral and ethical problems with the way Amway was conducting its business, and suggested that they meet in person to address those issues. That was the beginning of the end. Amway summarily ignored Orrin's pleas for change, and the relationship began to deteriorate.

In 2007, Quixtar announced that it was changing its name to Amway Global. Disheartened by this move and the failure of Amway to satisfy his moral and ethical concerns, Orrin had a falling out with Amway which resulted in three years of litigation and millions of dollars in attorney's fees. The lawsuit ultimately settled.

In 2011, Orrin launched a new multi-level-marketing organization called LIFE Leadership which provides (principle-based) leadership training, motivation and education to those who want to change their lives for the better. Orrin offers a way to change your financial destiny while still maintaining your integrity. Although TEAM lost half its members in the lawsuit, by 2012, Orrin had built up his membership to approximately 42,000 members. By July 2013, he had 70,000. That's what you call affirmation. People vote for winners with dollars.

Orrin Woodward did not invent the multi-level marketing system. Nor did he invent a revolutionary gadget, or the concept of selling motivational CDs. Nor did he invent the concept of leadership. But he took what somebody else had built and found a way to *do it better* while still maintaining his integrity and sticking to his principles. He found a seam in the armor and created his own mini-empire in the process.

When I visited his lovely lake-front home that sits on two hundred wooded acres, I asked him, "Orrin, did you ever dream you would have all this?" He said, "You know Dan, when I was on the high school track team, I used to run by this lake and dream that one day I would meet the owner of this land so I could ask him if I could go fishing here." Now he owns that lake along with 200 surrounding acres. He also owns nine acres of ocean front property. All because he found a seam in the armor.

Tacos

There are more tacos *per capita* in Austin, Texas than any other city in the U.S. So what would possess a gourmet chef who was used to serving diplomats and dignitaries from every country at the World Bank in Washington, D.C. to buy a used air stream trailer and start selling tacos on the streets of Austin? It was Mike Rypka's desire to be his own boss and his obsession with really good food. "Even though there are taco shacks on every corner in Austin, there was really nobody doing what I wanted to do. I wanted to make a gourmet taco masquerading as a street taco," Michael Rypka said. In 2006, Rypka quit his job, and started his own business. He maxed out his credit cards and took out a second lien on his house. He named his taco trailer "Torchy's Tacos"—a name that came to him in the middle of the night.

He parked his food trailer at 5th Street and Baylor in downtown Austin. But he knew from years of working in the food industry that marketing and advertising alone don't work. "You have to get the food in people's mouths," he said. He bought a used Vespa scooter and started delivering free chips and salsa to office buildings downtown. Then he started selling tacos to those customers who ordered his chips and salsa. Having a trailer gave him lots of flexibility to move around until he found just the right spot. Rypka says, "Imagine if we had taken out a loan and had built at the wrong spot."

The next year, he moved his operation into an old building on South First Street—just south of downtown. Rypka did not take a salary for the first eight months, and he was three months behind on his phone bills. But he kept persevering. By the end of 2012, he had thirteen locations throughout Texas.

So, what's the secret of Rypka's success in a town where there is a taco shack on every street corner? "We decided early on that we wouldn't put anything on the menu that didn't come from an inspired place." It was never about the business or the money. "It's all about the food. You have to be passionate about the food. It's about making people happy with tacos."

When I asked Rypka what he does to take back his focus in troubled times, he said, "I go back to my roots. I drive to one of our shops, and join the line cooks, and start joking and cutting up with them while slinging tacos. If you can't have fun doing what you're doing, why are you doing it?"

Over the years, Torchy's has developed a cult-like following. With such favorite tacos such as, the *Trailer Park*, and the *Brushfire*, Torchy's has always had an edgy feel to it. They also sell a deep fried chocolate chip cookie called a *Little Nookie*. Who can resist the urge to get a *Little Nookie* after dinner? What other successful business do you know of that has the word "damn" in its tag line? Torchy's management kept hearing their customers say, "Man, these are damn good tacos!" So they incorporated the tagline "Damn Good Tacos" into their logo, and put it on all their signs, t-shirts, mugs, and marketing materials. They also sell a "damn good" hot sauce that comes in a bottle shaped like a flask of whiskey. One year, there was a kid in Austin dying of brain cancer. The Make A Wish Foundation got involved and asked him what he really wanted before he passed. He asked that Torchy's Tacos be his last meal.

Rypka succeeded because he found a seam in the market between the average ordinary street taco and an expensive gourmet taco. "There is something inside of us that wants to get away with something," said Rypka. "This is a place you can come and get away with something."

When I asked Rypka why legendary entrepreneurs can see solutions that are invisible to others, he gave me a five-point response that was simple, yet profound: (1) They are always looking; (2) They are never satisfied; (3) They take a 360 degree look at the problem; (4) They analyze other successful businesses to see *how* and *why* they work; (5) They see both the macroscopic view and the microscopic view of the problem—at the same time.

Nevertheless, Rypka admits that he does not "see" solutions in the same as others. "I don't really see the solutions as much as *I feel them*. It's kind of like seeing by braille. The discovery process is half the fun." I compare Rypka's technique to a blind man trying to penetrate the stone wall of a very secure castle. He feels his way along the castle wall, looking for a way to get in. His fingers can feel the bumps and rough-hewn texture of the cold hard stone. He finds the edge of the stone and then a groove between the stones. *Must be the mortar*, he concludes. On to the next stone. Then the next. Then the next. Stone. Mortar. Stone. Mortar. Then . . . *What's this? This stone feels loose*. His fingers move to the edge of the stone where the mortar should be. But he doesn't feel the sandy grit of the mortar between the stones. *It's a crack. This crack runs deep . . . and long*. He quickly finds his crow bar and begins to dig and pry until the stone pops loose. This is how legendary entrepreneurs find the seam in the armor. It is as much about intuition as it is intelligence.

What advice does Rypka have for others who want to start their own business? (1) You have to have a burning passion for what you do; (2) It has to be fun; (3) Be open minded to all kinds of possibilities—even if they come from someplace you weren't expecting;

(4) Don't limit your beliefs about where the answers might come from. Open yourself up to the possibility that the answer might come from anywhere or anyone; (5) Always have faith that things are going to work out somehow; (6) Always believe that you are a success—even if your business is not; (7) Don't make decisions out of fear, greed, or anger. Nothing good comes of it.

Advertising

In 1971, a kid with a tie-dyed T-shirt and a scraggly pony tail walked into a banker's office in Austin, Texas and asked for a $5,000 loan to start an advertising agency. When the banker asked, "What's your business plan?" the kid said, "To make money. What's yours?"

Upon realizing that he was about to graduate from college, Roy Spence had gotten together with some of his friends and talked about what they would do next. They had three goals: (1) To stay in Austin; (2) To stay together; and (3) To make a difference. But they had no clue how do accomplish any of those three things. And they had no money.

Before graduating from the University of Texas, one of Roy's friends named Steve had worked part-time for the college newspaper called *The Daily Texan*, selling advertising. One day Steve said, "Why don't we go into advertising?" "What's that?" Roy responded. Together they went around town asking people "Hey, what's an ad agency?" and "How do you build one?" They didn't know what the rules were so they made them up.

They weren't looking for clients. They were looking for purpose. They wanted to change the world. They didn't know any better. Roy and his friends regularly volunteered to work in the campaigns of the politicians they believed could make a difference. In 1972, a couple of 25-year-old kids named "Bill" and "Hillary" came to Texas to run the George McGovern presidential campaign in Texas, and surrounding areas. They regularly slept on the floor of Roy's apartment after a long day of work. That began a life-long friendship with the Clintons.

Roy's first clients were politicians whose mission he believed in. A friend of Roy's named George Shipley was a political consultant who knew the players in the Democratic party. Shipley introduced Roy to Robert Krueger who was running for U.S. Congress. Despite Roy's lack of experience, Krueger hired him because he could feel his sense of purpose and his passion.

Roy was successful at getting Robert Krueger elected to Congress. As a result of that success, local millionaire Red McCombs took notice of Roy and his fledgling advertising agency called GSD&M. McCombs hired GSD&M to promote his car dealerships all over Texas. McCombs also had a good friend named Herb Kelleher, founder of Southwest Airlines. Herb Kelleher hired Roy over a mayonnaise jar of smuggled tequila complete with worm.

Eventually, GSD&M had a list of clients that read like the Who's Who of corporations. Its clients included such powerhouses as Southwest Airlines, Wal-Mart, AT&T, MasterCard, BMW, John Deere, L.L. Bean, AARP, Coca-Cola, Hallmark, Lennox, the United States Air Force, Compass Bank, Norwegian Cruise Line, the PGA Tour, the American Red Cross, Chili's Restaurants, and the State of Texas (for the "Don't Mess With Texas" campaign).

After the 9/11 attack on the World Trade Center, GSD&M teamed up with the Ad Council to help bring perspective and unity to a torn country. Roy and his team came up with the innovative "I Am an American" campaign. The TV ads featured the individual faces of people from all walks of life and every culture (Asians, blacks, whites, Native Americans, Jews, Arabs, Persians, Iraqis, and Latinos) looking intensely into the camera and simply saying, "I am an American." The spot ended with *"E Pluribus Unum,"* the first official motto of the United States. *"Out of many, one."* We were reminded that—all of us is one of us.

Roy Spence has been named Ad Man of the Year, and the Idea Man of the Century. The offices of GSD&M are not merely in an office building. They are housed in a complex called Idea City.

Roy has been interviewed by the *Wall Street Journal, USA Today,* the *New York Times, BusinessWeek, U.S. News and World Report, Esquire, Fast Company,* and *Fortune.*

How did this kid with a pony tail and a tie-dyed T-shirt accomplish all this? He did it with the power of purpose. He said to me,

"Dan, I never was a good salesman because I couldn't sell something I didn't believe in." All through the years, he has focused on helping clients like Wal-Mart and Southwest Airlines realize their true purpose. He starts out by asking his clients, "What business are you in?" He helped Sam Walton realize that he was not in the retail business. He was in the business of helping regular people afford what rich people could afford. He helped Herb Kelleher realize that Southwest Airlines' purpose was to democratize the skies—to make the cost of flying affordable for everyone at a time when only the top 15% of the people in America could afford it. "Southwest Airlines is not in the transportation business. It's in the freedom business," says Roy. He challenges anyone who owns or operates a business to stop and figure out what business they're *really in*. To figure out what their higher calling is. Then he builds a branding and marketing campaign around that purpose.

But going back to 1971, the banker gave Roy that $5,000 loan. It was not until many years later that Roy discovered that the father of a friend of his had called the banker and told him he would guarantee the loan. But he swore him to secrecy. Today, experts estimate annual revenues of GSD&M to be approximately $1 billion.

When I asked Roy to explain why legendary entrepreneurs can see solutions that are invisible to others, he replied, "It's because they are actively creating them. They combine two totally unrelated things to form something that has never existed before." The ad-man in him couldn't resist adding, "Then they find a way to explain it to 'Bubba.'"

What advice does Roy Spence have for someone who wants to start his own business? "What is your reason for being?" asks Roy. "Whatever it is, elevate that purpose above all else, and build a business around that purpose. Purpose sets you apart from the competition, authenticates your brand, inspires passion in your people and helps you achieve the impossible."

> *The biggest obstacle I ever had to overcome*
> *was realizing that there were no obstacles.*
>
> —Roy Spence

Iced Tea

Clayton Christopher was a charter boat captain in the Florida Keys. He had a lot of fun, but wasn't making any money. One day he realized that the people who owned those boats made a lot more money than the guys that sailed them. One day in 1998, as he was driving home through Mississippi and Alabama, he came across several front porch shops selling sweet southern iced tea like the kind his grandmother used to make. It brought back all kinds of warm childhood memories of his grandmother. He wondered why no one sold a bottled tea that actually captured that kind of sweet southern flavor.

He went home and bought two garden hoses from Home Depot and used a pillow case for a tea bag. Then he started brewing tea in a giant crawfish pot. Using his grandmother's recipe as a starter, he experimented with lots of recipes until he got just the flavor of his grandmother's tea in such a way that would stay sweet long after it was bottled. He filled the bottles with the garden hoses and twisted the caps on by hand. When he got tired of twisting the caps on by hand, he hung drills from the ceiling of his home to twist on the caps. He got his first break into the retail market after begging a local convenience store for shelf space. There were many months when he had to decide whether to pay his employees or his vendors. He lived in a one bedroom apartment and drove a used car. He called his tea *Sweet Leaf Tea* and put a picture of a smiling grandmotherly character on the bottle.

Soon, he got shelf space in more and more convenience stores. In 2000, he had 14 employees, two filling lines, and one refrigerated van to distribute iced tea to convenience stores throughout Southeast Texas. In 2002, he relocated to Austin, Texas, where he got into some huge grocery store chains, like H.E.B, Kroger, and Safeway, and finally into the organic grocery store Whole Foods. In 2008, he got private funding of $18 million. In 2009, Nestle invested $15.6 million in Sweet Leaf Tea. Eventually, he was selling his bottled sweet southern tea in all 50 states. Now he sells a variety of flavors of bottled teas all over the world.

When I spoke with Clayton, the first thing I asked him was, "Why tea? Didn't it ever occur to you that this was already a very crowded field and that Lipton, Snapple, and all the other major bottled beverage producers would eat you up in the market? Even if you had a better tasting tea, what was to stop them from coming up with something almost identical?" He paused a moment, and said, "Wow, I never thought about that. I guess I should have."

It's probably better that he didn't. If he had thought about it, if he had actually taken the time to write out a well-thought out business plan, if he had done a true risk-analysis, fear would have crept in, and he never would have taken the time to brew that first crawfish pot full of sweet southern tea.

Health Care

Bob Fabbio grew up in an average home of 1,200 square feet in upstate New York. When he was 4 years old, he walked around the neighborhood selling toy car tires for one penny each. At the age of 11 years, the public school he attended shut down its hockey program for lack of funds. He went to the principal and asked to buy a set of hockey equipment since the school wasn't going to use them anymore. Fabbio's request prompted a public auction where he was allowed first dibs on anything he wanted for $25. He still has the jersey and socks he bought back then. As a teenager, he decided he wanted Black Panther hockey skates, which his parents could not afford. So he began shoveling snow out of driveways until he earned $50 and bought them himself.

Upon graduating from college, Fabbio held a series of software engineer positions and senior architect positions at various companies, including Eastman Kodak, Computer Consoles, Applix, Prime Computers, and finally IBM.

Even though he enjoyed great success, and rose up through the ranks quickly, Bob Fabbio was one of those serial entrepreneurs who simply could not sit still. In 1989, he founded Tivoli Systems, which later went public and was then acquired by IBM. He later founded DAZEL Corporation, which was acquired by Hewlett Packard. Then he founded Ventix Systems, which later merged with Motive Communications and went public. After that, he was a venture capitalist with Austin Ventures and with TL Ventures.

Already a multimillionaire at the age of 49 years, he didn't need any more money. He was simply getting bored. He was sitting in Rudy's BBQ in Austin when he decided he needed more mountains to climb, more problems to solve. That's when he happened to have a bad experience at a doctor's office which gave him the revolutionary idea that launched *WhiteGlove Health.*

If you've ever sat in the waiting room of a doctor's office for at least an hour waiting to be seen, you can relate to the frustration Bob Fabbio experienced one day while he was waiting for his doctor. The times I have experienced this, I remember thinking, "What other professional could treat his clients this way and get away with it?" If you had a pre-scheduled appointment and your lawyer, your dentist, your accountant, your real estate agent were an hour or more late, would you really tolerate it? But we allow this kind of treatment from our doctors all the time. Not Bob Fabbio. He decided to take matters into his own hands.

It was while he was sitting in Rudy's BBQ that he decided to launch WhiteGlove Health. Bob calls it the "Costco of health care." It is a membership based service. People pay $300–$400 per year, plus $35 per visit in exchange for the right to have medical professionals come directly to their home or office anytime they need to see one. Typically the professional is a nurse practitioner who can prescribe medication. The service operates from 8 a.m. to 8 p.m. seven days a week. This virtually eliminates the need to ever visit a general practitioner's office. If you need a blood test, the nurse practitioner draws your blood at your house or office, and sends it to the diagnostic lab where the results are digitally communicated to the patient. They will also deliver to your door chicken soup, crackers and Gatorade. The concept was so brilliant Fabbio easily secured $37.5 million in venture capital. Over 500,000 members have access to the service in Texas alone. White Glove is now operating in five states. Fabbio says "we're experiencing triple digit growth." It is my prediction that Bob Fabbio will revolutionize the health care industry. In the end, it will not be the government, or doctors, or hospitals, or insurance companies who take care of you. It will be the entrepreneurs of the world who find a way to provide affordable, high quality health care to the masses.

Tortillas

Felix Sanchez arrived in the United States in 1970 with nothing but the clothes on his back. He came from Puebla, Mexico with only a fifth grade education. He spoke no English. Felix spent his days driving a forklift at an electrical equipment factory and his nights making tortillas. On weekends, he would sell them door to door in Latino neighborhoods. Eventually he was able to save up $12,000. In 1978, he and his wife Carmen bought a tortilla press and an industrial dough mixer in Los Angeles and moved it to a warehouse in Passaic, New Jersey. He continued selling his tortillas door to door in Latino neighborhoods, but this time he was selling in New York City. As his business grew, he formed a company called *Puebla Foods* and was soon distributing tortillas and dried chilies to bodegas and restaurants throughout the Northeast. Today, he makes $19 million per year and has factories in Los Angeles, Miami, Pittsburgh, Toronto and Washington.

Now think about this for a moment. Felix is not a rocket scientist. He speaks broken English and he sells tortillas for a living. Tortillas! It's not like he introduced anything new or revolutionary to the food industry. But he did do something no one else was doing. He went door to door delivering his warm tortillas to one family at a time until he had built up a cult-like following. When his tortillas finally hit the shelves of the local grocery stores, it was the most natural thing in the world to reach for the *Puebla* brand. Felix penetrated the castle walls with a warm tortilla.

Credit Card Processing

Eric Cohen started his career at the age of twelve with a newspaper route that quickly became the largest paper route in Central New Jersey. At the age of fourteen, he started a lawn mowing service which quickly grew to include 30 yards per month. After college, he got a job at a giant corporate bank. But he quickly realized that he was working longer and harder than everyone else, including his boss, and was not being rewarded for it.

Soon thereafter, he joined a multi-level marketing organization selling all natural products. He had great success for five years, and it

was during this time that he was exposed to the credit card processing business. He realized that every small business that takes credit
cards needs a credit card machine and something called a "merchant
account." A "merchant account" is set up by a middle man called a
"processor." The processor connects the issuing bank and the merchant and facilitates the flow of money.

Cohen began selling credit card machines to small businesses and
made $50,000 in six months. Then he discovered that once he sold a
credit card machine to a store, or restaurant, he could also make a
percentage of every sale that the customer paid for with a credit card.
Now all he needed was to recruit an army of sales representatives to
sell credit card machines to stores and restaurants everywhere, and
start collecting a percentage of every credit card sale they made.

Cohen aligned himself with a successful credit card processor in
Texas and began recruiting sales representatives and teaching them
how to earn residual income with credit card machine sales. After
two years, Cohen became disillusioned with the ethical practices of
his business partner and, after a heated lawsuit, branched out on his
own, and moved back to New Jersey to be near his family.

For the next four years, Cohen built his business and was making
so much residual income that he was able to take two years off to
watch his children grow. During the interim, he saw that the credit
card industry was growing increasingly unethical and unscrupulous.
In order for credit card processors to maximize their profits, they had
to charge high fees, but in order to recruit new business, they had to
promise low fees, and then slowly raise them over time. It was during
this time that Cohen realized that no one was truly looking out for the
interests of the merchants. Most stores and restaurants are too busy
running the day to day operations to take the time to analyze their
credit card statements and the fees they are being charged. They also
don't know the difference between a low fee, an average fee, and an
excessive fee. But Cohen does.

Cohen changed his business model so that he only makes money
if he can find ways to save the merchants from excessive charges by
unscrupulous credit card processors. Today, his company, Merchant

Advocate, reviews and analyzes the fees that credit card processors charge merchants. With his many years of experience in studying credit card statements and fees, he and his staff can quickly spot excessive fees, negotiate with the credit card processors to reduce their fees, and if that doesn't work, transfer the merchant to a processor who does charge lower fees. Cohen is not a giant credit card company like Visa, American Express, CitiBank or Chase. He is also not the largest credit card processor in the country. But he saw a seam in the armor and penetrated it with a razor sharp edge. Today he grosses approximately $2 million per year simply by working hard to save small businesses money.

The people in this chapter are no smarter than you. In fact many of them are *less smart* than you. But intelligence does not equal innovation. High IQ does not equal creativity. All of these people saw, felt, and intuited ways to penetrate the armor of the corporate empires by identifying and penetrating the weak spots. Even if you don't think you are creative enough to come up with a whiz-bang new idea for a business, can you at least find a seam in someone else's?

THINGS TO PONDER

+ You don't have to invent anything from scratch, or create a whole new industry.

+ Just find the seams in the armor.

+ Legendary entrepreneurs don't look for money. They look for problems that match their skills and passions.

PART THREE

Now Look Around You

------------ -‹‹‹‹•››› - ------------

CHAPTER 24

What If You're Out of Options?

Idon't know where you are in life right now. But I know that at times you may have felt that you were completely out of options—that you were at a dead end—your wit's end. After studying the lives of people who overcame extreme adversity for the last twenty years, I can tell you with great confidence that when heroes and legends are out of options, they all did the same thing. They chose to create *more* options.

In the Bible, young David (yes, the one who killed Goliath) was on the run from King Saul who was trying to kill him. He was captured by Achish, King of Gath. Achish thought his new captive had a strange resemblance to David, the great warrior who had killed "his tens of thousands" and considered him a threat.[180] David was trapped and out of options. He had no army, no weapons, no armor—not even a slingshot to defend himself. He was helpless. But David did what all great heroes and legends throughout history have done when they are out of options. He created more options. David threw himself on the floor, and started screaming and hollering, foaming at the mouth, and coughing. King Achish, said "Wait, this isn't David. This is some crazy guy you've brought me. Get him outa here!" So they did, and David was released.

Even when you think you are out of options, you always have the option to do something so irrational, illogical and downright crazy that it is bound to create more options. The legendary Roy Spence, co-founder of powerhouse advertising agency GSD&M, and *Idea City*, in Austin, Texas told me that his staff had once fallen into a stagnant state and he was not satisfied with the solutions they were coming up with. On that occasion, he ordered the entire inside of his office building painted bright yellow and rearranged all the furniture during the night. The next day, the staff showed up and was shocked. The office was all abuzz with excitement and confusion. When I asked Roy why he did that, he said "to create mass chaos." Sometimes when you have run out of options, the best thing you can do is disrupt the status quo by creating mass chaos. Anthony Robbins calls it "interrupting the pattern." The founder of Amazon.com, Jeff Bezos, says, "Innovation is disruption."

> *I like nonsense. It wakes up the brain cells.*
> *Fantasy is a necessary ingredient in living.*
>
> —DR. SEUSS

Leonardo da Vinci used to stimulate his own creativity by splashing paint on a wall to see what interesting patterns it formed. He explains that, "in order to excite the mind to various inventions [one should contemplate] walls covered with shapeless stains or made of ill-assorted stones, one can find in them mountain landscapes, trees, battles, figures with lively movements, faces, and strange costumes."[181]

Over a period of several years, a friend of mine had been telling me he felt trapped in his marriage and in a job he hated. He didn't know what to do. He couldn't afford to divorce his wife because he would lose half of everything he'd worked for his whole life. He couldn't afford to quit his job because there were no better alternatives out there. He was stuck and extremely frustrated. For years he had been telling me the same frustrations over and over. I had given him all the encouragement, support and advice I could possibly think of and I was starting to repeat myself. One day, when he started pouring out his soul to me yet again, I opened my mouth and these words popped out, "Dude, sometimes, you just gotta shake the globe." "What?" he asked. "You know, shake the globe," I said shaking an imaginary snow globe with my hands.

You have probably seen one of those glass snow globes with the cute little houses and the white picket fences, and the trees and the snow covering the ground. Most of the time, it just sits there. It's cute, but pretty boring right? Sometimes that's how our lives get. Everything looks fine on the outside to the casual observer. But on the inside our lives are stagnant, or worse, frustrating, and depressing. We are out of ideas. Nothing is happening. There are no possible solutions in sight. We have gotten into a rut that is difficult, if not impossible, to get out of. It may be a job you hate. It may be a marriage you are not happy with. It could be your *whole life* you are dissatisfied with. Whatever it is, it looks just fine to people on the outside of the globe, right? It's picture perfect. But you are miserable on the inside. It's in times like this that I strongly suggest that you "shake the globe." Do something to create mass chaos. When you shake the globe, you automatically create more options than you currently have. And out of those new options, there is always a chance that one of them may be better than what you are experiencing right now. Sometimes, it's worth a shot.

In 1987, Richard Branson and his buddy Per Lindstrand decided to do something that had never been done before—cross the Atlantic Ocean in a hot air balloon. Seven people had tried. Five had died in the process. They would have to soar high up into the jet stream at 30,000 feet, the same altitude at which airplanes fly. The winds in the jet stream would push the balloon across the sky at 100 to 200 miles per hour. In case you don't know what 200 miles per hour feels like, it's the same speed at which you fall when you jump out of a perfectly good airplane *without a parachute.*

On July 2, 1987, they launched from Maine and set out across the Atlantic. In just 29 hours, they caught sight of the coast of Ireland. But then trouble hit. They began to sink. Fast. They were just above the surface of the ocean when a strong wind started pushing the balloon horizontally across the water. The capsule which held the two men started bouncing from wave to wave tossing the men inside like a bag of marbles. Per Lindstrand jumped out of the capsule and into the icy cold Atlantic. Without his body weight, the balloon soared upward with Branson still in it. He was in the biggest balloon ever built and he was rapidly heading toward Scotland. But he could not control the balloon by himself. "Whatever I did in the next ten minutes would lead to my death or survival. I was on my own. We had broken the record but I was almost certainly going to die."[182]

Branson had on a parachute and a life jacket. He knew he had to jump out of the capsule, open his parachute, and hope to survive the giant waves without the ropes from his own parachute entangling him, and the weight of his equipment drowning him. Even if he did not drown, the freezing cold water would surely cause his body to seize up with hypothermia.

He reached for the parachute release handle to make sure he knew which side of his body it was on, and steadied himself to jump. He knew if he jumped from that high, he would likely be injured from the impact and drown in less than two minutes. "Give yourself more time," he said out loud. Then he looked up at the balloon and realized that he was standing beneath the world's largest parachute. If he could find a way to bring the balloon back down, perhaps he could jump at the last minute before the balloon crashed into the water. He checked the fuel gauges. He had enough fuel to last another thirty minutes.

"It must be better to live for thirty minutes than to jump off with my parachute and perhaps live for only two minutes. While I'm alive, I can still do something. Something must turn up."[183] He turned off the burners to let the balloon sink. When he was fifty feet above the water, he turned on the burners again to slow his descent. Then he jumped. Without his weight, the balloon quickly soared up again. He was now bobbing up and down in the ocean like a cork. He looked up as the giant balloon got smaller and smaller as it sailed away. Then out of the corner of his eye, he saw a Royal Air Force helicopter headed toward him with a long rope ladder dragging across the sea. Branson did what all heroes and legends do when they are out of options. He chose the option that created more options.

Linus Pauling was awarded the Nobel Prize in Chemistry in 1954. In 1962, he was awarded the Nobel Peace Prize for his peace activism. At Linus Pauling's sixtieth birthday party, a student asked him, "Dr. Pauling how does one go about having good ideas?" He replied, "You have a lot of ideas and throw away the bad ones."[184] This is similar to how nature decides which tree in the forest gets to live to be 2,000 years old. Trillions of seeds fall the ground and germinate, but only a few are chosen to grow to the size of a giant redwood. Only a few are chosen to live 2,000-plus years. At first it appears to be random, but it's not. It's a numbers game. The more chances you give yourself, the more likely you are to survive and prosper.

When I was in college, my buddies and I used to play pool almost every day after class. After a while we got pretty good, and we always made each other "call our shots." In other words, we couldn't just shoot and hope something fell in. We had to identify what ball was going to go into which pocket and how. If I was going to use more than just the cue ball to make the chosen ball fall into a certain pocket, I would have to say "Combination. Six off the Four into the corner pocket." This way, everyone knew that if the chosen ball actually went into the corner pocket, it wasn't luck, or what we called "slop."

Every now and then, the guy who was "breaking," (taking the first shot at the pile of balls at the other end of the table), didn't get a very powerful shot off and the pile of balls just kind of stayed in the center of the table instead of dispersing to all parts of the table. This made the second guy's job quite difficult because his options were very limited. All the balls were bunched up in the center, and there were no "sitting ducks" (balls lined up very close to a pocket). That guy would do what he could, but typically the next four or five shots would be misses or result in "slop." Finally someone would walk up to the table and boldly shout, "combo-bombo!" This meant he was going to shoot the cue ball into the heart of the bunched up balls as hard as he could and hope something fell in. Usually two or three balls fell (both his own and his opponent's) into some pocket or another. But at least now the balls were spread out all over the table. This started a whole new ball game because now there were lots of options, including some "ducks." Even if it helped his opponent, it at least made the game more interesting.

Wherever there's adversity, wherever there's change, where ever there's uncertainty, entrepreneurs see opportunity.
—MARK CUBAN

I didn't realize it, but back then we were using the same techniques that Roy Spence and Leonardo da Vinci used. Creating mass chaos solely for the purpose of creating more interesting options. I asked Roy Spence, how do you stimulate your brain to come up with creative ideas when you are completely out of ideas? "You don't get more creative ideas by trying to think more creatively," he said. "You get them by *acting* more creatively."

Professor Evangelina G. Chrysikou agrees. She says that, "Exercises that shake up people's typical ways of thinking can help put them in a creative mind-set."[185]

It takes massive action of the sort that you are not used to taking. You have to do things you've never done before, and perhaps never even *considered* doing. In short, if you want things you've never had before, you have to do things you've never done before.

Trina Paulus once said, "In order to become a butterfly, you must want to fly so much that you are willing to give up being a caterpillar." You will not change your life until the discomfort of staying the same is greater than the discomfort of changing. Most people never reach that point. They just learn to tolerate a greater and greater degree of discomfort right where they are—watching their dreams die . . . slowly . . . one . . . at . . . a . . . time.

The point is when you feel you are out of options, you always have the option to create more options. But this requires that you take massive, disruptive action to change the status quo. You never know what you will get when you do something as crazy as I am suggesting. Not all of the newly created options will be good ones, but some will. Just wait and see. Better yet, *just act*—and see. Sometimes you just gotta shake the globe.

✳ THINGS TO PONDER

+ You are never out of options.
+ You always have the option to create more options.
+ If you want things you've never had before, you have to do things you've never done before.
+ Sometimes you just gotta shake the globe.

CHAPTER 25

What If You Could Change Your Brain?

In doing the research for this book I asked several hundred entrepreneurs whether the ability to see solutions that are invisible to others could be taught, or whether a person had to be born with this ability. The answers were almost evenly split. But each person who answered this question was equally adamant in their position. None of them knew for sure *why* they believed as they did. They just did. The question of *nature v. nurture* is always the underlying question whenever we study the lives of people who excel at what they do. This is my attempt to answer that question where the ability to see hidden solutions is concerned.

For many years, neurologists told us that the brain was like a computer. You could fill it with information and instructions, but that was about it. You were born with a certain amount of brain power and could never do anything to increase it. A computer presents a picture of something rigid, static and unchanging. The storage capacity, the processing power, and the random access memory are fixed and finite. You can change the programming, but not the hardware itself (unless you physically yank it out and replace it, which is not really an option when it comes to the brain). In other words, you can change what you think about all day, but you cannot change how the brain processes that information or add any more brain cells to your brain. They told us we were born with a certain IQ and no more.

Neurologists thought they had discovered the Holy Grail when they discovered the part of the brain the controlled speech. In 1861,

Paul Broca studied one of his patients who had had a stroke. The stroke had rendered him unable to speak—except for one word. No matter what you said, or what you asked him, his response was always just, "tan, tan."[186]

When the man died, Broca dissected his brain and found damaged tissue in the left frontal lobe. Broca continued his research and found that other patients who had lost the ability to speak also had damage in the same location. Neurologists started calling that area "Broca's area" and concluded that this must be the part of the brain controls the muscles of the lips and the tongue.

Over the next hundred years, neurologists mapped out the entire brain and declared that each part of the brain was "hard wired" to perform only one function. One part of the brain could not perform the function of any other part of the brain. Just like the video card in your computer cannot do what the random access memory chip does. Neurologists lived by the mantra, "One location = One function." You have undoubtedly seen cross-sections of the brain that map out each part of the brain's functions.

Neurologists told us that the visual cortex in the occipital lobe was responsible for vision. The audio cortex in the temporal lobe was responsible for hearing, and so on. Neurologists also told us that once a certain part of the brain was damaged due to a head injury or a stroke, the functions of that part of the brain were gone forever. They also told us that our brains only had a certain number of brain cells and that as brain cells were destroyed, they could never be regained.

However, recently neurologists have discovered new evidence that turned everything we thought we knew about the brain on its head. In 1959, a 65-year-old professor from Catalan named Pedro Bach-y-Rita had a disabling stroke that paralyzed half his body, and his face, and left him unable to speak. He had to be physically placed on the toilet and bathed with a sponge. After going through four weeks of physical therapy at one of the best rehab hospitals in the area, the therapists told his two sons there was no hope for recovery. One of his sons named George brought Pedro home to live with him in the United States. He knew absolutely nothing about physical therapy or how to rehabilitate a stroke victim. But he was determined to help his dad any way he could.

George recounts the early stages of the process. "I decided that instead of teaching my father to walk, I was going to teach him first to crawl. I said, 'You started off crawling, you are going to have to crawl again for a while.' We got kneepads for him. At first we held him on all fours, but his arms and legs didn't hold him very well, so it was a struggle."[187] George then had Pedro crawl by leaning next to a wall which acted as a support for one side of his body. Soon, his paralyzed arm and leg seemed to be regaining strength and their ability to move. After a while, George started playing games on the floor with marbles. He would roll the marbles across the floor and his dad would try to catch them. Then he turned to washing pots. He would make Pedro hold the pot with his good hand and make his weak hand go round and round by flopping it over and over at the shoulder. Fifteen minutes in one direction. Fifteen minutes in the other. The shape of the pot kept the weak hand in a small confined space and offered some support. Little by little Pedro began to regain the use of his arm and hand and could make his hand go in the direction he wanted it to go in without flopping it around with his shoulder.

Soon Pedro was able to sit down and eat dinner with both hands. Eventually, he was able to move both legs as well. Then he began standing and walking. Pedro also tried with all his might to speak, and eventually his ability to speak came back. Then he tried to regain his ability to write. He would sit at the typewriter with his middle finger hovering over the desired key. The he would drop his entire hand from the shoulder to try to hit that key. Once he was able to hit the desired key consistently, he began dropping just his wrist, and finally one finger. Eventually, he regained the ability to type just as well as he used to.

Three very difficult years later, Pedro was able to start teaching at City College in New York. He was thrilled that he was able to do anything again—especially doing what he loved most. He taught until he resigned from that position at age seventy. Then he got another teaching job at San Francisco State. He also remarried and kept working, hiking and traveling the world. Ultimately he went hiking high up in the mountains of Bogotá, Columbia. He had climbed to nine thousand feet before he had a heart attack and died. He was 72 years old.

Pedro's other son Paul Bach-y-Rita was a doctor. But in 1965, there were no brain scans and no ability to see what was actually going on inside the brain. A fellow doctor named Dr. Mary Jane Aguilar performed an autopsy. A few days later, Dr. Aguilar called Paul very excitedly and said, "Paul, come down here. I've got something to show you." When Paul got there, he saw slices of his father's brain spread out on glass slides. It turned Paul's stomach to see his father's brain displayed like that. But he swallowed hard and began to study the slides.

The brain slices revealed that his father had several huge lesions from the stroke that had never healed. There was severe damage in the brain stem which is the part of the brain that connects the spinal cord to the rest of the brain. Ninety-seven percent of the nerves that run from the cerebral cortex to the spine had been destroyed. This was what caused the paralysis. Paul stared in disbelief. How was his father able to completely recover the use of his entire body, including his ability to speak with that much damage to his brain?

Paul later explained, "I knew that meant that somehow his brain had totally reorganized itself with the work he did with George. We didn't know how remarkable his recovery was until that moment, because we had no idea of the extent of his lesion, since there were no brain scans in those days. When people did recover, we tended to assume that there really hadn't been much damage in the first place."[188] What Paul Bach-y-Rita saw that day changed his life. He became an expert in neurology and rehabilitation, and began studying *neuroplasticity*—the ability of the brain to rewire itself.

In 1969, Bach-y-Rita published an article explaining the results of his experiments with a little known device called a "tactile-vision device." The people chosen to use the device were blind from birth. In the 1960s, the device was huge and weighed four hundred pounds. The blind person would sit in a chair behind a large camera the size of a television. The person would turn the camera with a hand crank to survey the room around him. The camera sent electrical signals to four hundred vibrating stimulators situated along the back of the chair so that the person's skin could feel them. The electrical signals vibrated to show the dark parts of the scene, and were quiet for the brighter parts of the scene. The intensity of the electrical signals varied according to all shades of gray in between. The resulting image was similar to what you see when you place a photograph on the copier and make a copy, only not as sharp or detailed.

Simply by receiving electrical stimulus that separated the darkest and brightest areas in the room through the skin, the subjects could actually make out objects in the room. They could also identify faces and could tell which objects were closer and which were further away. They could also see perspective and discern how an object changed shape when it was viewed from different angles. They were able to identify such random objects as a telephone, a chair and a table. Ultimately the subject's "vision" got so good that they would duck or hold their arms up if someone threw a ball at them. The subjects retained this same visual perception even when the vibrating stimulators were moved from their backs to their stomachs. Eventually, the subjects were able to move the camera around the room and say such things as "That's Mary. She is not wearing her glasses today. Now she is yawning. Now she is waving at me." The images they saw were not as clear or as sharp as that of a person with 20/20 vision. But it was vision nonetheless. This led Bach-y-Rita to utter the now famous phrase, "We see with our brains, not with our eyes." In this case, the subject's eyes were still completely useless to them. He declared that the doorway through which the information enters the brain is not important. In this case, the skin was a suitable substitute for the retina.

Doctor Normal Doidge, who has spent many years studying neuroplasticity, explained it this way:

> It's one thing to find a new data port, or way of getting sensations to the brain. But it's another for the brain to decode

these skin sensations and turn them into pictures. To do that, the brain has to learn something new, and the part of the brain devoted to processing touch has to adapt to the new signals. This adaptability implies that the brain is plastic in the sense that it can reorganize its sensory perceptual system.[189]

In the case of the blind subjects, this meant that signals from the sense of touch (normally processed in the sensory cortex near the top of the brain) were routed to the visual cortex (at the back of the brain). The brain had created *new* neuropathways for the purpose of transmitting the input from the skin to the visual cortex. The brain had changed itself.

Thirty-three years later, neuroscientists succeeded in creating a tiny version of the tactile-vision device that patients could place on their tongues. Stimulus that entered through the tongue also triggered the visual cortex, allowing the patients to "see" the darkest and brightest parts of the room and all shades of gray in between. It matters not what doorway the brain uses to gather its information. The brain is capable of rewiring itself to turn that stimulus into real images in the visual cortex.

Today, scientists are also able to replace a damaged cochlea (the part of the ear that picks up sound and transmits it to the audio cortex) with a cochlear implant that transforms speech into electrical impulses which it then transmits to the brain. Our body's natural cochlea is connected directly to the audio cortex through a series of nerves and neurotransmitters. But if the cochlea is damaged beyond repair, the brain can no longer receive input through that portal. The electronic cochlea has its own tiny receiver and a converter that translates sound waves into electrical impulses and an electrode connected to the nerves that connect to the brain. But the brain still has to rewire itself to be able to accept those electrical impulses from the artificial source and then translate those electrical impulses into words, music and other useful information. An artificial cochlea only works because the brain is able to create new neuropathways coming from the artificial device to the brain.[190]

But what is the triggering mechanism that causes the brain to rewire itself? Mark Rosenzweig of the University of California at Berkeley conducted studies of rats who were born and raised in stimulating environments and compared them to rats who were born and raised in non-stimulating environments. The rats raised in highly enriched environments were surrounded by other animals, novel objects to explore, toys to play with, ladders to climb, and wheels to run on. The rats in the second group were only given food and water with nothing to explore, no wheels to run on, and no incentive to exercise.

When the rats eventually died, he studied their brains. He discovered that the brains of the rats who were raised with lots of stimulus had more neurotransmitters, weighed more, and had a better blood supply than those raised in non-stimulating environments. Rosenzweig was one of the first neuroscientists to explain that environmental stimulus and physical activity can and does produce changes in the structure of the brain.[191] The brains of the rats with rich environments developed 25 percent more neuron branches, had much higher neuroconnections per neuron, and had a much higher blood supply.

Expanding upon this research and applying it to humans, Erik Kandel of Columbia University won the Nobel Prize in 2000 for his experiments that showed conclusively that as humans learn, our individual neurons alter their structure and strengthen the synaptic connections between them. When we form long-term memories, neurons change their anatomical shape and increase the number of synaptic connections they have to other neurons.[192] It turns out that learning does not simply give us more information, the process of learning itself actually increases our brains *capacity to learn*. A new analogy was born. The brain is not like a machine at all.[193] It is more like a muscle.[194]

It is well known that a muscle must have regular exercise or it will begin to atrophy and eventually be of no use. Two neurologists wanted to determine if the brain worked the same way. At Johns Hopkins, David Hubel and Torsten Wiesel were attempting to "micromap" the visual cortex to better understand how the brain processes stimulus entering through the eyes. They inserted microelectrodes into the visual cortex of kittens. Then they sewed one of the kitten's eyelids shut at birth so the eye received no visual stimulation at all from birth. After eight weeks, they opened that eye. They discovered that the micro parts of the visual cortex responsible for processing vision from that eye had failed to develop, leaving the kitten blind in that eye for life. The conclusion was that during the first eight weeks after birth, the kittens had to receive visual stimulation in both eyes in order for the visual cortex to fully develop.

In 1895, Sir Charles Sherrington conducted a series of experiments on monkeys in which he cut the *sensory* nerves in a monkey's left arm just before they entered the spinal cord. The *sensory* nerve's purpose is to transmit impulses from our skin and muscles to the brain. But it is the *motor* nerves that transmit impulses from the brain to our muscles, which causes them to move. Sherrington had purposely left the *motor* nerves coming from the brain to the muscles intact and fully functioning. The monkeys were fully capable of moving the left arm. Yet, a few days after the surgery, the monkeys stopped using the left arm. So why did the monkeys stop using that arm? Sherrington was perplexed.

Acting on a hunch, Sherrington put the monkey's perfectly good right arm in a sling to prevent the monkeys from using it. Unable to use their one good arm, the monkeys started using the left arm whose *sensory* nerves had been cut. They were able to do so because the *motor* nerves were still functioning. He concluded that the monkey's previous failure to use its left arm was due to the fact that it could not receive any sensory input that provided confirmation of action. In other words, when you tell your arm to reach out and pick up an ice cold glass of tea, the *motor* nerves send the signal, but it is the *sensory* nerves that transmit the actual feeling of the cold glass and the weight of the iced tea back to the brain to confirm that the task was accomplished. Without this positive reinforcement, the animal gives up and starts to use the good arm instead. Neuroscientists call this phenomenon "learned nonuse." This nonuse also causes the real estate in the brain that was responsible for moving that arm to go unused, and ultimately lost.

But what happens to the part of the brain that was originally allocated to controlling the left arm in the monkeys and to processing vision from the sealed eye of the kittens? Does it die? Does it truly atrophy like a muscle? It turns out that when one part of the brain is not receiving information from its normal sources, it does not die. Instead, that part of the brain will reallocate itself to receive and process information coming from other sources.

For example in the human hand, the *median* nerve transmits information from the palm of the hand to the brain. The *radial* and *ulnar* nerves transmit information from the back of our hands to the brain. A neuroscientist named Jon Kaas of Vanderbilt University conducted experiments with adult monkeys in which he cut the *median* nerve but left the *radial* and *ulnar* nerves intact. Two months later, he went back to test what had happened inside the brain itself. With electrodes connected to the brain, he saw that when he touched the monkey's palm, there was no activity in the part of the brain that normally processes information from that nerve. This is what Kaas was expecting to see. But then something amazing happened.

When he touched the outside of the monkey's hand, the part of the brain that was supposed to be receiving information coming from the palm through the median nerve lit up! But how could this be? There was no information coming from the median nerve because it had been cut. Where was this information coming from? As he dug deeper, he noticed that the part of the brain that receives information from the *radial* and the *ulnar* nerves had almost doubled in size and had invaded the part of the brain that was once allocated to processing information from the *median* nerve. Kaas concluded that the various parts of our body are constantly competing for precious real estate in the brain. It was as though the back of the hand had claimed "squatter's rights" in the part of the brain previously allocated to receiving information from the palm of the hand. A new mantra was born, "use it or lose it."[195]

We do not simply forget things like how to play the piano, how to play the violin, how to bowl, how to ice skate, or how to dance. The part of our brain that was once allocated to those movements is literally taken over by the other things we do instead. You must constantly practice the things you learned in your youth in order to keep those skills sharp. If you don't, that real estate in the brain will be taken over by whatever else you do regularly.

As an avid salsa dancer, I can tell you that when I first learn a new dance pattern, if I don't go out and practice that pattern in a social setting with various partners at least three times that week, I will completely forget it, and will have to start over with my instructor the following week. All intermediate salsa dancers I know have experienced this same thing. No one "gets it" completely after just one lesson without having to practice the pattern immediately in a social setting several times within the next seven days. My buddies who go golfing regularly tell me the same thing applies to your golf swing.

The process of repeating the dance pattern over and over is actually creating new neuropathways in the brain. It's kind of like taking a machete and hiking through the Amazon jungle for the first time. The very first time you cut a path through the jungle is always the most difficult. If you only pass that way once, the jungle will grow back quickly and hide the trail you just cut. But the second time you go down that path, it's a little easier. By the 1,000th time down that path, you don't even need a machete. The trail is permanently embedded in the brain. It turns out the old saying "practice makes perfect" is true, but not for the reasons we were told. When we repeat any new skill over and over, we are literally creating new neuropathways in the brain. This is a startling revelation if you think about it. It means that our experiences have the ability to literally mold and shape our brain simply by what we do with our bodies. Pedro Bach-y-Rita's amazing recovery from his debilitating stroke is a perfect example. His forced daily exercises literally forced the brain to rewire itself.

But what about our thoughts and feelings alone? Are these sufficient to create new neuropathways in the brain? Recently, neuroscientist Alvaro Pascual-Leone of the Harvard Medical School conducted an experiment with two groups of people who had never played the piano before. He asked both groups to play a series of notes, instructing them which fingers to use and letting them hear the notes as they played. Then he asked the first group to sit at an electric keyboard, but not to touch the keys. They were only to *imagine* touching the keys and hearing the sounds in their heads. They were to do this for two solid hours each day. He asked the second group to actually physically practice playing the notes on the electric keyboard for two hours a day. Both groups practiced for two hours a day for five days straight. Pascual-Leone took brain scans of each subject's brain both before and after the experiment. Then both groups were asked to play the piece on a real piano and a computer measured the accuracy of their performances.

When Pascual-Leone studied the brain scans of the two groups, both groups showed the exact same brain-map changes. The students who practiced only with their minds had the same changes in their neuropathways as the students who physically practiced with a real piano. The group that practiced with their minds did not score quite as high on the final test as those who practiced with a real keyboard. But after only two hours of physically practicing on a real keyboard, the "mental group" scored just as high as the other group.[196] Dr. Doidge explains it this way, "When people close their eyes and visualize a simple object, such as the letter *a,* the primary visual cortex lights up, just as it would if the subjects were actually looking at the actual letter *a.* Brain scans show that in action and imagination, many of the same parts of the brain are activated. That is why visualizing can improve performance."[197]

Basketball coaches have been vaguely aware of this phenomenon for a long time—even if they didn't understand exactly why. In similar tests, basketball players who were only allowed to visualize shooting free throws scored nearly as high as those who actually practiced shooting free throws with a real basketball. All top level athletes use the power of visualization to improve their performance.

Neurologists Miguel Nicolelis and John Chapin of Duke University taught a rat to press a bar which sent an electrical impulse to a small tank of water. When it pressed the bar, a drop of water was released. A part of the rat's skull was removed and electrodes were attached to the motor cortex. The electrodes recorded the activity of forty-six neurons in the motor cortex which were active during the pressing of the bar. Each time the rat pressed the bar, those forty-six motor neurons sent an electronic firing pattern to a computer. The computer recorded that pattern and was soon able to "recognize" it whenever the rat pressed the bar.

Then Nicolelis and Chapin disconnected the wire from the bar to the water tank. The rat became frustrated when it pressed the bar because nothing happened. But the neuroscientists now connected the bar to the same computer that was still attached to the electrodes coming from the rat's brain. Whenever the rats had the thought "press the bar" the electrodes on the brain would send that same firing pattern to the computer, which would then yield a drop of water. After a few hours, the rat learned that it didn't have to press the bar at all. All it had to do was imagine pressing the bar, and presto, there would be water. Nicolelis and Chapin repeated the test with four separate rats. All four of the rats were able to make the tank yield water with the *power of thought*.[198] These same two neuroscientists used a similar method to teach a monkey to play video games using only its thoughts to move a cursor on a video screen and shoot at various moving targets.

All of this is very interesting, but what impact does it have on humans? In 1996, John Donaghue of Brown University used a similar technique on a human being named Matthew Nagle. Nagle had been stabbed in the back of the neck and was now paralyzed in all four limbs. Doctors implanted a tiny silicone chip with a hundred electrodes in Nagle's brain and attached it to a computer. After practicing for four days, Nagle was able to move a computer cursor on a screen, open email, change the channel on his TV, raise and lower the volume, play a computer game and control a robotic arm—all with the power of thought.[199]

Dr. Doidge explains that, "Each thought alters the physical state of your brain synapses at the microscopic level. Each time you imagine moving your fingers across the keys to play the piano, you alter the tendrils in your living brain."[200] It turns out that *thoughts are things*.

It is very common, and now almost passé, to praise the imagination when we discuss creativity and innovation. There are hundreds of now overused quotes out there about the power of the imagination. But the overwhelming scientific evidence now arms you with something you may have never considered before. With the power of our imagination, we have the ability to create new neuropathways in our brains. Literally. These new neuropathways are what enable you to get to the top of the next hill mentally to achieve a higher vantage point where you can see things you've never seen before. The smart get smarter.

On April 17, 2012, the *New York Times* reported that Cathy Hutchinson, who is paralyzed from the neck down, is able to manipulate a robotic arm *using just her thoughts*. She can use the robotic arm to reach out and grab objects. For example, she can pick up a cup of coffee and bring it to her mouth where she can sip it from a straw. Hutchinson had suffered a disabling stroke fifteen years earlier, which caused enough damage to separate her brain from her limbs. But now a tiny chip implanted just below her skull in the motor cortex in her brain allows her thoughts to travel down neural pathways to transmit an electrical signal to a computer that controls the robotic arm. All she has to do is *imagine* that she is controlling the arm.

The chip is a sensor that contains 96 pinprick electrodes that connect to a patch of neurons. When she imagines herself moving the arm, the neurons transmit a pattern to a computer through a tiny wire. The computer records those patterns and translates them into an electronic command, such as *move left*, or *down* or *up*. John P. Donoghue, a neuroscientist at Brown University explained that even though her brain is no longer connected to her limbs, "it is still able to generate all the neural activity necessary to make movements."[201]

We have known for a very long time that the brain can change our thoughts. But now we know that our thoughts can also change our brain. Ponder the magnitude of this new truth for a moment. Something *intangible* can affect something concrete and *tangible*. Imagine the various ways this can change your health, your career, your income, your wealth—and in fact, your entire life.

This new evidence puts to rest the philosophy submitted by René Descartes over 400 years ago when he argued that the mind and the brain were two entirely separate beings. Descartes argued that the mind was an intangible, spiritual being that existed outside the realm of the physical brain, and that it was subject to an entirely different set of principles, non-physical in nature. Descartes can be forgiven because he didn't have the tools or technology we have today. He was not able to observe the profound impact of *intangible* thoughts on the *tangible* brain. If he had he would have known without a doubt that thoughts, in fact, are things.

Once you grasp the magnitude of this truth, it opens up all kinds of possibilities for growth, change and rebirth. This is a true game changer. It turns out that we can actually rewire our own neuroconnections and mold our own brain *at the speed of thought.*

Like a muscle, the brain must be exercised in order to retain its ability to form new neuropathways. The brain craves new and interesting situations like a ravenous hunger. When you get that feeling of being "bored out of your mind," it's your brain telling you *it's starving.* Please feed it. This is also why solitary confinement is the worst form of punishment that can be used on a prisoner. Prisoners confined in a small 10 x 10 room with no light, no human interaction, no music, and nothing to do for extended periods of time often go crazy—literally.

> *The brain is like a muscle. When it is in use we feel very good. Understanding is joyous.*
>
> —CARL SAGAN

In order to retain your brain's ability to rejuvenate itself and create new neuropathways, it is critical that you be constantly learning something new that requires intense concentration for extended periods of time.[202] Neurologists recommend learning a foreign language, taking dance lessons, learning to play a musical instrument, learning one of the many available martial arts, interacting with new and different kinds of people in different social settings, and taking on new and challenging projects at work or at home.[203] The process of learning a new skill that requires intense concentration actually triggers what scientists call *neurogenesis*.[204] It is a rebirth of neurons.[205]

Recent studies have also confirmed that regular physical exercise strengthens existing neuron connections because it increases the flow of oxygen to the brain. Walking, cycling, hiking, mountain climbing, and running all strengthen the heart and the blood vessels, which keeps oxygen flowing to the brain, which keeps the neurons healthy and strong.[206] It has been confirmed that people who regularly do these things are sharper mentally and have better memories as they get older.[207] Frank Lloyd Wright designed the Guggenheim Museum at the age of ninety. Benjamin Franklin invented bifocal glasses at the age of seventy-eight. Internationally known cellist, Pablo Casals kept practicing the cello well into his nineties. When a student asked him why he continued to practice when he was already a master cellist, he replied, "Because I am making progress."[208]

> *The brain is a muscle, and I'm a kind of body-builder.*
>
> —Karl Lagerfeld

Even dealing with extremely stressful situations that require creative problem solving on your part keeps the brain young and moldable. Over the years, whenever I was dealing with a huge problem or a tragedy, my Dad's way of helping me deal with it was to say "It's gonna be okay son. It builds character." It turns out that diligently looking for and finding creative solutions to problems does more than just build character. It builds new neuropathways in the brain. It strengthens the existing synaptic connections, and creates new ones—assuming you don't just give up and walk away. When you give up and walk away, you are not only robbing yourself of the "character building" opportunity, you are robbing your neurons of the chance to grow and become stronger. You are robbing your brain of its *capacity to learn.*

> *What you get by achieving your goals is not as important as who you become by achieving your goals.*
>
> —Zig Ziglar

In short, if it is possible for the blind to see, the deaf to hear and the lame to walk, then certainly it is possible for a person of average intelligence to learn to be innovative and creative, and, more importantly, to see the solutions that are literally all around them. As with the game of basketball, you will always have a few "Michael Jordans" who have more raw talent than others. But even Michael Jordan admits that raw talent alone is not sufficient.[209] You need coaching, hard work, discipline, focus and the power of repetition to create new neuropathways in your brain.

> *Be transformed by the renewing of your mind.*
> —ROMANS 12:12 (NIV)

In fact, there is a group of young men who live in the tropical islands in the Burmese archipelago off the coast of Thailand who have a rare ability to see clearly underwater and to read placards without the blurred vision caused by refraction.[210] They can do all this without the use of goggles. They learn to swim before they learn to walk. They spend most of their lives living on boats and diving over thirty feet deep (without scuba gear) for clams and sea cucumbers. Scientists call them Sea Gypsies because they are nomadic tribes that move from island to island.

One particular tribe, the Sulu, can dive over seventy feet to search for pearls. Genetically, they are identical to you and me. But the neuropathways in their brains have adjusted to their life in the sea. When they are diving at great depths, their brains automatically change the shape of the internal lenses in their eyes, and constrict their pupils by 22 percent. This is the exact opposite of what most people's pupils do under water.[211] Most people's pupils get larger under water.

But their ability to see better than we do isn't limited to *under* the water. On December 26, 2004 a tsunami hit the Indian Ocean, killing hundreds of thousands of people. But not a single Sea Gypsy was injured.[212] Why not? They should have been the people *most affected* by the tsunami. They survived because they can also read the messages sent by the sea. They saw that the sea had receded in a strange way.[213]

They saw the dolphins head for deeper water. They saw the elephants stampede to higher ground. They heard the cicadas become deathly quiet. They began to recount ancient stories about "The Wave That Eats People" and started warning each other that it was coming again. Long before the tsunami hit, they had either fled to higher ground or had sailed far out to sea. They connected the dots long before all the oceanographers and earthquake experts did with all their sophisticated electronic technology.[214]

Ironically, thousands of Burmese fishermen who live in the same area, but use traditional fishing and harvesting methods perished. After the tsunami, an investigator asked one of the Sea Gypsies why so many of the Burmese fishermen had died in the tsunami. He answered, "They were looking at squid. They were not looking at anything. They saw nothing. They looked at nothing. They don't know how to look."[215] Likewise, ordinary people appear to be geniuses, not because they know *what* to look for, but because they know *how* to look.

The same may be true of you and someone living down the street from you. You can be living in the same neighborhood. Performing essentially the same type of function in society. Reading the same newspapers and books. Going to the same seminars and workshops. Listening to the same motivational speakers. Going to the same or similar places of worship. But one of you may have a superior ability to see solutions and opportunities than the other. Why?

It has little to do with education. It's because one of you has learned "how to look." The one who is obsessed with improving his life. The one who disciplines his mind and body to practice daily what he has learned in all those workshops and seminars. The one who has intense focus. The one who, through years of practice, has developed a heightened awareness. The one who knows that *thoughts are things*. The one who actually commands his brain to look for and find solutions. The one who walks around with the shape of the problem in his head—always looking for a key that fits. The one who has taught himself to see the hidden connections between unrelated objects. The one who can see that "this" is like "that." The one who has taught his brain to see the "tool in the bush."

The molecular structure of your body and your neighbor's body is essentially the same. You are both within the same class, genus and species. *Homo sapiens.* But the one who has learned how to mold and shape his own brain at the speed of thought will always be able to see more solutions. The beauty is that you can now start molding and shaping your brain and creating new neuropathways any time you truly get serious about it, and you can do it at the speed of thought. All it takes is that you start making the daily critical choices designed to get you there.

So, what's the common denominator that compels people to concentrate so hard on finding solutions that they actually end up rewiring their brains? What compels people like Pedro Bach-y-Rita to force their bodies, by the sheer force of their will, to keep struggling against all odds in order to create those new neuropathways that causes neurogenesis? What's the secret ingredient?

THINGS TO PONDER

+ The brain is more like a muscle than a computer.

+ When you walk away from a problem because it is too big for you, you are robbing your neurons of the chance to make new connections and become stronger.

+ It is possible to learn exercises that will open the eye of the brain.

+ Thoughts are things.

+ Something intangible can affect something tangible.

+ You can achieve neurogenesis.

+ In order to see hidden connections, you have to learn "how to look" all over again.

CHAPTER 26

When Is it Okay to Be Obsessed?

In the Summer Olympics of 2012 in London, Manteo Mitchell ran 400 meters of the men's 4x400 relay with a broken leg. His time was 45 seconds. In case you're wondering how long 400 meters is, it's 1,312.34 feet. There are 5,280 feet in a mile. So, that means Mitchell ran about a quarter of a mile in 45 seconds—with a broken leg! Mitchell says, "I was thinking I just didn't feel right. As soon as I took the first step past the 200 meter mark, I felt it break. I heard it. I even put out a little war cry, but the crowd was so loud you couldn't hear it. I wanted to just lie down. It felt like somebody literally just snapped my leg in half."

When asked why he kept running, Mitchell replied, "I knew if I finished strong we could still get it (the baton) around. I saw (teammate) Josh Mance motioning me in for me to hand it off to him, which lifted me. I didn't want to let those three guys down, or the team down, so I just ran on it. It hurt so bad. I'm pretty amazed that I split 45 seconds on a broken leg." The rest of the world was amazed too. Due to Mitchell's valiant effort, the U.S. team finished second in that heat and qualified to run in the finals, where it won a silver medal.

At the same Olympics, U.S. Olympic gymnast McKayla Maroney won a gold medal and a silver medal with a broken big toe on her right foot. "I've worked so hard to be here, I can ignore the pain," she said. Her teammate Jordyn Wieber won a gold medal with a stress fracture in her right leg. "It's the Olympic Games," she said. "It would take wild horses to drag me out of here."

Who can forget the words of U.S. women's gymnastics coach Bela Karolyi when he cupped Kerri Strug's face in his hands, stared her in the eye and said "You can do it Kerri!" It was the 1996 Summer Olympics. The Russian women's gymnastics team came into the team competition with a very narrow lead over the U.S. womens' team. The competition came down to one final event on the final day of the team competition. The vault.

The first four U.S. women landed their vaults, but struggled to land them cleanly. Teammate Dominique Moceanu fell twice on her landings. Strug was the last to vault for the United States. But on her first vault, she missed her landing, causing her to fall and damage her ankle badly. She received a lousy score. The whole world saw her limp off the mat. But she still had one more vault to go.

Just before her second vault, her coach uttered his now famous words, "You can do it Kerri!" She limped to the starting point. Millions of people around the world watched in disbelief and held their breath. Oblivious to the pain, she ran like a gazelle down the runway and hit the vault which launched her high up into the air where she performed a perfect aerial somersault with the kinds of twists and turns that only an Olympic gymnast can perform. But she still had to stick the landing. *Could she do it?* When her feet hit the mat hard, she winced in pain, but remained standing, hopping only slightly on her good foot, and saluting the judges instantaneously. The crowd went wild. Then she collapsed in pain. She scored a 9.712, which guaranteed the U.S. women's team would win the gold. Like an affectionate father, Bella Karolyi carried her tenderly in his arms like a baby to the medals podium to join her team for the awarding of the gold medals. It was an unforgettable moment.

At the 1976 Olympics, the Japanese men's gymnastics team was in a close race with the Soviet Union for the gold. Shun Fujimoto broke his knee during the floor exercise. But he continued to compete, not willing to let his teammates down. His dismount from the rings meant he would have to launch himself eight feet into the air and land on his bad leg, and remain standing perfectly still when he landed. Forgetting completely about the pain, he performed a flawless routine on the rings and flew into his dismount. He winced when he landed hard, and wobbled a bit. But he did not fall. He scored a 9.7. Afterward his doctor said, "How he managed to do somersaults and twists and land without collapsing in screams is beyond my comprehension." The Japanese won the gold by only 0.4 points.

Obsession is like putting a razor sharp edge on your mission. Trying to accomplish something great without it is like trying to cut leather with a butter knife. Nothing is quite as powerful as obsession put to a good cause. It cuts through obstacles like a laser beam. I remember when my Dad was trying to teach me how to play the guitar. I was a teenager. He said to me, "Son, you will never get good at anything unless you become obsessed with it." I have found that to be true throughout my life. It was true when I went to law school. It helped me graduate with honors from a top ten law school. I found it to be true when I wrote my first book. I found it to be true in each and every one of the countless numbers of lawsuits I won against corporate giants. I found it to be true when I took up running. I found it to be true when I took up salsa dancing. I found it to be true when I needed to lose weight.

Was anything great ever accomplished until someone became so obsessed with a fantasy that they turned it into a reality? Consider the following quote by expert stock trader Jim Rodgers.

> Most of us don't have the discipline to stay focused on a single goal for five, ten, or twenty years, giving up everything to bring it off, but that's what's necessary to become an Olympic champion, a world class surgeon, or a Kirov ballerina. Even then, of course, it may be all in vain. You may make a single mistake that wipes out all the work. It may ruin the sweet, lovable self you were at seventeen. That old adage is true: You can do anything in life, you just can't do everything. That's what Bacon meant when he said a wife and children were hostages to fortune. If you put them first, you probably won't run the three-and-a-half-minute-mile, make your first $10 million, write the great American novel, or go around the world on a motorcycle. Such goals take complete dedication.[216]

Throughout history, the power of obsession has driven ordinary women and men to accomplish incredible feats, and overcome otherwise immovable obstacles. Estée Lauder, the queen of skin care and perfume, describes her early days in the skin care industry like this: "Good was not good enough—I could always make it better. I know now that 'obsession' is the word for my zeal. I was obsessed with clear glowing skin, shining eyes, beautiful mouths. It was never quiet in the house. There was always a great audible sense of industry, especially in the kitchen, where I cooked for my family and during every possible spare moment, cooked up little pots of cream for faces. I always felt most alive when I was dabbling in the practice cream. I felt as though I was conducting a secret, absorbing experiment—a real adventure."[217]

The famous author Sir Walter Scott had been trying to compose a particular sentence all day. He finally decided to take a break and go hunting. Suddenly the right words leapt into his head. But he had no pen or paper with which to write. Afraid he would forget the sentence when he got back home, he shot a crow, plucked one of its feathers, used his hunting knife to sharpen the end into a quill, dipped it in the bird's blood and wrote the sentence down on the sleeve of his canvass hunting jacket.

While the famous artist Henry Matisse was lying sick in bed recovering from abdominal surgery near Nice, France, he longed to be able to get back to his canvas. Unable to get out of bed, he attached a piece of chalk to a long bamboo stick to draw pictures all over his bedroom wall.

Leonardo da Vinci would often paint from sun up to sun down never putting down his brush, forgetting to eat, forgetting to drink and painting without pause. Michelangelo would often sculpt and paint for days on end without sleep and with only very little to eat or drink until he fell over exhausted. He would not wash himself for days, and often slept on the dusty, dirty floor alongside his work. He once got his nose broken in a fist fight with another man over who was the better sculptor.

Albert Schatz, who discovered an effective treatment for tuberculosis, would often work eighteen hour days working in a dungeon-like laboratory to concentrate on the experiments he was working on, sleeping on the cold concrete floor with only two torn blankets for comfort.

Thomas Edison typically worked eighteen hour days for weeks on end, eating at his desk, refusing to stop for sleep or even showers. He did not like bathing and usually smelled of sweat and chemical solvents.[218]

In seeking a solution to the problem of bacteria killing people, Alexander Fleming said, "I was consumed by the desire to discover ... something which would kill these microbes."[219] Fleming would eventually discover penicillin for which he was awarded the Nobel Prize in Medicine.

When Syracuse fell to the Roman General Marcellus in 212 B.C., the great mathematician and physicist Archimedes was drawing geometric figures in the sand as he was surrounded by the turmoil of the massacre. His last words after being stabbed by a Roman sword were, "Noli turbare circulos meos" ("Pray, do not disturb my circles"). Geniuses and entrepreneurs have often found themselves under the grip of a powerful obsession that prevents them from focusing on anything else.

The great astronomer and mathematician Tycho de Brahe's nose was cut off by another Danish man in a fight over who was the better mathematician. That's what you call obsession.

On August 22, 1741, Handel was reading the Bible when he was so overcome in his spirit that the music came pouring out of him. He says that he could literally hear music from another world in his head, and that all he could do was write it down. He could not write fast enough. Several sources close to him record that Handel was so caught up in God's Spirit during the three weeks that it took him to write *MESSIAH,* that he actually locked himself within his study, refusing food and writing music amid periods of crying and moaning in that same spirit. Handel's servant described him as follows:

He was praying, or he was weeping,
or he was staring into eternity.

Another servant explains that at the end of this three-week period, Handel burst out of his study with tears in his eyes and the *Messiah* script in his hand declaring, that he had a great vision, and had seen God seated upon His throne;

> *I did think I did see all Heaven before me,*
> *and the great God Himself seated on His throne,*
> *with his Company of Angels.*

Powerful obsession often leads to divine inspiration.

When he was only 29 years old, doctor Werner Forssmann was so consumed with coming up with a way to perform a human heart catheterization, he actually performed it on himself while he was fully conscious. First he convinced an unwitting nurse to give him access to the surgical instruments. Then he injected a local anesthetic into the crease of his left elbow to deaden the pain so he could cut a hole big enough in his own artery to insert a thin sterile rubber tube. This kind of tube was typically used by urologists to drain urine from the kidneys. He then pushed the 26-inch long catheter up his artery and toward his heart.

Once the catheter was deep in Forssmann's arm, he walked down two flights of stairs to the X-ray department where he pushed the catheter into the atrium (upper chamber) of his own heart. He used a fluoroscopic fluid to allow the X-ray to reveal exactly where the tube was at all times. He documented the whole thing with a series of X-rays. He completely ignored the fact that the insertion of the tube into the sensitive endocardium (the inside lining of the heart) could cause fatal heart rhythms.

Forssmann recalls that a half-asleep bushy-haired young intern burst into the X-ray room and yelled "You idiot, what the *#@* are you doing?" He was so desperate to pull the catheter out of my arm. I had to give him a few kicks to the shin to calm him down."[220] Rumors soon spread that Forssmann had tried to commit suicide. But it was his obsessive passion for finding a solution to a problem that drove him forward. This sole act of determination, willpower, and incredible courage is what was required to demonstrate to doctors everywhere that a catheter could, in fact, be injected directly into the heart without significant risk of inducing a heart attack. Without this amazing feat of absolute obsession, the life-saving angioplasty procedure would not be possible today. Forssmann was awarded the Nobel Prize in medicine.

New York Times writer Joe Nocera describes the power of obsession as the thing that "caused Bill Gates to drop out of Harvard to start Microsoft, that drove Steve Jobs to build the first home computer in a garage, that motivated Marc Andreessen to create the first commercial browser while still in school."[221] I would also add that it was the thing that drove Mark Zuckerberg to ignore his studies at Harvard to start Facebook, and Michael Dell to ignore his studies at the University of Texas to start a small computer company.

Orrin Woodward said, "The word 'fanatic' is a loser's excuse for a winner's commitment."

Christopher Columbus described his passion to find a way to the Far East by traveling west as a "fire that burned within me." In 1490, a committee of the king's most learned men said Columbus' proposal was "mad" and that his errors were "colossal."[222] He lobbied King Ferdinand and Queen Isabella for fifteen years until they finally said "yes" to his request for funding and sponsorship.

The Wright brothers bicycle shop went broke because they would not give up on their incredible passion to build the first manned flying machine.

The brilliant playwright and movie producer, Tyler Perry lost everything he had and ended up sleeping on the streets for years until his first play "I Know I've Been Changed" finally became a success.

During one of Niccolo Paganini's great violin performances, each string of his violin began to break until only one remained. Paganini continued to play and finished the entire concerto on just one string. He received a standing ovation.

Even now as I write, a good friend of mine named Joe Barrero is sleeping (it's noon) because he was up till 5:30 a.m. writing code for his new project. Whatever it is you are doing, or trying to get good at, I can tell you from personal experience, but more importantly, from the historical record, that you will not excel at it—until you become obsessed with it. Until your life becomes so out of balance that it starts affecting your health, your relationships and perhaps your sanity—in order to see it succeed.[223]

Once it succeeds, you can gain all those things back. Then you will tell everyone, including your therapist, your pastor, your rabbi or your spiritual guru, that you are trying to live a more "balanced" life. And they will hug you and smile . . . knowingly.

The author of the best-seller *Outliers*, Malcolm Gladwell, claims you need to invest at least 10,000 hours into any craft in order to master it. In support, he cites a few isolated examples.[224] However, few people have the discipline and commitment and persistence required to invest that kind of time and energy into any craft. Most of us are willing to take a class or a workshop and try something for a few weeks, a few months, or even a few years. But when we realize that rising to the top of the industry is going to take a lot more time, energy, and money than we ever anticipated, we soon become disenchanted and move on to the next project.

The missing ingredient that Gladwell does not talk about is obsession. When you are obsessed with something, wild horses can't drag you away from it. The words, *discipline* and *commitment* aren't even part of your vocabulary. These may be the words others use to describe what you do. But the words you use are *love, excitement, thrilling,* and *fun*. Michael Jordan explained it this way:

> When you love anything, you'll go to extremes to maintain that love. That's what love does. It drives you to do everything you can to maintain that connection. . . . Only love can make you overcome all the obstacles that will be thrown your way.[225]

As I surfed through Facebook today to see how my friends were doing, I stumbled across the "status" of a good friend and legendary artist named Michelle Dunaway. Her status was as follows, "Stopped and did a quick painting on the way back home from Carmel, California. It was very cold and windy outside. My fingers were numb, my hair tangled, and I felt blissfully happy!"

When you are obsessed with something, you think about it while you are eating, drinking, talking, walking, working, playing, driving and sleeping. Everything seems to remind you of it. You simply can't turn it off. Thinking about doing it again tomorrow does not evoke the kind of pain we think of when we hear the word "discipline." This is something you would do even if no one were paying you. Unless have that kind of obsession, you will never invest 10,000 hours into anything.

Here's a litmus test. If you have to grit your teeth, and tighten your gut, and listen to motivational CDs in order to muster up the strength to perform the task again tomorrow, this is not your passion.[226] On the other hand, if you could spontaneously, without preparation, give a ten minute motivational presentation that explains what you do and how you do it, this just might be your passion.

I will no doubt, catch some flak from people who will send me a list of their personal friends who have succeeded just fine without any degree of obsession. I know they exist. I even have such friends. I applaud those people. I tip my hat to them. But they live their lives in relative anonymity.

The people whose names we remember, the people they write books about, the people they make movies about, are the people who became so obsessed with the task at hand that they change entire industries, change lives, and indeed, change history.

The following quote is from a friend of mine named Teresa Castle, a consummate entrepreneur, who read this chapter when it appeared as one of my blog posts.

> It's even more than that. If you have to talk yourself into becoming obsessed with something, then that thing is probably not going to be your Apple, Inc. It's more like something clicks and you just CAN'T be stopped. And I don't mean like an "oh, isn't that great ... she's so motivated" kind of can't be stopped. I mean like a semi-truck barreling down the side of a double black mountain kind of can't be stopped. Even you

can't put on the brakes. That gravitational force has taken over and you WILL get down that mountain and you WILL barrel through whatever obstacles get in your way.

Whatever force is driving that truck is different for different people but it's similarly and dangerously powerful. The obsession is only what is observable to others. It is you gripping the wheel like it's your life (and at that moment, it is) that they see. What they don't see is what's driving that obsession.

Psychologist John D. Gartner, of Johns Hopkins Medical School, describes the kind of obsession that drives legendary entrepreneurs as "hypomania"—the point closest to the edge of sanity before you step over into craziness: "Yet without their irrational confidence, ambitious vision, and unstoppable zeal, these outrageous captains would never have sailed into unknown waters, never discovered new worlds, never changed the course of our history."[227]

But be careful. There is a difference between obsession with a worthwhile goal that will benefit humanity and naked, self-serving, neurotic ambition. Neurotic ambition is self-centered. Neurotic ambition eventually destroys the soul. Neurotic ambition may temporarily reach its goals, but it destroys everything in its path in order to get there, and eventually destroys itself. You may have met someone like this.

The kind of obsession I am talking about is obstinate optimism in the face of immovable obstacles. It is dedicated toward creating something of value in the world where it did not exist before—not simply taking already existing value from others. It is the application of massive action onto the simplest and narrowest of goals. This kind of obsession gives you a kind of hyper focus, and laser-like vision to see solutions that are invisible to others. Leonardo da Vinci said, "Those who are obsessed with practice, but have no science are like a pilot setting out with no tiller, or compass, who will never know for certain where he is going."[228] This kind of obsession requires discipline, a system and a methodology. It is not simply a random explosion of energy in all directions. Only when you are absolutely obsessed with finding a solution, and you use a systematic approach, will you begin to see the solutions that are all around you.

Sam Walton was in a meeting with the local manager and the staff of one of his stores. He posed this question to his team. "A single mom walks in at five minutes till closing time. She's looking for three pairs of socks. How can we save her $1.50?" Sam Walton was obsessed with saving his customers money.

A.G. Lafley, the CEO of Proctor & Gamble from 2002 to 2010 was obsessed with the learning and understanding the customer's experience. He required his upper level executives to actually go and spend time in the homes of individual consumers and help them do laundry using Tide and other Proctor & Gamble products. Proctor & Gamble had just spent millions of dollars redesigning and repackaging the Tide box, and had shipped it out to all the stores. Shortly thereafter, an executive was having dinner in the home of a woman who was a long-time Tide user.

After dinner, she happily said to him, "Let's go do some laundry!" She walked him into her laundry room, picked up a screw driver from a shelf and began violently stabbing the top of the Tide box over and over. It was a like a scene from a bad horror movie. Like blood squirting, Tide sprayed out everywhere. His mouth hung open as he stared in disbelief. She was absolutely destroying the new box and the graphics of the new box they had spent millions developing. He swallowed hard and faked a smile, "May I ask what are you doing?" he finally asked. "Oh, it's nothing. The stuff inside is great once you get to it. But this is the only way you can get the box open." But for A.G. Lafley's obsession with the customer's experience, the executives at Proctor & Gamble would never have known about this little problem.

Think about how a knife works. The entire weight and heft of a knife is designed to put all the pressure onto the narrowest part of the knife. Not the blade, but the tiny edge of the blade. If you ever look at the edge of a blade under a microscope, you will see that the edge of the blade is honed down to just a few molecules. It is when there is massive weight behind those tiny few molecules and they are applied to an apple, or a steak, or a tough piece of leather that the knife's edge does its best work.

The edge of a sharp knife is so narrow that it literally slips between the molecules of the thing it is cutting and separates them from each other, dividing the thing in two. This is how the power of obsession works. Massive power and energy focused on a single task.

When I was in college, my best friend Chris Webb gave me a very expensive camping knife for my birthday. It was the coolest and most expensive knife I had. It had a polished wooden handle, and the blade glinted like lightning in the moonlight. It was so sharp it easily but painlessly cut me when I slid my finger across it for the first time. I remember staring at my bleeding finger thinking to myself—*wow*. I was so proud of it I didn't want to use it. I didn't want the blade to get dull. So, I put it back into its black leather sheath and hid it away in a safe place. For years, that knife stayed hidden, sharper than ever, but never used. I always took cheaper knives on my camping trips. Eventually, I forgot I even had it. Twenty years later, I stumbled across it. A smile came across my face. I pulled it out of its black leather sheath. I unfolded it. I gently ran my finger across the blade. It was just as sharp as the day I first opened it. I felt no pain as I watched my finger bleed. The beautiful polished wooden handle was still as shiny as before. But then it hit me. I had never actually allowed myself the pleasure of using this knife to do anything fun. Never took it camping. Never took it hunting. Never took it fishing. All these years, I had been robbing myself of the joy of using it. But a knife left in the drawer can never do its job. It can never fulfill the purpose for which it was created. In my efforts to preserve it, I had denied myself the enjoyment of it. It was wake up call.

What else in my life was I holding back, saving it for a special occasion? Waiting for just the right moment? What gifts, talents, and treasures lie within me, like an unfolded pocket knife, begging to be released? Why was I depriving myself and the world of these gifts?

The most successful athletes in the world leave nothing in their gas tank when they are in the heat of the battle. They leave it all out on the field. They are absolutely spent by the end of the contest. Many of them collapse on the field just after the event. There is nothing left. And if you think about it, there *should be* nothing left. If you are holding something back for a better day, then why are you on the field to begin with? If you are not in it to win it, then why are you playing the game?

In 1950, Red McCombs walked away from a promising career as an attorney because he found the law "too confining." At the end of his second year of law school, the assistant dean at the University of Texas School of Law told Red he was making a great mistake by walking away because the legal profession was such an "honorable profession." Red simply said, "Well, let someone else have that honor," and walked out. Red only meant to sell cars for six weeks while he was waiting to start his training as a sales representative in the heavy construction industry in Jackson, Mississippi. He sold a car his first day on the job, and quickly became the best car salesman in Corpus Christi, selling 30–35 cars a month. The average sales representative sells between eight and ten cars a month (both then and now). Red was hooked.

Because he was raised during the Great Depression, Red had a natural tendency to save every penny he earned. During his time in Corpus Christi, he had partnered with a friend to buy and then sell a small local "farm team" baseball team for a profit. He had saved up around $100,000 combined from his commissions and the profit he made from selling the baseball team. A struggling Ford car dealer in San Antonio heard about Red and invited him to partner with him on a hand-shake deal. The first thing Red did was commit the entire $100,000 to a massive radio campaign that aired over the most popular radio station in San Antonio—KTSA. Red's business partner tried to talk him out of it because the dealership was struggling. "That's a lot of money Red," he said. "And we might still lose everything." But Red was undaunted. In his mind, he wasn't taking a risk at all. He wasn't betting on the business. He was betting on himself.

In addition to the radio spots he bought, he paid the most popular disc jockey a bonus to mention Red's car dealership every time he got the chance. Then he retrained the sales reps in his own way of selling. Soon, sales began to explode. The struggling car dealership was saved and became the biggest car dealership in San Antonio. When the upper management at Ford headquarters in Michigan heard about Red's success, they asked him if he was interested in taking over other struggling Ford dealerships in Houston and Dallas. Red, of course, said yes, and soon owned Ford dealerships all over Texas. Then he repeated the process and ended up owning car dealerships all over the United States.

That was the stepping stone to Red's incredible success, including owning the San Antonio Spurs, the Minnesota Vikings, the Denver Nuggets, and Clear Channel Communications, the biggest radio production company in the U.S. When I asked Red how he did it, his answer was simple. He never went home unless he sold at least one car. If he had a slow day, he would take one of the used cars on his lot and drive it over to another dealer, and sell it for a few hundred dollars, or whatever he could get. He did anything and everything he could do to generate a little cash flow every single day. "Cash flow is the mother's milk of any business Dan," he told me. "Without it, you're dead in the water." I learned a great lesson that day.

Red was absolutely obsessed with daily cash flow. Not for the sake of greed, but for the sake of surviving and succeeding. He grew up dirt poor in the tiny town of Spur, Texas. He said, "I'm not as smart as you are Dan. I never did anything special. Never invented anything. Never came up with anything all that innovative. I'm just a peddler." I was speechless . . . and humbled. Red succeeded beyond his wildest dreams because he applied massive action to a single, narrowly defined goal. Selling cars. It was not all that sexy, not very cutting edge, not very earth shattering. But it worked—as nothing but obsession can.

The famous preacher Gerald Mann explains about how he had once prepared what he believed would be an amazing sermon that would move thousands to action. But on this particular Sunday, only a few people showed up. He thought about changing the sermon at the last minute so he could save his best sermon for a bigger crowd. But he remembered a bit of advice an old retired preacher had given him years before. "Always give 'em your best stuff. Never hold anything back. There will never be a better time than this." So Gerald let 'em have it with both guns blazing. He preached to that handful of people like he was preaching to a hundred thousand people in a giant football stadium. Sunday after Sunday he did this. Staying faithful to the mission. Always giving 'em his best stuff. Never holding anything back. Eventually, that small handful of people became hundreds and the hundreds became thousands. Eventually, they had to build a bigger church. Eventually, the bigger church was not big enough and they had to build an even bigger church, which became one of the biggest mega-churches in Austin. That same preacher eventually touched my own life in ways he will never know—because he never held anything back. In pouring his entire heart, mind and soul into each and every sermon, he ended up touching the lives of millions of people throughout his career.

Subrahmanyan Chandrasekhar was an astrophysicist from India. He left India in 1933 by slow boat from Calcutta to England. On the boat ride, he wrote a paper that led to the theory of black holes. He eventually immigrated to the United States. While living in Williams Bay, Wisconsin, he was asked to teach a seminar at the University of Chicago. But only two people showed up. Everyone thought he would cancel the seminar. But he didn't. Instead, he drove back and forth to Chicago from Wisconsin twice a week to teach that class. Eventually both of his students won the Nobel Prize for Physics.[229] In 1983, Chandrasekhar himself was awarded the Nobel Prize for Physics.

What special gift or bit of knowledge do you have that you are saving for a "special occasion?" Whatever it is, the time to use it *is now*. The time to share it with your guests *is now*. The time to unleash it on the world *is now*. You aren't getting any younger. The people who need it are waiting for you to take massive action focused on a single, solitary goal—*now*. The life you've always dreamed of living wants to be born *now!* Can you feel it kicking inside you like a baby longing to get out? Can you feel the labor pains deep inside you telling you to take action *now*? It *cannot* wait. It *will not* wait. However, before you can ever become *sufficiently obsessed* with a goal to make it come true, you have to have a "big enough reason why."

THINGS TO PONDER

+ Before you can achieve anything great, you have to become obsessed with it.

+ Only the "love of the game" will push you past the obstacles thrown in your way by self-doubt, by the naysayers, by lack of money, by lack of education, and early disasters. Nothing else can. Nothing else will.

+ Powerful obsession in pursuit of a worthy cause often leads to divine inspiration.

CHAPTER 27

⫷⫸

What's Your Big Enough Reason Why?

It was 1912, and the Mexican Revolution was raging throughout Mexico. Thousands of refugees were fleeing Mexico to the safety of Texas, New Mexico, Arizona and California. Juan Salvador Villasenor Castro was 11 years old.[230] The village founded by his grandfather Don Pio Castro in Los Alto de Jalisco had been destroyed by the war. Juan and his family had saved for months and months to be able to afford the train tickets that would lead them to El Paso, Texas. They were so poor that little Juan had no shoes. But eager to escape the slaughter, they had traveled for weeks on foot with all of their earthly possessions being pulled by burros and carts. Along the way, they passed burned out villages, and the bloated bodies of soldiers and carcasses of horses. Eventually, they ran out of food and had to eat their own burro. Little Juan cried and ran and hid while the others ate. He couldn't eat a single bite.

When they got to the little village of Leon where the train would pick them up, they had to wait a few days. Juan met some other little boys and they began to run foot races to see who was the fastest. On the day the train arrived, they decided to have one last foot race, but they threw in an element from the game of "chicken." There were five boys, and the challenge was to stand behind the train and when the train took off to see which boy would chicken out first and run to catch the train. It was extremely dangerous because to miss the train meant they would be separated from their families during the middle of the revolution and would have no means to take care of themselves.

The giant iron wheels of the train began to turn. Slowly at first. Then a little faster. The first little boy took off like a shot and caught the train. A bead of sweat ran down Juan's face. A tremor pulsed through his body. The train was going faster now. Two other little boys took off and caught the train. Now it was just Juan and another boy named Eduardo standing there crouched in a runner's stance watching the train. Juan watched as the train picked up speed. His fingers started to twitch. He glanced at Eduardo nervously and then back at the train. Then at Eduardo. Then at the train. Then both boys took off as fast as they could. Huffing and puffing, little Juan held onto his hat as he ran faster and faster. He reached out and could barely touch the hand rail at the end of the train, but his fingers were not long enough to grasp it.

Juan fell over face first in the tracks, ripping open his mouth. He lay there in the dirt and the rocks, spitting blood and dust. When he looked up, he could see the train getting smaller and smaller in the horizon. Tears welled up in his eyes. Eduardo stood up and laughed at Juan. "Why are you laughing?" said Juan. "There goes your family. There goes my family, and we're never going to see them again!" Eduardo turned to walk away. "Pendejo!" he said. "My aunt and uncle live here in Leon. I can always stay with them and catch the next train." He left Juan lying there in the dust and the blood.

Little Juan stood up. He dusted himself off. He looked around at the vast desert all around him, and did the only thing he knew to do. Catch that train. He ran. He ran, and he ran. He stopped to rest and saw that his feet were swollen and cracked and bleeding. But he kept running, running, and running. Then he walked for a while. His grandfather had taught him how to survive in the desert by eating the fruit of the cactus, which is a purplish color, and looks like a small heart shaped fig. When Juan found the fruit of the cactus, he picked it off and ate some and put the rest in his pocket. He spent a cold night in the desert and threw rocks at a mountain lion to keep it away.

The next day, he got up and ran, and walked and bled some more. Twenty-four hours after he started, he finally got to the next village where the train had stopped. His lips were white and his tongue was swollen. He was staggering through town asking "Have you seen my family? Have you seen my family? At first people said, "No." But finally, someone said, "Yes, they are over there." When he saw his Mom, he ran to her and jumped into her arms. "Mijito, mijito! How did you get here? Es un milagro!" his Mom cried. But all Juan could do was hold her and cry because, you see, even he did not understand how he had gotten there. It truly was a miracle.

When I first read that true story in the book *Rain of Gold* by Victor Villasenor, who is the son of the man little Juan grew up to be, I was in awe. "Now *that's* motivation," I said. Then I wondered, what if I had offered little Juan a huge gold medal and said, "Juan, what I want you to do is run barefoot through the desert for twenty-four hours with no food and no water. If you can do that and survive, I'll give you this gold medal." Would that have been enough? Somehow I knew the answer was *no.* But Juan did it. Why? Because he had a *big enough reason why.* That's the kind of burning, overriding passion you need to accomplish your goals. Whatever it is you are working toward, if you are doing it with any less commitment, discipline, passion and obsession, then it's just a hobby. You are simply a participant in someone else's game.

Limits, like fears, are often an illusion.[231]

—MICHAEL JORDAN

Without enough motivation, you will not have the discipline to daily engage in the very strenuous mental, emotional and physical activities that are required to rewire your brain in a way that will open the eye of the brain. If you are doing it just for the money, then when you stumble, when you suffer a setback, or when things get too difficult, you will quit because somewhere along the way, when the going gets tough, you will say to yourself, "I've worked hard. I'm doing fine now. Why do I need to do more?" Then you will start quoting Jesus or some other spiritual leader that taught us how to be content with what we have. But if you are obsessed with a higher purpose, a purpose you can't put a price tag on, then nothing, and *I mean nothing,* can stop you.

Shannon Sharpe's acceptance speech into the NFL Football Hall of Fame is one of the best descriptions of the driving force that compels people to achieve great things that I have ever heard. When I first heard it, I was moved to tears. I will let him describe his big enough reason why—in his own words.[232]

> You need to walk 20 years in this body and feel this raging *inferno* that I felt to get out of Glennville, to leave that thousand square foot cinder block home with the cement floors, to leave what my grandmother said, 'Baby, is it going to be the gas this month that I'm going to pay or is it going to be the lights? Do you want to eat or do you want light to see so can you do your homework? Son, do you want the phone just in case there's an emergency we can call somebody? What is it going to be this month?' ***That drove me. That drove me!***
>
> Nobody ever knew how much this *five alarm fire raged inside of me*. My sister didn't know, my brother didn't know, *but it raged*. I had to leave Glennville. I had to make a better way for my brothers, for my sister, for my mom. I didn't want my kids to live one night, not one hour, not one hour in the life that I had, let alone a day.
>
> And I neglected my kids. I missed recitals, I missed football practice, I missed graduations because *I was so obsessed with being the best player I could possibly be* that I neglected a lot of people. I ruined a lot of relationships. But I'm not here to apologize for that because it got me here and it got them to a life they never would have enjoyed had it not been for that.
>
> I want to leave you with this: My position coach who is sitting right there in the stands, Les Steckel once asked me, '*Son, why do you work so hard? Every time at lunch you're not eating, you're in the gym, you're working out.*
>
> You study harder, you practice harder, you have more fun.' I said, 'Les, I never want to eat cold oatmeal again." I said, '*You don't know what it's like, Les, to grow up like I grew up. To eat the animals that I ate. I remember eating raccoon. I*

remember eating possum. I remember eating squirrel and turtle. I remember those days.' I said, 'I ate that now as a kid, but I'm not going to have to eat that when I become an adult.'

The one story I want to leave you with, to tell you why I became this person: When I was 12 years old I told my mom, 'Mom, I'm going to have some money one day, and I'm going to buy you a Mercedes, and I did.'

When I came and I asked my grandmother, what do you want? She always called me her baby. She never called me by my name. I said, 'You want me to buy you a car and teach you how to drive?' She said, 'No, son, I don't want that. I said, 'Granny, do you want jewelry?' She said, 'No, son, I don't want that. She said, 'Son, I want a decent house.'

And I'm thinking well, my grandmother wants 7,000, 8,000 square feet. But then I knew my grandmother, knowing her like I know her, after pausing for five or six minutes. I said, 'Granny, what is a decent home?' And I remember it like yesterday, and it was 30-plus years ago.

She said, son, I want a decent home and her words verbatim is 'Son, I want to go to bed one night,' and she said, *'I want God to let it rain as hard as he possibly can, and I want him to let it rain all night long.' She said, 'I want to wake up and not be wet.'* That's a decent home for my grandmother. That's all she wanted! For 66 years, my grandmother never went to bed and had it rain and not be wet the next morning. I remember those days of putting those plastic coats on the bed and I'm going to date myself and call them croaker sacks but now we call them burlap bags. I remember that.

I remember putting the pots and pans on the floor to catch the rain water. The very pots and pans that we're going to cook in the next day. *I remember that.* It broke my heart that my grandmother, all she wanted was . . . look here, she's got two grand boys that are making millions of dollars, and she wanted a house that wouldn't leak. That's all she wanted! That's all my grandmother wanted!

For two boys that are making millions and all you want is a decent house. You want to go to bed and not get wet when you wake up. ***That's what drove Shannon. That's what got me here.***[233]

But that kind of motivation is not limited to genetically gifted superstar athletes. In September 2004, in the little town of Beslan in Russia, a group of masked men stormed a middle-school and took the whole school hostage. A young 17-year-old girl named Karina Bega-yeva had a chance to escape with other children who hid in the boiler room. But she turned back and ran into the school gymnasium where most of the kids were being held. Why would anyone flee safety and knowingly run headlong into danger? Because she *saw something no one else could see.* Her little brother was in there.

She knew that her brother could not walk because of his withered leg. Over the next three days, the terrorists made all of the children strip down to their underwear and refused to give them food or water. When the children cried, they shot rifles into the air and threatened to kill them if they did not stop crying. They forced them to drink their own urine. After three days without food or water, the children began to grow weak and sick.

Outside the building, 10,000 Russian troops kept watch, waiting for an opportunity to strike or to negotiate a peaceful solution. But then the sounds of an explosion and gunfire filled the air. Naked school children ran from the school being shot at by the terrorists as they fled. Russian special-forces stormed the building. Relatives screamed in helpless horror.

When the first bomb blast happened, a piece of shrapnel tore through Karina's left foot. Half blinded by the blast and choking on the dense smoke, she could barely stand. But she knew she only had a few seconds to get herself and her brother to safety. She somehow managed to reach for her brother's arm and half-carry, half-drag him along in the midst of the chaos as the firefight between the terrorists and the Russian special-forces erupted all around them. She managed to scramble out through a broken window where Russian police ran up and whisked them away.

What would possess a frail young 17-year-old girl to run back toward terrorists carrying machine guns and bombs when other kids were running to safety? It was the love for her brother. When you focus on a purpose that is bigger than yourself, you see things that others cannot see. You see the "big enough reason why" that is invisible to others. Nothing else matters. It's what you alone can see that matters. When you believe in a cause that is worth fighting for, you can do almost anything. Age, size, gender, skills and equipment do not matter. If you have a big enough reason "why," you can always find the answer to "how?"

As a business litigation attorney, I have seen business partners deceive, betray, and backstab each other over money more times than I can count. You can only be in business for so long before, sooner or later, someone will do something so despicable you wouldn't believe it unless it actually happened to you. You can only live life for so many years before one of your closest friends or family member will betray you. You need to make up your mind now how you will handle it because eventually, if it hasn't happened already, it will. In the heat of that moment, you will be too angry, too depressed, or too vengeful to think straight.

The following is a note I posted on Facebook a few years ago after I had been betrayed in business. I wrote it in an attempt to regain my focus and drive myself forward toward my goal instead of letting those who had betrayed me continue to steer my brain cells and energy off course. I share it with you only because I hope it will give you some resolve to keep going *in the right direction*—no matter what.

Just Keep Walking

Nobody ever said life was fair ....
Nobody ever said life was just ....
Okay, maybe they did, but they were *pretty stoopid*.
And they never got anywhere in life.

Truth is, life is not very fair at all. That's why we have revolts in third world countries all the time.

That's why we have *always had revolts* ... throughout the history of mankind.

Fact is:

Truth does not ALWAYS win out ....

Justice does not ALWAYS prevail ....

Right does not ALWAYS win over wrong ....

Sometimes the bad guys really do win .... and get the last laugh.........

Great riches do not ALWAYS go to the smartest and hardest working among us

The best-selling authors are not always the best writers.................

The Grammy does not always go to the best musician ....

The Oscar does not always go to the best actor ....

The contract does not always go to the lowest bidder ....

So what are we to do?

Crawl under a rock and die?

Moan and weep and seek counseling?

Get drunk?

Get drugs?

Get laid?

Go to church?

Pray?

Meditate?

Ok, sometimes all of the above.......... and not necessarily in that order...........

But in the final analysis, all we can do is acknowledge that the world does not revolve around us and our petty wants and needs and desires.

When we find ourselves face down in the dirt, all we can do is slowly stand up, dust ourselves off, wipe our tears and slowly put one foot in front of the other.

And look up toward the horizon.

Yes, that's it. Pick a point on the horizon, and start walking
 towards it.
Yes, just one foot.........now the other.....
That's it............
And keep walking ....even though your feet are bleeding, and
 blistered and bruised........
Keep walking.......

And keep looking up toward the horizon..........
Not at your feet..........
Not at those who have gotten in your way......
Not at those who have knocked you down.....
Not at how far you've come........
But ahead to where you are going........

Focus on it.
Form a picture of it in your mind......
Yes, cement that picture firmly in your mind so that after the sun
 goes down and you can no longer see it, you can still see it
 with your mind's eye.
So that you can keep walking, guided only by the stars and the
 light of the moon.

And when someone asks why you keep walking, you just look at
 them and smile, and point your finger toward your goal and
 say *THAT* is the reason......
And keep walking..........

Even if "they" can't see what you see.......
And keep laughing........
And crying.........
And persevering........
Because only you know the reason.........
You will always . . . keep walking.......

Obsession with a worthy cause can do more than change your life.
It can change the course of history.

THINGS TO PONDER

- Identify your "big enough reason why," and embrace it with all your heart.

- When you suffer a crisis, don't focus on what you've lost. Focus on what you have left.

- When you fall, try to fall forward in the direction of your goal.

CHAPTER 28

————— ⊰⊱ —————

Is There a Way to Level the Playing Field?

Innovation, creativity and entrepreneurship have always been and will always be the great equalizers. No matter what your race, your social class, your income, your pedigree, your education level, if you can identify and solve problems, you can write your own ticket in this world. The co-founder of the global advertising agency, GSD&M, Roy Spence says, "Entrepreneurship is the purest form of lifting people up there is." But entrepreneurship is first and foremost about solving other people's problems. If you can do that, you can change the world.

One of the oldest and best known examples comes from approximately four thousand years ago. Like the black slaves who would come several thousand years after them, an entire race of people, the Hebrews, were enslaved in Egypt. They were born slaves. They were not allowed to read or write. They spent their entire lives doing back-breaking work, and they died slaves.

But along came a lowly slave who had been kicked out by his own people. He had a gift for solving problems. He could interpret dreams. The book of Genesis describes him as a guy who couldn't stay out of trouble. His own brothers hated him because he was his father's favorite. They sold him as a boy into slavery and told their father a wild animal had killed him.

The boy was traded as property again and again until he ended up a slave in the house of a high Egyptian official named Potiphar. He worked hard, and was gracious and very intelligent. He did such a good job that eventually Potiphar put him in charge of his entire household, managing all the other slaves, and running the daily affairs of the villa. At some point, Potiphar's wife took a liking to the now young man and tried to seduce him. When he refused, she accused him of rape, and had him thrown in jail.

In jail, he developed a reputation for interpreting dreams. When Pharaoh had a dream that none of his spiritual advisers could interpret, word came to him about a Hebrew slave in prison who might be able to help. Pharaoh sent for the slave. He accurately interpreted the dream as a premonition of seven years of great harvests followed by seven years of great famine. He advised Pharaoh to store up as much grain as he could during the seven good years. Pharaoh followed his advice and when the famine hit, Egypt was the only country for thousands of miles that had enough food to survive. Pharaoh promoted him to his second in command.

Eventually, the slave's own family was forced to travel to Egypt to trade goods for food. In a heart wrenching reunion, the slave forgave his brothers with the words, "What you meant to me for evil, God meant to me for good." The slave believed God had sent him ahead of his family to Egypt to prepare them for the great famine. His name was Joseph. His family eventually settled in Egypt and became the worker bees of the Egyptian society. They were ultimately enslaved for approximately four hundred years. Then came Moses.

Throughout the ages, those who were oppressed, tortured, enslaved, and discriminated against found a way to overcome by solving problems. The stories of Harriett Tubman, Rosa Parks, Martin Luther King, Jr., Nelson Mandela, and Oprah Winfrey are well known. But here are a few heroes whose stories you may not have heard.

Cathy Hughes was an employee at a small AM radio station in Washington, D.C. She was a high school dropout, and a single mother who had a child at age seventeen. Because she was so poor, she was evicted from her apartment and had to sleep in the radio station. Most people would have given up, gotten on welfare and said, "That's it! I quit! I have no opportunity in this country. Too many rich white people. I have no education. I'm oppressed. I'm a single mom." The list of excuses could have gone on and on, including "The government owes me this."

But when the station was on the brink of going under, she offered to buy it with the little bit of money she had saved as a down payment. But when she tried to get a loan, she was turned down by 32 separate banks. Seriously, would you have loaned her $1 million if you had a few million extra dollars lying around? Finally, someone said yes and loaned her $1 million to buy the station. She called her radio company Radio One. She changed the programming from R&B music to a 24-hour talk radio format. But she didn't stop there. Radio One now owns at least 53 radio stations in nine major markets in the U.S. In 1999, Radio One became a publicly traded company, listed under the NASDAQ stock exchange. It was her ability to solve problems, not government aid or affirmative action that lifted her up.

Tyler Perry was abused as a child. He grew up angry, bitter and disillusioned. As an adult, he discovered from watching an episode of *Oprah* that journaling was very therapeutic and could help him resolve old issues. He learned to forgive. Then he turned his journal into a play called *I Know I've Been Changed*. For several years he worked at trying to produce the play in Atlanta, Georgia. But when the show aired, it was a total failure. Still he did not give up.

He worked hard to improve the play. He became obsessed with it to the point that he ran out of money and was jobless. His friends and family urged him to give up on this senseless project and get a real job. Driven by his passion and little else, he ended up living on the streets for several years in order to save enough money to produce the play. When the play finally opened at The House of Blues in Atlanta it was a smash-hit and played every night to sold-out audiences. The success of this one play led to the production of a movie called *Diary of a Mad Black Woman*. This led to other movies, like *Madea's Family Reunion*, *Daddy's Little Girls*, *Meet the Browns*, *The Family That Preys*, and *I Can Do Bad All By Myself*. In 2011, *Forbes* named Tyler Perry the highest paid man in entertainment, earning $130 million between May 2010 and 2011.

Oseola McCarty was an 88-year-old African-American woman who had been a washerwoman all her life, living in Hattiesburg, Mississippi. She lived in a small home left to her by her uncle, doing laundry for others out of her house for a few dollars at a time. She had a dog named Dog, a hog named Hog, and a cow named Hazel. She had lived by herself since 1967, working every day for a meager income. But she had a great gift—the gift of generosity. Osceola possessed the gift of wanting to help others succeed. On July 26, 1995, she did a very simple thing. She made a decision to give what she had to others, not knowing it would change the rest of her life. Over the years, she'd been saving the little money she made, never wanting much and never needing much. Knowing that she was getting up in age, she decided to dedicate her life savings to the University of Southern Mississippi to finance scholarships. She walked into her bank and asked them to give away her life savings, which amounted to several hundred thousand dollars. She did so without fanfare, without press conferences, without press releases, and without expecting anything in return. It was a simple act of generosity.

Oseola's generosity made her a national celebrity. Within weeks of her gift, Oseola had been interviewed by every major news organization in the nation. She was on the front page of the *New York Times* and the *Hattiesburg American*. She was on *Good Morning America* and named one of Barbara Walters' 10 Most Interesting People of 1995. She was interviewed by *Tiempo Nuevo*, a "live" Argentine television show and featured in magazines such as *Ebony, Jet, People, Guidepost,* and *Glamour.* She was on the BBC and MTV and she carried the Olympic torch a short distance during the 1996 Olympics in Atlanta.

Oseola has received countless humanitarian awards and has met with the President of the United States. Roberta Flack and Patti LaBelle have sung her songs. Harvard University gave her an honorary degree. Whoopi Goldberg knelt at her feet.

Before her gift, Oseola McCarty had been out of Mississippi only once and she had never been on an airplane. Now she flies all over the country to receive plaques and awards and to eat dinner with celebrities. Her friends say that the transition in her life has been like watching the petals of a flower open. People have called her holy. People who talk to her say she makes them feel "clean." They say they feel peace when they're with her. She wrote and published a book of her sayings called *Simple Wisdom For Rich Living.*

Oseola McCarty is no miracle worker. She had no extraordinary talent, athletic ability, musical ability, mental genius, status, or social connections to speak of. But she did have the ability to see and hear the world around her as only heroes can. She was not angry at society for her station in life. She did not pity herself. She did not ask for government handouts. She did not spend all her time complaining and griping against the top 1% of wealthy Americans. Instead of hoarding what she had to get her through her golden years, she made a decision to *give away* what she had. To give it away? Are you serious? Who gives away everything they have when they need it most? Oseola was born into poverty. She had no more opportunities in life than you do. She probably had *much less* opportunity than you do. But she was rich in spirit and has enriched the lives of everyone around her. It's not all about how much you can gather and horde up for your golden years. It about whether you leave the earth a better place than you found it. Oseola McCarty did just that.

Jeff Henderson was a crack dealer in San Diego. At the age of 21, he was making $35,000 per week. Until the law caught up with him. He spent the next 20 years in jail. But it was in that jail that he learned his calling in life. He learned how to cook—from scratch. He had never made homemade biscuits and gravy before. He had never made homemade pancakes before. He had never made homemade cinnamon rolls before. But being in the kitchen got him out of his cell. He fell in love with both the process of cooking and the smiles on the faces of his friends when they ate his food. It was extremely therapeutic. He had found his true love. One day he read an article in *USA Today* about the top black chefs in the U.S. When he saw pictures of them standing proudly in their tall white hats and starched white suits, he made the most critical decision of his life. He said to himself, "One day, I'm gonna be like one of them."

Most people who've spent the last twenty years in jail would simply be happy to get a job at the local McDonalds. But not Jeff Henderson. After he read that article, he said, "I knew then that I would be more than just a cook at some fast food joint." At first no one would hire him. Think about it. Would you hire a rather large black felon who had been in prison for the last twenty years? Finally, a dive restaurant hired him—but only to wash dishes. Every day, he would show up early and stay late. He spent his breaks hanging out with the cooks and asking them questions. Watching every move they made. He was like a sponge. Eventually, the manager let him try his hand at cooking. Henderson knocked it out of the ballpark. Everyone loved his cooking.

But he knew if he was going to break out of that greasy spoon, he needed to cook at a more prestigious restaurant. He also needed a role model, a mentor. He tracked down Robert Gadsby who had just opened up a luxurious restaurant in Los Angeles. Gadsby too offered him a job as a dishwasher. Henderson knew he was better than that. He knew he had real talent. But he wasn't insulted. He didn't walk away in disgust. He didn't go live in a tent in front of City Hall with a sign that said "Down with Corporate Greed!" Instead, he said, "Thank you! Thank you sir! I won't let you down. I will make you proud!" He continued to show up early and leave late and spend all the time he could with the cooks.

Eventually Gadsby let him try his hand at cooking a few dishes. He worked his way up to become the head chef there. He kept moving further up the food chain as he went from one fine white tablecloth restaurant to another until he finally landed a job as the head chef at the Bellagio, one of the most expensive and prestigious hotels in Las Vegas. Eventually, he went on all the talk shows and became a best-selling author.[234]

So, when I hear about people saying "Hey, I just got laid off and I can't find a job. There are no more opportunities for people like me in America. This is not the America I grew up in. Things have definitely changed for the worse," I think of Jeff Henderson, and I ask them: "Are you a rather large black male convicted felon? Does your resume show that you spent the last twenty years in jail?" Then I tell them Jeff Henderson's story, and they just walk away with their head bowed, all their weak excuses kicked to the curb. Or they walk slowly back to their tent in front of City Hall.

Every decision is like a murder, and our march forward
is over the stillborn bodies of all possible selves
that will never be.[235]

—ARTHUR KOESTLER

Once, when I was in Johannesburg, South Africa on business, I was getting ready for my early morning meeting with a partner of the Werksmans law firm. A maintenance man was in my room messing with the air conditioning. There was a knock at the door. When I opened it, this huge radiant smile greeted me. A tall, young black man instantly grabbed my hand in both of his hands aggressively. "Hi, my name is Peter," he said. "They sent me to fetch you." Then he rushed over to the maintenance man, grabbed his hand and began to shake it violently. "Nice to meet you," he said. "I'm Peter. They sent me to fetch you."

Then, he turned to me and said, "Can I help you with your things?" Before I could say, "No, I can manage," he had already walked passed me with his long gangly legs and found three of my bags and was already carrying them toward the door. "Wait," I said. "That's my luggage. Those things can stay here. I'm coming back tonight. All I really need is my briefcase." Seeing that I was already carrying my briefcase, he bounded over to me and reached down for the briefcase, "Here allow me," he said. "I insist." I had never been greeted with such enthusiastic service from a chauffeur anywhere in the world. He was eager to please so I said, "Well okay, if you insist."

He drove us in a shiny black BMW to the Werksmans law firm where I was to meet with one of the partners to discuss filing a lawsuit against a South African corporation for fraud and breach of contract. I was there to interview various law firms to hire as local counsel. When we walked into David Hertz's office, he said, "I see you've met my associate Peter." To my surprise, Peter actually sat in with us during the entire meeting and did not say a word. He just took notes. He seemed to be scribbling down everything I said. I presumed that aside from being a driver, he was Mr. Hertz's personal assistant.

After a while we broke for lunch and the three of us went to a very posh restaurant in downtown Johannesburg. Again Peter did not say a word. When the food arrived, I noticed that even after Mr. Hertz and I had started eating, Peter had not touched his food. "Go ahead and eat Peter," David finally said. At that, with his usual zeal and enthusiasm, Peter dove into his food.

At the end of a very long day, Peter drove me back to my hotel. In the parking lot, I began to ask Peter a few questions. "Where were you born? How long have you worked for the Werksmans law firm?" It turned out Peter was actually a young attorney working for the law firm.

Peter Tshisevhe was born in South Africa during the worst of apartheid—the total segregation of blacks and whites. He was from a small village in the Northern Transvaal. His mother was Zulu. His father was Venda. When he was 11 years old, he only had one pair of pants, and no shoes. He was 16 years old before he owned a pair of shoes. He went to junior high school under a tree. He experienced extreme poverty, discrimination and abuse at the hand of the whites. His first job was at a Pick-n-Pay packing fruit and vegetables. He used the money he saved from working to pay for school. It turns out Peter was brilliant. He spoke eleven languages, including English, and Afrikaans, the language of the descendants of the Dutch colonists.

He eventually put himself through college and then law school at the most prestigious law school in South Africa—the University of Witwatersrand. While he was in college, he worked three jobs to make ends meet. One day he was so tired, he actually collapsed and fell asleep in the shower. But he survived and eventually made it. Now he was working for one of the most prestigious law firms on the African continent. He was also driving a new BMW.

He told me that one year when he went to see his mom in the village where he grew up, the entire village gathered around his beat up old car as he was unpacking it. The car was used, but it was his, and he was proud of it. Seeing the people gathered around him and snickering, he looked up and said, "Why are you all standing around looking at me?" They all laughed, "Because," they said, "we know you stole that car, and we are just waiting for the police to come and arrest you." They couldn't believe someone from their village could afford such a luxury.

One day some white policemen stopped him, suspicious that he was driving a stolen car. While they checked their computer records, they talked about him in Afrikaans and laughed and made fun of him. When Peter spoke back to them in Afrikaans, they were shocked.

As my conversation with Peter went on late into the night, I finally asked him, "How did you do it? How did you come so far having started with so little? How did you overcome all of this oppression and discrimination?" "Because, Danny, I am like a tennis ball," he said. "The harder you hit me up against a wall, the harder I bounce back." I had never met anyone who had been through so much suffering who had such a radiant smile, such a zest for life and such an obsession for overcoming.

Today, the legal industry in the United States is in an industry wide downturn. Some of the biggest and most prestigious law firms in America have gone bankrupt and no longer exist. Many of the lawyers I know are struggling to survive from month to month. I hear them griping and complaining about how the legal industry is no longer what it used to be. But then I always think of Peter.

"Have you ever seen a lion in the wild, Peter?" I asked. He jumped back and with wide eyes said, "Are you crazy! Lions eat people from my village. I never want to see a lion!" I laughed. "Peter, I'm going into the bush this weekend to look for lions. Why don't you come with me?" He stared back at me in stunned silence. He knew there was a thriving business in taking rich white people on photo safaris, but the thought of being able to afford this kind of luxury had never even occurred to him. Plus, he knew lions were a very real danger. "It's perfectly safe. We'll be in a jeep and there will be a ranger with a gun," I said.

I was shocked that the very people who were native to Africa could not even afford to see the lions, leopards, cheetahs, rhinos, and the other wildlife for which Africa is famous. "Tell you what, come with me and I'll pay your way. Don't worry about the cost." Now he had only his fears to stand in the way. Something within him couldn't resist. "Okay, I'll come . . . *No wait*, I can't come! It's too dangerous!" After much cajoling and teasing on my part, he finally acquiesced.

That weekend, he met me at Tshukudu game lodge near Hoedspruit, in the northern province of South Africa. We ate our meals on the veranda of the luxurious lodge. Hanging on the walls were pictures of the lodge owner's grandfather standing with a rifle proudly over various big game animals he had shot in the early 1900s. There were old black and white photos of him standing next to dead elephants, dead lions, leopards, cheetahs, and rhinos. But when Peter's eyes fell on one particular picture, he froze in horror. There on the wall was an old black and white, cracked photo of a great white hunter standing over a dead Bushman he had just killed. Back then, the great white hungers used to shoot the native Bushmen for sport. They were considered wildlife. Peter was sick to his stomach. But he didn't say a word until late that night when we were alone. He had learned when to speak and when to keep his mouth shut. He did not want to start a fight. He did not want to ruin my moment.

Every morning, we went for long walks with two lion cubs (Tsabo and Tawana) padding alongside us like little puppies. Little kids were petting them. But Peter wouldn't dare go near them. "Even the children are not afraid of the lions Peter," I taunted. "Come on pet one so I can take a picture. You can send it to your mom." After a while, he finally relented, got down on one knee and very gingerly put his hand on the head of the lion cub, then snapped it back quickly. "That was too fast. Do it again so I can get a good picture. Leave your hand there for a few seconds." He faked a smile and lightly brushed his hand over the head of the lion cub. I snapped the picture.

That night, we sat around a bonfire and were entertained by Zulu dancers in traditional tribal dress, dancing and chanting to the rhythms of ancient drumbeats. When the music and dancing stopped, our hosts asked us to be silent and listen. At first we heard nothing, but after a while we could make out the chuffing, grumbling and roaring of lions in the bush nearby. It was nighttime, and they were hunting. I discovered that lions are like cats. When one roars, they all roar. A chill went up and down my spine. The rangers offered to walk us back to our hut with a gun and a flashlight. There was nothing separating us from the bush. Attacks had been known to occur in the dead of night.

By the time we went to bed, it was storming badly outside. Peter was my roommate. We were each lying on our bunks talking about all the animals we had seen that day and listening to the wind howl. Suddenly, a hard gust of wind blew open the screen door to our cabin and slammed it against the outside wall. Peter jumped up and pulled the blanket over him. "A lion!" he shouted. I nearly fell off the bed laughing.

The next morning, one of the rangers showed me the huge paw prints of lions that had been walking in the midst of our camp during the night. I didn't bother to tell Peter.

Peter later went to work for Africa's largest law firm—Edward Nathan Sonnenbergs, where he became a Senior Director. Recently, he and some friends formed a boutique law firm with five partners who handle corporate tax law, transactions, mergers and acquisitions. His law firm, *Tshisevhe Gwina Ratshimbilani Incorporated* (TGR Attorneys) now has 24 attorneys, and is the biggest black law firm in South Africa. The firm specializes in all aspects of commercial law, including corporate law, mergers and acquisitions, banking and finance, commercial litigation, and property law. His high rise office in Sandhurst overlooks Africa's richest square kilometer, Sandton City, Sandhurst, Hyde Park. The most desired real estate in Africa. A few days after Nelson Mandela passed away, I called Peter to tell him I was thinking of him. "You don't know it yet Peter," I said. "But you're going to be the next Nelson Mandela."

Another group of people who have risen above tragedy after tragedy, massacre after massacre are, of course, the Jews. If you don't know what Queen Isabella did to the Jews during the Spanish Inquisition, long before Hitler came along, it's worth the reading. The Spanish Inquisition lasted 350 years, and it was gruesome.

And yet despite their suffering, the Jews have contributed to the history of the world brilliant scientists like Einstein, and brilliant doctors like Julius Axelrod who won the Nobel Prize for discovering the neurotransmitters epinephrine, norepinephrine, and dopamine. Baruch Blumberg won the Nobel Prize for developing the hepatitis B vaccine. Carl Djerassi won the National Medal of Science for developing the birth control pill. Jonas Edward Salk developed the polio vaccine. Richard Feynman won the Nobel Prize for his research in quantum physics and sub-atomic particles. The list goes on and on.

The very foundations of Hollywood were funded and operated primarily by Jewish people.[236]

The list of Jewish lawyers and judges reads like the *Who's Who* of the legal industry.

Louis Brandeis, U.S. Supreme Court Justice (1916–1939)

Stephen G. Breyer, U.S. Supreme Court Justice (1994–present)

Benjamin N. Cardozo, U.S. Supreme Court Justice (1932–1938)

Abe Fortas, U.S. Supreme Court Justice (1965–1969)

Felix Frankfurter, U.S. Supreme Court Justice (1939–1962)

Ruth Bader Ginsburg, U.S. Supreme Court Justice (1993–present)

Arthur J. Goldberg, U.S. Supreme Court Justice (1962–1965)

William Kunstler, lawyer famous for defending controversial "radical" clients such as the "Chicago Seven" protesters of the 1968 Democratic National Convention.

Samuel Leibowitz, lawyer, defender of the Scottsboro Boys.

Edward Levi, U.S. Attorney General (1975–77)

Laurence H. Tribe, Professor of Law, Harvard University.

Marcia Clark, prosecutor in the trial of O.J. Simpson.

Roy Cohn, chief attorney for Joseph McCarthy.

Ed Koch, Judge on *The People's Court* and former mayor of New York.

Robert Shapiro, lawyer, known for the trial of O.J. Simpson.

If you've ever worn perfume by Estée Lauder or Coco Chanel, you owe thanks to the Jewish perfumeries in Europe and New York who created and supplied those luscious scents that wafted across the seas and into your local department store. If you've ever bought a diamond for someone, or received one as a gift, it is likely that before you found it, it made its way through the Jewish diamond cutters of Antwerp, Belgium where most of the world's diamonds are sent for cutting and polishing.

Every culture, every ethnicity, every race of people has its list of heroes who rose above tragedy and oppression to make a positive impact on the world. More than any other single factor, the ability to solve problems has helped them overcome a history of oppression, discrimination and stereotyping that is thousands of years old. Women entrepreneurs are a perfect example.

In 2000, Sara Blakely was selling fax machines door to door, and had only $5,000 in savings. One evening while she was getting dressed for an event, she put on a pair of cream-colored dress pants. She looked at her rear end in the mirror and saw ugly panty lines and couldn't figure out how to get rid of them. Spontaneously, she decided to cut the feet out of her control top panty hose and wear what was left of the panty hose as panties. "I wore them all night," Blakely said. "My rear looked firm, my cellulite had been smoothed out, but they rolled up my legs all night." It was a problem in need of a solution. "I thought, I got to figure out a way to comfortably keep this just below the knee, and I will have a home run for women," she said.

She used her $5,000 in savings to create a support panty made of nylon, cotton, and lycra that was unlike anything else on the market. Because it was almost sheer, it was much thinner than all of those other thick and bulky slimming products on the market.

She had never taken a business class. She had never worked in fashion or retail. She simply saw nagging problem in need of a solution. She worked on this project for two years in her apartment in Atlanta, Georgia. Because she was still working a full time job, she worked on her pet project at night and on weekends. She called all the big hosiery manufacturers about her idea, but they all rejected it. Except one, which helped her create a prototype.

She was even forced to write her own patent. She spent weeks researching pantyhose patents at the Georgia Tech library at night after work. Her mom drew the original product drawing for the patent, using Sara as the model. She called her underwear *Spanx* and applied for the trademark herself online.

She called the buyer at Neiman Marcus and begged for 10 minutes of her time. When the buyer agreed, she put her prototype in an ordinary zip lock bag from her kitchen, threw it in her red backpack and flew to Dallas to meet the buyer. After a first-hand demonstration of Spanx in the lady's room, the buyer said, "It's brilliant. I'm buying them for seven of my stores." Then Blakely repeated the process at Saks, Nordstrom and Bloomingdale's.

She also sent a gift basket to Oprah Winfrey that included a pair of Spanx. A few weeks later, she received a phone call from Oprah's staff telling her that Oprah had chosen Spanx as her favorite product of the year. An avalanche of orders came rolling in. She has never had to advertise her product in newspapers, magazines, TV, or radio. All of her sales have been driven by word of mouth via the "tell-a-woman" network. Today her product is selling in forty different countries around the world. At 41 years of age, Blakely is youngest female self-made billionaire in history. All because she found a problem in need of a solution—and solved it.

Coco Chanel was born in France to a single mom in 1883. She was raised in an orphanage by strict nuns. Her first job was that of a shop assistant at a mom and pop lingerie and hosiery shop. At the age of 22, she started putting ribbons and lace in the hats of her boyfriend's mistresses to decorate them for when they went to the horse races. The mistresses would wear the hats to high society events, and soon other women began to notice and asked Coco to arrange their hats as well.

Her first commercial success came from selling hats out of her boyfriend's apartment in Paris. Again, her first clients were her boyfriend's high society mistresses.[237] Her second boyfriend helped her rent a storefront in Paris. The first dresses she sold were other people's dresses, which she merely altered and rearranged. "I cut the front of an old jersey so I wouldn't have to pull it over my head," she said. Then she added a ribbon, a collar and a knot. "Where did you find that dress?" a friend asked. "I'll sell it to you," was Coco's reply. Later she recounted, "I sold ten dresses like that. My dear, my fortune is built on that old jersey that I'd put on because it was cold in Deauville."[238]

On July 15, 1915, her wealthy British boyfriend helped her opened a dress shop in Biarritz, France near the border of Spain, and soon had to hire sixty sewing girls to keep up with the demand. Harper's Bazaar was the first American magazine to write an article featuring Coco Chanel. One year later, she had 300 sewing girls. By 1917, she reimbursed her boyfriend 300,000 francs cash and owned the dress shop outright. In 1918, her boyfriend announced that he was engaged to marry another woman. He married the other woman but kept Coco as a mistress. Keep in mind that Coco's business was born and actually thrived while World War I was raging throughout Europe.

Before Coco Chanel, women only wore black as a sign of mourning. It was Coco Chanel who created the "little black dress" and turned the color black into a fashion statement. She was not selling clothes. She was selling an attitude. In 1923, she introduced Chanel No. 5 perfume by having her staff mist the dressing rooms where clients were trying on dresses. When the clients came back, they asked about the scent and where they could get some. For a solid year, Coco's reply was the same "My dear, I don't sell perfume. But since you are a dear friend, perhaps I could give you small sample of it." When the clients were hooked, she then agreed to sell them larger bottles.

When the Germans marched into Paris at the outset of World War II, they went straight to Coco's store to buy some Chanel No. 5 to send back to their wives and girlfriends. Over the years, Coco regularly entertained and became good friends with Winston Churchill, Igor Stravinsky, Picasso, Renoir, Van Gogh, and the Grand Duke of Russia, Dmitri Romanov. When, in her opinion, World War II was getting completely out of hand, she actually tried to broker a peace treaty between Churchill and Hitler, and was later accused of being a Nazi spy. She was 60 years old.

After World War II ended, Coco Chanel's fashions and perfume would cross the Atlantic and hit America like a storm. Hollywood movie stars would not be seen in public unless they were wearing Chanel designs. Grace Kelly, Lauren Bacall, Ingrid Bergman, Elizabeth

Taylor and Rita Hayworth were just a few of Coco's disciples. In the 1950s, Marilyn Monroe became famous for saying "All I wear to bed is Chanel No. 5." In 1963, Jacqueline Kennedy was wearing a raspberry wool Chanel dress on the day her husband, John F. Kennedy was assassinated. Coco Chanel's legacy survives her. As I was writing this chapter, I came across a full page ad in the *New York Times* with a very sexy young woman wearing Chanel perfume. Coco Chanel not only survived, she prospered through two World Wars, and the Nazi occupation. She did all this without a husband. Innovation and entrepreneurship were her only weapons.

The same is true of Jodi Pliszka of Muskego, Wisconsin. Pliszka started losing her hair in 1979 at 13 years old. "We found a bald spot while braiding my hair. I looked like a cancer patient losing hair from chemotherapy. But I wasn't sick at all," she says.

Pliszka's mother took her from doctor to doctor. "They had no idea what was wrong with me," she remembers. "I had every allergy test, every solution applied and then they started injecting my scalp with cortisone, which worked. I seemed to be fine." When she was 20 years old, she started losing her hair again. "My hair started falling out in clumps," she says. "My eyelashes fell out all at once. They looked like a big spider lying there in the sink. Within a few weeks, I only had a few tufts left. Within a month, all my hair was gone."

The cause was a rare autoimmune disorder called *alopecia areata.* Only one percent of the entire population has it. People with *alopecia areata* produce too many white blood cells. Her body thinks her hair is an infection, so it kills off the hair cells. In her early twenties, when most women are discovering their femininity, Jodi went through a very dark time, coming to the realization that she would never have any hair.

She was forced to wear wigs. But the wigs were hot and uncomfortable. The sweat consistently ran down into her eyes. She tried a variety of moisture absorbing materials to line her wigs to keep it out of her eyes, including panty liners. But nothing seemed to work properly or on a consistent basis.

Pliszka began to experiment with various materials in 2001. One day, she folded a synthetic car chamois into various shapes, and glued the final shape to the inside of her wig. It worked like a charm. But she wanted a more hi-tech material. She worked and experimented with various materials and three years later succeeded in obtaining a patent on her product.

Soon after, the producers of a new TV show called *American Inventor* heard about her invention and invited her to participate as a contestant. She was selected as a finalist in 2006 and received $50,000 in prize money to further develop her product. For two and a half months she had access to top scientists who helped her to find a material that is breathable and lightweight, and does not irritate the scalp. She then found a manufacturer in China, and designed the logo herself. The material she finally settled on is a high tech wicking material that captures perspiration and keeps the person's head dry. It is an ultra-thin, breathable material that allows the air to ventilate. It also protects wigs and caps from unsightly sweat stains, dirt, and oil. It is also disposable, which guarantees that she will always have repeat customers.

Today, she markets her product as *Headline It!* and sells it to firemen, construction workers, soldiers, policemen, cancer patients, and of course, women all over the world. She has major accounts with QVC London, Valero Energy Corp., Alliance Energy, Pepsico, the U.S. Marine Corps, and has distribution centers in seven countries.

> ***An entrepreneur is someone who jumps off the cliff***
> ***and builds the wings on the way down.***
>
> —ROY SPENCE
> Co-Founder of GSD&M Ad Agency

Summer Knight was raised by a single mom in a trailer park in Florida. The most sophisticated person she knew as a kid was the manager of the trailer park. Drugs were pervasive and all around her. As a teenager, she ended up in the hospital due to stress because her step-mother accused her of stealing from her. Her biological mother died when Summer was 19 years old.

But, she remembers lying in the grass one beautiful afternoon, staring at the clear blue sky, knowing that she was going to do something great. In her early twenties, she got a job as a firefighter/ paramedic and discovered she had a passion for medicine. So, she went to college at the University of Wisconsin and graduated *summa cum laude*. Then she went to medical school at the University of Illinois at Chicago and became a doctor. Then she got her MBA from the University of Florida.

She began her career as a family physician, and then became a partner in an urgent care clinic. She founded the State Government Physical Leadership Council and was appointed by the Governor to the Florida Cancer Control and Research Advisory Committee. A few years later, she was appointed as Chief Medical Officer of the State of Florida. In that position, she saw problems with the flow of Medicaid funds and in the quality of care in that system. Soon thereafter, she created IntegriCor, LLC for the purpose of detecting and preventing fraud in the long term care Medicaid systems. After aggressively growing that business, she sold it for ten times the annual cash flow. She agreed to stay on board of the new company for a few years as Executive Vice President and Chief Medical Officer. Today, she runs a new company called *DSK*, which teaches disruptive innovation to companies and individuals.

In 1998, Ali Brown was working at a small New York City ad agency. "I was working in a tiny company and was doing everything from talking to clients, to servicing accounts, to getting coffee for people, to fixing the fax machine. That was when I realized that I had the skills I needed to do this on my own." She quit her job, and started selling her services as a copyrighter, writing brochures, ads and newsletters for people.

She had no mentor or coach to guide her. She had no website. She had no business plan. She had no clue. In the beginning, she had trouble finding clients because she didn't know how to market herself. Soon she was out of money. "I remember one night going to the ATM," she says. "I was meeting some friends for drinks, and I couldn't even take out a $20 bill. My balance was $18.56. I will never forget that number. I had to call them and cancel and go home. I had maxed out my credit cards. I had been putting all I had into my little start-up business."

But she hung in there. She loved her independence too much to give it up. "I trusted myself. This was my path. I listened to my heart and knew that this was what I was supposed to do. Soon enough I figured it out, one day at a time."

Ali created an online magazine called an "e-zine," and anointed herself the "Ezine Queen." She started to land projects with prestigious clients such as New York Times Digital, Adweek Magazines, Scholastic Books, and Dun & Bradstreet. Eventually other women started asking questions like, "How do you market yourself? How do you get clients? How do you use the internet? How do you publish an ezine?"

In response, Ali created her first e-book, titled *Boost Business With Your Own Ezine.* She published it online and sent an offer to a very small e-mail list, using AOL and a dial-up modem. She was terrified that her friends might reject her because she was selling to them. She took a break and went to the gym. When she got back, she was shocked to see that her inbox full of orders. "I'll never forget that feeling," she says. "There were dozens of orders that had come in. And I realized, I'm not working right now! I had done the work, and income was coming in. I thought, I want to learn more about this and teach it to others."

Ali's following grew, and she began to expand her offerings to include courses, programs, seminars, events, and mentoring. Eventually, Ali was ranked on the *Inc. 500* list of fastest growing companies in the nation and was named one of Ernst & Young's Winning Women Entrepreneurs. She has also been named as one of the Enterprising Women of the Year, and one of *Forbes'* Women to Watch. She has been interviewed by every major TV network, and was also featured in the season finale of ABC's *Secret Millionaire.* She became a millionaire by age 35. Today she has a subscriber based training program with approximately 40,000 members. Ali also presents workshops, keynote speeches, and offers coaching and mentoring services for entrepreneurs who want to start or grow their own business.

The point is—innovation, creativity and entrepreneurship knows no boundaries. It penetrates the deepest seeded racial barriers, gender barriers, ethnic barriers, economic barriers, and educational barriers. These people know that it's not about the money. Andrew Carnegie, one of the richest men in history, said, "He who dies rich, dies disgraced." He believed the purpose of being rich was to give away or spend all your money on good causes. Mark Zuckerberg said, "The ultimate payday is not a priority. Changing the world is." Coco Chanel put it best when she said, "It's not about money for money's sake that I'm interested in, but money as the symbol of success."[239] Money is simply a way to keep score. In reality, it's always and only about solving problems. Money is the way people grade how well you solve their problems. If you can do that often enough, for enough people, the money will come. You can count on it.

In my first book, I touted the virtues of a book called *Do What You Love, The Money Will Follow* by Marsha Sinetar. I have since come to believe that if you truly do only what you love, *to the exclusion of all else*, you will starve to death. But if you do what enough *other people* love, you'll be rich. That's what problem solvers do. What are *you* doing to level the playing field?

✳ THINGS TO PONDER

+ No matter where you came from, or what obstacles are before you, remember that innovation and creativity level the playing field.

+ Your current obstacles may become your greatest assets.

+ Entrepreneurship is first and foremost about solving other people's problems.

CHAPTER 29

Can You Create Value Out of Thin Air?

Every tree casts a shadow. Money is not the tree. It is merely the shadow of the tree. Money is not real. It is but the shadow of the things that are real. Too many people spend their entire lives chasing shadows instead of planting seeds that will grow into trees.

So where does real money and wealth come from? Most people believe that money exists separate and apart from themselves. That money is "out there" and is something to be obtained. They feel that it has intrinsic value of its own, and that in order to be wealthy, they must do something to "go get it." They feel that it is like some kind of fruit hanging high in the branches of a distant tree—if only they could reach it.

They feel poor without it and powerful with it. It is as though this external, tangible substance is their life force. Without it—they are empty. Powerless.

But the truth is that all the money, all the power, and all the wealth in the universe is not "out there" waiting to be gotten. It is within us, waiting to be released from our inner being, like sweat, secreted from our very pores.

Steve Jobs, Michael Dell, Bill Gates, Oprah Winfrey, Tyler Perry, Cathy Hughes, Red McCombs, J.K. Rowling, and Mark Cuban did not go out and "get" money. They exuded it. It flowed out of them as from a hidden wellspring. They created value by *what they did*. They brought something of value to everyone around them. But that value started out—inside them. In their soul. In their spirit. In their brains.

That's why there are millionaires who have lost everything and then came back and became millionaires yet again—after starting over. Some have lost it all and won it all back *several times*. That's also why most people who win the lottery are poor again after just a few years.

True wealth... always and only comes... from within.

A mere one hundred years ago, Las Vegas was just a barren desert covered with rocks, sand, coyotes, cactus and buzzards. The elegant buildings, hotels, restaurants, and casinos in Las Vegas weren't simply "out there" waiting to be plucked. No one had a secret map to go "find them." The wealth of Vegas came from *inside of us*. It flowed out of us and into the sand, and onto the streets, and into the sky. Without us, it would still be rocks and sand.[240]

We created the wealth in Vegas, New York, Los Angeles, Moscow, Tokyo, Bangkok, Paris, and Johannesburg.

All wealth, in fact, comes from within.

It is not "out there" waiting to be obtained.

It is *in here*, waiting to be released.

Entrepreneurs and innovators know how to create value out of thin air. They also know the difference between value and money. Value is something that makes someone else's life better. Money is the way we measure how we are doing at the task of making other people's lives better. It's how we keep score. It is merely a symbolic representation of value.

Everything you need to create value out of thin air is already inside you. When Walt Disney was dirt poor and living in his uncle's garage, he drew a picture of a rabbit and put it in human clothes, and gave it a human voice. His cartoon character was a smashing success. When Universal Studios hoodwinked him and effectively stole that creation, he simply did it again. But this time, he drew a picture of a mouse and put it in human clothes and gave it a human voice. Have you seen this mouse?

You see, when you have the ability to create value out of thin air, there is no financial setback too great to overcome. When Carl Stanley, from the tiny town of Burleson, Texas, suffered a huge financial set back that destroyed his credit rating, he slowly began to rebuild his life by figuring out for himself how credit scores work, what specific factors were driving his credit scores, and how to correct them. Once he discovered that he had the ability to take charge of his own credit scores, he looked around and saw that lots of other people were having the same problem, and he began offering to help them. Today his company, Rising Point Solutions, helps thousands of people all over the U.S. take charge of their credit scores and rebuild their lives.

Howard Schultz created value out of thin air by taking a normal cup of coffee that would normally cost fifty cents at a convenience store, and turning it into a warm, comforting experience. Whenever I meet a new client for the first time, I always say, "Which Starbucks would you like to meet at?" Starbucks has stores in so many locations around Austin, Texas, it has become my branch office. It provides a warm, inviting, relaxed atmosphere in which to meet. If I like the client, and the client likes, me, then I invite them back to my office to talk business.

Colonel Sanders created value out of thin air by selling a simple chicken recipe.

Walter Frederick Morrison created value out of thin air by turning a simple aluminum pie tin into the Frisbee.

Bette Claire McMurry created value out of thin air by turning simple tempera paint into White Out.

Art Fry created value out of thin air by turning glue that wasn't quite sticky enough into Post-it Notes.

Roy and Bert Sosa created value out of thin air when they taught poor people without bank accounts how to store money on a flat piece of magnetic plastic.

When I was 12 years old, I created value out of thin air by mowing lawns. As an attorney, I create value out of thin air by putting black ink on white paper in a particular order. All litigation throughout history comes down to one thing—words. Litigation has always and only been a *war of words*. I discovered that if you can artfully put words onto paper and persuasively present an oral argument, you can shift public policy, defeat unjust laws, right wrongs, and change people's lives.

In 1463, the Florence Cathedral acquired a sixteen foot tall boulder of white marble. Two separate sculptors tried to work it into a piece of art and gave up. The badly damaged block of marble was put in storage. Other sculptors were brought in to see what they could do with it. They took one look at the mangled stone and said it was worthless and demanded a new stone. Forty years later, Michelangelo saw the damaged block of marble and fell in love with it.[241] He took it out of storage and within eighteen months carved it into the statue of young David. The statue of young David is one of the greatest sculptures ever created. Michelangelo saw what was invisible to all others. The magic is not in *what* you see. It's in *how* you see.

When you have the ability to create value out of a badly damaged rock, or even out of thin air, it doesn't matter what "they" take from you. They can take your house, your car, your wallet, your credit cards, your driver's license, and your job. But they can't take away your creative mind, the energy in your soul, the bounce in your step, the smile on your face, the warmth of your handshake. They can't take away your empathy for people, and your willingness to go out of your way to solve problems.

You see, all of the entrepreneurs and innovators throughout history who went from rags to riches did so, not by looking for and acquiring the great wealth that was "out there." They did so by enhancing people's lives, solving other people's problems, one person, one problem at a time. In short, they did it by turning themselves inside out. They did it by giving themselves away. One of the most entrepreneurial things ever uttered by a spiritual leader was this: "Give and it shall be given to you, good measure, pressed down, shaken together, and running over."[242] There has never been a greater formula for abundance and riches than this. Zig Ziglar modernized it when he said, "You will only get what you want when you've given enough other people what they want."

I often chuckle when I hear people criticizing the extremely wealthy simply for being extremely wealthy. If a professional basketball player or a musician makes $30 million per year, it doesn't take any money out of your pocket. In fact, we help pay their salaries every time we go to the movies or watch a basketball game. You vote for who gets to be in the top 1% every time you buy a cup of coffee at Starbucks and every time you login to Facebook. You are voting with your dollars. You are voting with your time and attention. The extremely wealthy don't steal from us. We give them our hard earned cash voluntarily every time we buy goods and services from them. We choose who gets wealthy every time we decide what TV program to watch or not watch, and what website to visit or not visit. People who gripe over who got the biggest piece of pie come from a philosophy of scarcity, not of abundance. If there is an endless supply of pies, isn't the question of who got the biggest piece of pie quite irrelevant?

It is not simply a matter of seeing the glass "half full" or "half empty." It is the failure to see that you are sitting next to a fountain with fresh spring water flowing at a million gallons per minute. Entrepreneurship is the wellspring of eternal ideas bubbling forth from within every moment of every day. It never runs dry.[243] There are new opportunities and new solutions all around us all the time.

What is it that is *within you* waiting to be released? You already have within you the seedlings of all the solutions you seek. Now go plant them. You might be shocked to see where they take root. The wind, and squirrels, and birds may carry them to places you never intended them to go. When you start getting phone calls, emails, and hand written letters from places you've never been to, from people whose names you can't pronounce, thanking you for solving their problems, you will know what I mean.

THINGS TO PONDER

+ Money is not real. It is but the shadow of the things that are real.
+ Money is not "out there" waiting to be obtained.
+ All the money and all the value you need is already inside you. To release it, you just need to start solving other people's problems.
+ There will always be enough money in the world because there will always be problems that need solutions.

CHAPTER 30

What Are You Willing to Walk Away From?

Would you leave a job earning more than $250,000 per year in the state where you grew up to move 3,000 miles away to work as a low level employee in an industry you knew nothing about?

Howard Schultz grew up dirt poor in the Bayview Projects in Brooklyn. He went to college on a football scholarship, which soon fell through because he wasn't very good. To get through college, he had to work part time as a bartender. He also sold his blood to earn extra money. As the first kid in his family to earn a college degree, Schultz had achieved his parent's dream for him. Within six years of graduating, he had become the vice president of a Swedish company and was earning enough money to buy his own apartment on the Upper East Side of Manhattan in New York City. He had a company car, an expense account, and unlimited travel to and from Sweden. He also owned a summer house in the Hamptons.

And yet one day, he came home and announced to his wife that he was leaving it all behind to go to work as a low level employee in an industry he knew nothing about for a company that no one ever had heard of in Seattle, Washington. His wife and his parents thought he had lost his mind.

Long after others have stopped to rest, I'm still running, chasing after something nobody else could ever see.

—Howard Schultz
CEO of Starbucks

Schultz went to work for a small coffee roaster called Starbucks. At that time, Starbucks did not sell brewed coffee in the cup at all. It didn't even have a place for customers to sit. It simply sold coffee makers and roasted coffee beans to go. One day, Schultz walked into the office of the president of Starbucks, and said, "Hey, I have a brilliant idea! Why don't we start brewing the coffee and sell espresso and offer our customers a place to sit?" To his utter surprise, the president said, "Howard, we're coffee roasters, not coffee brewers. We don't want to break outside of our area of expertise. We don't want to dilute our brand in the market." They turned him down flat. Schultz was depressed for months. He knew how much potential the company had. Why couldn't they see it?

After months of agonizing about it, Schultz decided to leave Starbucks to start his own coffee roasting and espresso company. He wanted see his vision come to life one way or another. Once again, his parents and his wife thought he was nuts. "Why leave such a good job to risk it all? You're doing great there?" But Schultz had already made up his mind that he would one day have his own chain of sit-down coffee shops.

He had no liquid cash to invest and knew nothing about how to raise venture capital. Nevertheless, on a whim and a prayer, he started beating the bushes for seed capital. His initial seed money of $400,000 came from friends and family.

He would model his first store after the old fashioned bistros he had seen in Italy. In 1985, he opened his first store and called it *Il Giornale*, giving it an Italian flare. By 1987, he had three stores. Around that same time, the owners of Starbucks decided to pursue other interests for personal reasons and sold its name and its six locations to Schultz. By August 1987, Starbucks was his. Now he could begin to build his dream of having his own chain of Italian style bistros. The response from consumers was absolutely rabid, and soon Schultz had Starbucks coffee shops in every major city in the United States. If you live in a big city, chances are there are multiple Starbucks locations in your town. It turns out, the most powerful people on the planet are those who act as though things the rest of us only dream about—are real.

I can't give you any secret recipe for success, any foolproof plan for making it in the world of business. But my own experience suggests that it is possible to start from nothing and achieve even beyond your dreams.

—HOWARD SCHULTZ

Anthony Robbins and other self-help gurus tell us that human beings will not change unless the pain of staying the same is greater than the pain of changing. While this may be true for many people, my research has shown that it is not categorically true. There are too many people throughout history who left perfectly comfortable jobs to embrace the unknown with no money, no training and, no experience, and succeeded beyond their wildest dreams.

In the 1960s Herb Kelleher was a small time business attorney in San Antonio, Texas. He was not wealthy, but he had a comfortable living. Back then, only corporate executives, movie stars, and the rich could afford to fly. Kelleher himself had only been on an airplane a few times when his clients paid for it. He had no education, training, or experience in running a commercial airline. Yet, he could see something the industry insiders could not see.

The airline industry ran its flights using a "hub and spoke" model in which airplanes flew out of the center hub to the destination cities, and then back again to the hub. Kelleher thought this was a very inefficient model. At the St. Anthony Club in downtown San Antonio, Kelleher and a buddy named Rollin King drew a grandiose business plan for a new airline on the back of a cocktail napkin. The entire plan consisted of a single triangle. Each corner of the triangle represented one of the major cities in Texas: (1) Dallas; (2) Houston; and (3) San Antonio. There would be no hub. Instead, the airplanes would fly round and round in a circle. The airline would only serve those three cities.[244] By staying small and efficient, they could keep costs low. This would bring the prices of tickets down to an affordable level so that anyone could fly. In short, Kelleher wanted to democratize the skies.

I imagine Kelleher coming home one day and having the following conversation:

Herb:	"Honey, I'm leaving it all to start my own airline!"
Wife:	"Excuse me? You want to start a what?"
Herb:	"An airline!"
Wife:	"Howard, have you ever been on a plane?"
Herb:	"Yes, twice!"
Wife:	"Do you own an airplane I don't know about?"
Herb:	"Nope."
Wife:	"Do you know anyone who owns an airplane?"
Herb:	"Nope."
Wife:	"Can we afford to buy an airplane?"
Herb:	"Nope."
Wife:	"Do you have any experience, education, or training in running an airline?"
Herb:	"Nope."
Wife:	"Herb . . . . . . have you been taking your medication?"[245]

Nevertheless, in 1967, Kelleher did exactly what he set out to do. He started gathering seed money from friends and investors and raised $750,000, which was enough of a down payment to buy three 737 airplanes from Boeing. Boeing gave them 90% financing for the balance owed. Kelleher called the airline Southwest Airlines.

But when Kelleher applied for a license from the Texas Aeronautics Commission, the application was bitterly opposed by the existing airlines. A lawsuit ensued, which lasted four years. The fledging airline almost died before it was born. But the license was ultimately approved. On June 19, 1971, Southwest Airlines launched its first airplane.

Braniff, Texas International and Continental Airlines would keep Southwest Airlines embroiled in multi-million dollar litigation for the next twenty years. In the courtroom, the other airlines would show up with fifteen high-powered attorneys flown in from New York, Chicago and Los Angeles. On the side of Southwest Airlines, there would be only one lone attorney—Herb Kelleher.

In the air, Southwest Airlines competed by putting beautiful stewardesses in tight hot pants and white knee-high go-go boots. It didn't serve drinks and snacks. It served "love potions" and "love bites." Before take-off, the head stewardess would take the microphone and crack corny jokes and soon the entire airplane would be laughing. Even if you were having a stressful day up to that point, the laughter always made you feel good. Despite the legal battles, and the intense competition, in its entire 42-year history, Southwest Airlines has never posted a loss for any single year. How many other airlines have filed bankruptcy during that same period or are no longer in business?

But the bigger question is this: What would possess an already successful attorney to leave everything behind to go into an industry in which he had no experience, education, or training—especially when he had no money to invest? The title of the biography of Herb Kelleher's life is called *Nuts!* and this explains quite a bit.

Moses asked the Hebrew children to leave their comfortable existence in Egypt to follow him into the wilderness in search of a land none of them had ever heard of, had never seen, and knew nothing about. Yes, they were slaves. But all their needs were provided for. They had plenty of food, shelter, clothes, transportation, and a guaranteed job for life. Moses was asking them to leave all that to go to a place he himself had never been before. There was no internet. There were no pictures, no brochures, no tour guides, and no travel insurance. Yet, somehow Moses was able to persuade the Hebrew people to follow him into the vast unknown. Howard Schultz and Herb Kelleher did essentially the same thing. Brilliant entrepreneurs have the ability not only to see a "promised land" that no one else can see, but also to motivate and inspire others to invest their time, their money, and their very lives into the great unknown.

Every great spiritual leader who has ever lived has taught by his/her words and example that if you are going to make it to the promised land, you have to leave the comforts of your current existence, and commit everything you have, and everything you are to one singular purpose. Jesus asked his followers to leave their parents, spouses, careers, wealth and everything they possessed and follow a new spiritual path. Today approximately 2.6 billion people (one third of the Earth's population) call themselves Christians.

Buddha led by example. He left a life of wealth and luxury behind and voluntarily become a pauper in search of a spiritual connection with the divine. His followers soon began doing the same.

Muhammad claims he received several divine revelations during a time of prayer and meditation in a desert cave on Mount Hira near Mecca. After receiving these revelations, he abandoned his former life and began preaching the things he had been taught in these revelations. His followers did the same.

Great entrepreneurs follow the same pattern. In late 2001, during the recession that followed the bombings of 9/11, Doug Guller took a trip to Australia. He was at a bar, when a very attractive waitress came up to him and said, "Wanna beer mate?" His eyes lit up. He straightened his posture, ordered the beer and proceeded to have a great time as this young lass treated him like royalty for the rest of the evening. It was that night that he realized there was an industry that was recession proof. It involved beer, beautiful young women, food and sports—all the things that make people feel good when times are tough. He vowed that day that he would one day own such a business. But he wasn't ready yet.

From 2002 to 2005, Doug was earning $400,000 working for World Wide Technology in Washington D.C. He was only 32 years old and single. He was living the great American dream. But he decided to leave it all behind and start a business in an industry he had never worked in, and had no education or training in. He decided to open a sports bar. But not just any sports bar—a sports bar where the waitresses were all attractive young women who wore "Daisy Duke" shorts, cowboy boots and bikini tops. He would call the bar "Bikinis."

When I interviewed him, I said, "Doug, at that time, there were already several huge chains of sports bars that dominated the 'scantily clad waitress' industry. There was *Hooters, Twin Peaks,* and the *Tilted Kilt*. What made you think you could compete with them?" His response was startling. "I only knew that Hooters existed. I didn't know about the others. I just knew what I wanted. So, I went for it."

In 2006, Doug's first sports bar opened on the heavily trafficked IH-35 in Austin, Texas. Within nine months, he had already recovered his initial investment. Then he started opening more locations. In 2008, as though to test Guller's theory, America was hit by the worst recession since the Great Depression. Experts began calling it the Great Recession. But Guller's theory proved correct. During tough times, people seek distraction and entertainment more than at any other time. Guller's business was exploding.

By 2013, he had fourteen Bikinis locations. During that same period, he also opened a Mexican food restaurant in downtown Austin, and eight other bars under different and unique names.[246] In 2013, he bought an entire town and renamed it Bikini, Texas. It is located very near the famous town of Luckenbach, Texas. Not surprisingly, Guller is the mayor of that town. Guller now lives across the river from Michael Dell.

It seems that true entrepreneurs can't leave well enough alone. They always want more. But it isn't more money they want. It's the thrill of the game. It's the thrill of winning. And once they've won, they're willing to walk away from everything they've accomplished and start over again with something they've never tried before. It's lunacy. But it's the best kind of lunacy.

> *When their time arrives, the ordinary become extraordinary. The rebels of the world are those who've had enough and decide, 'I'm going to bet all that I have and all that I am on something greater than myself.'*
>
> —BRIAN WILLIAMS
> *NBC Nightly News*

What can we learn from them? In baseball terms, you can't steal second base with one foot still on first. The question here is, what are you willing to walk away from in order to achieve your wildest dreams? If you are unhappy doing what you're doing, why do you keep doing it? The historical record is full of examples of spiritual leaders and entrepreneurs who left behind much more than you now possess just for the sheer pleasure of experiencing something they had never experienced before. What is it you are clinging to so desperately— *and why?*

THINGS TO PONDER

+ The most powerful people on the planet are those who act as though things the rest of us only dream about are real.

+ If you are not willing to walk away from everything you are doing and everything that you are, your goal is not big enough.

+ You will never arrive at your "promised land" until you are willing to embrace the unknown.

-·-‹‹‹•›››-·-

CHAPTER 31

What Solutions Are All Around You Right Now?

I don't know where you are in life right now. Life may have just dealt you a devastating blow. You may have lost your job. Your spouse may have just left you. You may have lost a loved one. A fire, a tornado, or a hurricane, may have destroyed the building where you operated your business along with all your equipment and inventory. Google may have just changed its algorithms and buried your website on page 1,000 of the search results. Changes in the economy may have "re-routed" all your customers elsewhere overnight. But regardless of your situation in life, you have a decision to make. This will be *the most important decision* you ever make. You can choose to believe that life as you know it is over and give up. Or you can choose to believe that *there is no such thing as a problem without a solution.*

You may think you're at a crossroads. But you're not. You are at an *omni*roads. It is not flat. It is three dimensional. In fact, when you add the element of time, it is four dimensional.[247] Your options look like a dandelion. They are not flat and linear. They are blossoming like a flower outwards in all directions all the time.

Whatever problem you are facing right now, the solution already exists. It is out there in the future waiting for you. Whether you get to experience it or not is up to you. You are choosing which reality in a dandelion of possibilities you get to experience by what you do right here, right now, today.

In fact, someone, somewhere on the planet is already living your dream. The reality you seek already exists for someone—somewhere in time. You will read about them in the newspaper. You will see them on TV. Books will be written about them. Movies will be made about their lives. Those same books, movies and news stories could be about you. What are you doing right now to be able to experience that reality?

The fact that we are first and foremost spiritual beings means that our life's experience is not limited to what we can see, hear, taste, touch or smell. It is not even limited to what we can imagine. Great thinkers have always told us, "If you can imagine it, you can achieve it." But this is too limiting. I believe we can experience and achieve things we are not even capable of imagining. The great physicists who first looked into the inner workings of the atom taught us that the world we can see is not as real as the world we cannot see.

There are possibilities and opportunities out there that you have not even considered. Things you cannot see, taste, hear, touch or smell because they *have not yet materialized.* They are just around the corner. The answers to your problems are already out there waiting for you in the future ahead of your problems. The universe is bigger than the present, the here and the now. The universe is already happening three or four steps ahead of where you are now. The future is already happening as we speak.

The most profound thing that the theory of relativity taught us is that there is no grand measuring stick against which you can measure your position in time or space. Because everything in the universe is in constant motion, there is no absolute, fixed time-space coordinate system where you can say a thing is located at this spot at this exact moment in time or space.[248] You may say you are currently located in Los Angeles, California, but your coordinates on the x and y axis, are located on a planet that is spinning at 1,038 miles per hour. That same planet is hurling through space around the sun at 67,108 miles per hour. Our sun and all of its planets are moving as one unit at the rate of 486,000 miles per hour in an orbit around a black hole in the center of the Milky Way Galaxy. If you were to take a giant step back into outer space and photograph the entire Milky Way Galaxy from the top down, our entire solar system would appear as a single dot of dust riding along on one arm of the Milky Way.

To visualize it another way, next time you are at the beach, take your shoes off and walk around in the sand next to the water. Let your feet sink into the sand. Now sit down and dust some of the sand off your toes. Isolate a single tiny grain of sand between your fingers. Now walk to the water and toss that grain of sand into the ocean. The grain of sand represents our sun and all of its planets. The ocean is the Milky Way.

Now take an even bigger step back. When compared to the size of the entire Universe, the Milky Way itself is the size of a marble tossed into an even bigger ocean. The Milky Way is also zooming through space like a baseball shot out of a cannon at the rate of 2,200,000 kilometers per hour.

How many galaxies like the Milky Way are there zooming around in the universe? If you hold your little finger up to the night sky and isolate a very dark spot the size of your fingernail, there are approximately 10,000 galaxies there. From where you stand, it looks like the darkest spot in the night sky. We only know they are thousands of galaxies in that spot because of the Ultra Deep Field photographs taken by the Hubble Telescope. These photos were produced by pointing our best telescope at what appeared to be one of the blackest spots in the night sky for an extended period of time. It took a long time for the light from those galaxies to even be absorbed by the telescope enough to generate a photograph. The photographs of the blackest part of the sky revealed a stunningly beautiful sea of galaxies that we didn't even know existed.[249] And that's only counting what exists *in that one spot*. The universe is so vast—how do you really know where you are in time and space?

In the grand scheme of the universe, what do you measure your location against?[250] What do you measure your place *in time* against? If you apply the theory of relativity to real life, you realize that all possible futures are already happening in all directions all around us.

Einstein concurred. When his lifelong friend Michele Angelo Besso died, Einstein wrote a letter to Besso's family, saying that although his friend had preceded him in death, it mattered not. Einstein explained, "for us physicists believe the separation between past, present, and future is only an illusion, although a convincing one."

Envision yourself sitting inside of a giant dandelion—at the very center. When you look around, you see millions of dandelion seeds pointing outward in all directions like arrows targeting all the possibilities at the same time. They are pointing to your options. You have options you don't even know you have, and they are ever expanding. Each dandelion seed is capable of flying across mountain ranges and oceans before it reaches its final destination.

The reality you want is out there in the future waiting for you. But which reality you get to experience is being determined right now by the thoughts you think, the words you speak, the books you read, the friends you make, and the actions you take.

It is like driving down a dark country road at night. You can't see what lies beyond your headlights. But it is already there, waiting for you. In order for you to experience it, you simply have to continue on the path you are on. If you continue on that path, the future is not only predictable, it is inevitable.

Did you know that the light you see when the sun comes up in the morning is already 8 minutes old? That's how long it takes for the light waves traveling from the sun to reach the earth. The future you will experience in 8 minutes *is already happening now.*

In baseball terms, does the home run happen when the ball goes over the wall or when the bat makes contact with the ball? If you take all the necessary steps to hit a home run, including waiting for the right pitch, the future is determined as soon as your bat makes contact with the ball. The future is determined by our present actions even though we can't see the outcome yet.

Even the future events we cannot see, predict or control are already in the process of happening because the events that have set them in motion have already occurred. Nothing really ever happens "out of the blue." Even unanticipated events like car wrecks, bombings, and shootings were not without some prior chain of events. To us, the event seems shocking and completely arbitrary. But in truth, there was a long chain of interconnected events that had to happen in order for the final "arbitrary" one to happen.

Right now, you are setting in motion atoms, molecules, sound waves, and vibrations that will cause some future event to happen, and you don't even realize it. You have already knocked down the first domino. As you sit inside the dandelion, looking around at all the possible futures that are available to you, we know that one of the possible realities in your future is prosperity, love, and happiness. Not a life without problems. But a life full of solutions that already exist three or four steps ahead of the problems. You are on a collision course with opportunities and solutions you don't even know exist yet.

Now look up again at that pitch black spot you isolated in the night sky. What do you see? The moment of enlightenment comes when you realize that the world you *cannot* see is as real as the world you can see. You are capable of accomplishing dreams you have not yet dreamed.

> ***It is possible to believe that all the past is but the beginning of a beginning, and that all that is and has been is but the twilight of the dawn. It is possible to believe that all the human mind has ever accomplished is but the dream before the awakening.***[251]
>
> —H.G. WELLS

✳ THINGS TO PONDER

- The solutions and answers you seek are already out there waiting for you—three or four steps ahead of your problems.
- It is a sin to do nothing because you can only do a little.
- You are never at a crossroads. You are always at an *omni*roads.
- Learn to look at the world from the center of a dandelion looking outward. The hundreds of long seeds pointing outward in all directions are pointing at your options.
- Because of the time-space continuum, you can never identify exactly where you are in time or in space.
- The future you want already exists. Go get it.
- Accept that the world you cannot see is as real as the world you can see.
- You are on a collision course with opportunities you don't even know exist yet.

Notes

Part I: The Eye of the Brain

CHAPTER 2
Can You Believe in Something You Cannot See?

1 Scott O'Grady, *Return With Honor*, (New York: Harper Collins, 1995), 101–102.

2 Carl Sagan, *In the Shadows of Forgotten Ancestors* (New York: Random House, 1992), 276–277.

3 Robert Kaplan, *The Nothing That Is: A Natural History of Zero* (Oxford University Press, 2000).

4 Herbert Butterfield, *The Origins of Modern Science* (New York: The Free Press, 1957), 16.

5 John Rowland, *Understanding the Atom* (London: Gollancz, 1935), 56; Brian Cathcart, *The Fly in the Cathedral* (Great Britain: Penguin Group, 2004), 6; Fritjof Capra, *The Tao of Physics* (Boston: Shambhala Publications, Inc., 1975).

6 Arthur Koestler, *The Sleepwalkers: A History of Man's Changing Vision of the Universe* (London: Penguin Group, 1959), 540, 541.

7 When John Cockcroft and Ernest Walton were finally able to split an atom, they noticed that the atomic weight of what remained—after the splitting—was less than what they had started with. "The lost mass did not manifest itself in any material particle or any ray, but it could not have simply vanished because no such thing is possible. Instead, it became energy. When the alpha particles flung themselves in opposite directions, the energy they expended was that missing mass expressed in a different form." Cathcart, *The Fly in the Cathedral*, 234.

CHAPTER 3
Are There Ideas in the Air?

8 John Gertner, *The Idea Factory: Bell Labs and the Great Age of American Innovation* (New York: Penguin Group, 2012), 203.

9 William Ogburn and Dorothy Thomas, "Are Inventions Inevitable? A Note On Social Evolution," *Political Science Quarterly*, Vol. 37, No. 1 (March 1922).

10 Nancy Forbes and Basin Mahon, *Faraday, Maxwell, and the Electromagnetic Field* (New York: Prometheus Books, 2014), 248-263; Chad Orzel, *How To Teach Relativity to Your Dog* (New York: Basic Books, 2012). 35; and Stephen Hawking, *The Grand Design* (New York: Bantam Books, 2010), 91.

11 Ibid.

12   Forbes and Mahon, *Faraday, Maxwell and the Electromagnetic Field*, 255-263.

13   Ibid.

14   Ibid.

15   Forbes and Mahon, *Faraday, Maxwell and the Electromagnetic Field*, 255.

16   Ibid.

17   During Rockefeller's day, gasoline was a by-product from the manufacture of kerosene, which was still being used to light people's houses. Gasoline was considered useless because it was too volatile to be used safely. Refineries regularly dumped millions of gallons of gasoline into the local sewers, creeks, and rivers. But in order to drive an internal combustible engine, you need a fuel as powerful and volatile as gasoline. The saying remains true, "One man's trash is another man's treasure."

18   Koestler, *The Sleepwalkers*, 213.

19   Ibid, 523.

20   Serge Bramly, *Leonardo: Discovering The Life of Leonardo da Vinci* (New York: Harper Collins, 1991), 77.

21   Morton Meyers, A. *Happy Accidents* (New York: Arcade Publishing, 2007), 79.

22   Royston M. Roberts, *Serendipity: Accidental Discoveries in Science* (New York: John Wiley & Sons, Inc.1989), 65.

23   This is one reason why there is such a huge effort to save the rain forests. We know that there may yet be thousands, if not millions, of undiscovered remedies in the jungles that may provide the cures to modern ailments.

24   So strong was Edison's belief that he could always find a solution that when it was announced that Edison was searching for a way to create electrical lighting, the stock prices of gas lighting companies lost one-quarter of their value. Gerald Gunderson, *The Wealth Creators,* (New York: Dutton, 1989), 177.

25   Gertner, *The Idea Factory,* 21, 22.

26   We call sunrise the "beginning" of the day, and sunset the "end" of the day. But in reality, there is no beginning or end. The sun simply moves in a circle. The word "beginning" is merely a descriptor we use to describe when the sun came into our view. This is also why it is futile to ask, "When did the universe begin?" Who says it has to have a "beginning"? Maybe it is constantly expanding and then contracting. The beginning of any thing is simply a matter of when it came into our conscious awareness.

CHAPTER 4

Why Do We Look Without Seeing?

27   Arien Mack and Irvin Rock, *Inattentional Blindness* (Cambridge: The MIT Press, 1998).

CHAPTER 5
Why Do Even Experts Miss the Obvious?

28 S.C. Gwynne, *Empire of the Summer Moon* (New York: Scribner, 2010).

29 Ibid.

30 Bell beat Gray to the patent office by only a few hours.

31 Ira Flatow, *They All Laughed* (New York: Harper Collins, 1992), 224.

32 Ibid., 143-144.

33 At around the same time, John W. Cropper separately and independently invented a new type of fabric from expanded polytetrafluouroethylene (PTFE), the chemical constituent of Teflon. A lawsuit ensued over patent rights. Gore won, but only for technical reasons.

34 Flatow, *They All Laughed,* 152-155.

35 Glenn Rifkin, "Ken Olsen, Who Built DEC Into a Power, Dies at 84," *New York Times* (February 7, 2011).

36 Flatow, *They All Laughed,* 205-212.

37 Ibid, 225-226.

CHAPTER 6
Does the Brain Have Its Own Eye?

38 Bruce Lipton, *The Biology of Belief* (New York: Hay House, Inc., 2005).

39 Ibid.

40 Ibid.

41 Ibid.

42 Further confirmation that single celled creatures such as bacteria are intelligent is the fact they often outwit the antibiotics we throw at them, and eventually overcome them. Tuberculosis claimed one billion lives between 1800 and 1950. But in 1947, researchers found an antibiotic called *streptomycin* which was effective against tuberculosis. Deaths caused by tuberculosis plummeted. But by 1993, the World Health Organization declared tuberculosis to be a global emergency. Deaths caused by tuberculosis have climbed to two million per year. The microbes are fighting back.

43 Meyers, *Happy Accidents,* 35.

44 Paul Scott Anderson, "Key Step in Evolution Replicated by Scientists With Yeast," *Universe Today* (January 23, 2012)

45 Lipton, *The Biology of Belief.*

46 Stephen M. Kosslyn and Wayne G. Miller, "A New Map of How We Think: Top Brain/ Bottom Brain," *Wall Street Journal* (October 18, 2013)

47 When Jesus said that the flowers of the field and the birds of the air do not worry about what they will wear or where their next meal will come from, he was right. But this is because they don't have a neocortex, and therefore, cannot anticipate the future.

48 Our punishment for enlightenment was not physical death. Adam and Eve were not struck down the moment they ate of the fruit. Our punishment was the conscious awareness of our inevitable physical death. No other animal appears to know that it will one day die.

Part II: Opening the Eye of the Brain

CHAPTER 7
Can You Enhance Your Sense of Awareness?

49 This is because I recently started taking bongo lessons!

50 David Klinger, *Into the Kill Zone: A Cop's Eye View of Deadly Force.* (San Francisco: Jossey-Bass, 2004).

51 You can find a video of Jason making these shots complete with the entire story dramatically told by him by searching for the title "J Mac Greatest Basketball Story Ever" on YouTube. There are many videos of this story, but this one is my favorite. It brought tears to my eyes. Jason eventually received hugs and congratulations by Oprah Winfrey, Magic Johnson, Dallas Mavericks coach Mark Cuban, Dirk Nowitski, and President George W. Bush.

52 Richard Branson, *Losing My Virginity*, (New York: Crown Business, 1998), 63.

53 Ibid., 192, 193.

54 Ibid., 399.

55 Estée Lauder, *Estée: A Success Story* (New York: Random House, Inc. 1985), 55.

CHAPTER 8
Three Choices You Don't Realize You're Making

56 Peter Godwin, *Mukiwa: A White Boy In Africa* (New York: Harper Perennial, 1996)

CHAPTER 9
How Does Your Focus Affect Your Beliefs?

57 Branson, *Losing My Virginity*, 194.

58 Currently, Branson is trying to make commercial space travel possible.

CHAPTER 10
How Do Your Beliefs Affect Your Biology?

59 Graciela Flores, "Paying for Pleasure," *Scientific American Mind* (April/May 2008).

60 Benedict Carey, "More Expensive Placebos Bring More Relief," *New York Times* (March 5, 2008).

61 Dan Ariely, *Predictably Irrational:* The Hidden Forces That Shape Our Decisions (New York: Harper Collins, 2008).

62 Anne Harrington, *The Placebo Effect: An Interdisciplinary Exploration* (Cambridge: Harvard University Press, 1997).

63 Ibid.

64 Ibid.

65 Ibid.

66 Gina Kolata, "A Little Deception Helps Push Athletes to the Limit," *New York Times* (Sept. 19, 2011).

67 I have been a business litigation attorney for twenty-five years.

68 Mack, *Inattentional Blindness.*

69 Ibid.

70 Charles Perrow, *Normal Accidents* (Princeton: Princeton University Press, 1999).

71 Steve Andreas and Charles Faulkner, *NLP: The New Technology of Achievement*, (New York: William Morrow and Co., 1994).

CHAPTER 11

How Do Your Beliefs Affect What You See?

72 In the metaphor, a group of prisoners live most of their lives chained to the wall of a cave, facing a blank wall. All they can see of the outside world is the shadows projected on the wall from behind them when things pass in front of a fire. They begin to ascribe meaning and form to these shadows. This is as close as the prisoners get to viewing reality. So, it is with us in the moment of enlightenment. When we are freed from the cave, we come to understand that the shadows on the wall do not make up reality at all.

73 Koestler, *The Sleepwalkers.*

74 Early in his career, Newton himself called the idea of gravity "in which one body acts upon another at a distance through a vacuum, without the mediation of anything else . . . a great absurdity." Letter from Isaac Newton to his friend Richard Bentley. Trinity College Library, Cambridge, England. Quoted by Koestler, *The Sleepwalkers*, 344. It must have seemed absurd that one object can make another object move without ever touching it. The law of inertia never occurred to the ancient Greeks, or to Kepler, despite the fact that their own experience with bows and arrows and sling shots demonstrated it to them.

75 Even as Kepler was writing his laws of planetary motion, his 73-year-old mother was being accused of being a witch and brought into a torture chamber and shown the instruments of torture that would be used on her body if she did not confess.

76 Despite his aggressive criticisms of his opponents, Galileo did not believe his own eyes (and the recorded observations of others) when it came to comets. He insisted that comets, which he actually saw, were not real, but merely optical illusions. Arthur Koestler, *The Act of Creation* (New York: Dell Publishing Co., 1964), 217.

77　Joshua 10:12, 13 (NIV).

CHAPTER 12
Are Your Words Limiting What You Can See?

78　B.T. Gardner and R.A. Gardner, "Comparing the Early Utterances of Child and Chimpanzee," *Minnesota Symposium in Child Psychology*, Volume 8 (Minneapolis: University of Minnesota Press, 1974) 3-23.

79　Quantum physics has recently confirmed that the words and mathematical formulas we use to describe reality are not reality itself, but creations of the mind. They are not the truth, only the approximation of truth.

80　Koestler, *The Sleepwalkers*, 545.

81　Author interview with Herb Kelleher (January 2011).

82　At a more fundamental level, how we describe a problem betrays what we believe about the solution.

83　Michael Michalko, *Cracking Creativity* (Berkeley: Ten Speed Press, 2001), 20.

84　Ibid. at 36.

85　The word "vaccine" is derived from the Latin "vacca" meaning cow.

86　Amy Mayer, "Rename It, Reuse It," *Scientific American Mind* (July /August 2012).

87　Ibid.

88　Ibid.

89　Thomas A. Kinney, *The Carriage Trade* (Baltimore: The Johns Hopkins University Press, 2004), 203-242.

90　In 1876, German engineer Nicholas Otto, developed the four-cycle engine. In 1885, Karl Benz used the four-cycle engine to power a three-wheeled carriage. In 1886, Gottlieb Daimler used the four-cycle engine to power a bicycle.

91　The combustible engine is based on the law of conservation of matter. This law says matter is neither created nor destroyed. It simply changes from one form into another. Roberts, *Serendipity*, 29.

92　Ibid., 203-242.

93　If you are working on a project at your company, ask yourself if you are suffering from this same kind of myopia. You can tell where your focus is by taking inventory of the kind of questions you are asking your team.

94　After suffering devastating losses in market share, film manufacturers such as Kodak and Fuji finally began manufacturing digital cameras. Kodak ultimately declared bankruptcy.

95　Likewise, the traditional real estate brokerage model is on the verge of obsolescence because for years, brokers have been asking, "How do I recruit more agents?" and "How do I get my agents to sell more real estate?" instead of asking "How can I make it easier for people to buy and sell real estate?" When we focus more on who we are and what we do instead of on the needs of our customers, we are begging the market to replace us.

96 Kinney, *The Carriage Trade,* 271.

97 This presents quite a challenge because it may require that we admit our entire life's work is now suddenly obsolete. Most people are unwilling to do this and will hold onto their life's work till they are completely bankrupt, emotionally, spiritually, or financially.

CHAPTER 13
Why Do We Create Our Own Truth?

98 This is another example of "confirmation bias"—the natural tendency to seek only that evidence which confirms what we've already chosen to believe and discount all evidence to the contrary.

99 In fact, the Bushmen of Africa believe to this day that every time they see a shooting star, it represents the death of a great leader.

100 The *Wall Street Journal* and the *New York Times* stock analysts consistently do the same thing the day after the stock market does something dramatic. It would be unheard of for newspapers of this magnitude to simply shrug their shoulders and say, "Sorry folks, we don't really know why the stock market did what it did yesterday." But the reality is, they often don't. It is often takes years of hindsight before analysts can figure out exactly why the market did what it did.

101 William Manchester and Paul Reid, *The Last Lion,* (London: Little, Brown and Company, 2012), 47.

102 Ibid.

103 Ibid, 63.

104 Ibid, 66.

105 Ibid, 62.

106 Carl Sagan, *Cosmos,* (New York: Ballantine Books, 1980).

CHAPTER 14
How Do We Turn Background Noise into Information?

107 Quoted in Victor Weisskopf, *The Joy of Insight: Passions of a Physicist,* translated by Douglas Worth (New York: Basic Books, 1991), 296–97.

108 Paul Gray, "Alan Turing—Time 100 People of the Century," *Time Magazine.* (March 1999)("The fact remains that everyone who taps at a keyboard, opening a spreadsheet or a word-processing program, is working on an incarnation of a Turing machine.")

109 Wolfgang Kohler, *The Mentality of Apes,* (London: Pelican Books, 1931).

110 Meyers, *Happy Accidents,* 33.

111 Helen Keller, *The Story of My Life* (London: Hodder & Stoughton, 1959).

CHAPTER 16

Is it Okay to Wander While You Wonder?

112 John S. Rigden, *Einstein, The Standard of Greatness*, (Cambridge: First Harvard University Press, 2005), 85.

113 Josef Donnerer and Fred Lembeck, *The Chemical Languages of the Nervous System* (London: Karger Publishers, 2006), 23.

114 Ibid., 23.

115 Koestler, *The Act of Creation*, 147.

116 Roberts, *Serendipity*, 81.

117 Koestler, *The Sleepwalkers.*

118 Flatow, *They All Laughed*, 193.

119 Psalm 16:7 (NIV).

120 Roberts, *Serendipity*, 82.

121 Andre Chastel, *The Genius of Leonardo Da Vinci* (New York: The Orion Press, 1961), 204.

122 Ibid.

123 Koestler, *The Act of Creation*, 211.

124 Norman Doidge, M.D., *The Brain That Changes Itself* (New York: Penguin Group, 2007), 24, 239, 328, 385.

125 Carl Sagan also points out that mammals dream, but reptiles do not. Carl Sagan, *Dragons of Eden* (New York: Tess Press, 2004).

126 This is why Google, Facebook, all of the gaming companies, and any company that depends on the creativity of its people for its success have ping-pong tables, Nerf guns, giant squishy balls, and lots of other toys randomly scattered about their complexes.

CHAPTER 17

Can You Think in 3-D?

127 Orzel, *How To Teach Relativity to Your Dog;* and Hawking, *The Grand Design.*

128 Bramly, *Leonardo*, 78-79.

129 Ibid, 374.

130 Chastel, *The Genius of Leonardo da Vinci*, 204.

131 Meyers, *Happy Accidents*, 40.

132 This region of the brain analyzes and understands space (i.e., the world around you) in two and three dimensions. It processes mental imagery and navigation, distance and depth perception, and visuo-spatial construction.

133 Evangelina G. Chrysikou, "Your Creative Brain at Work," *Scientific American Mind* (July/August 2012).

134 Proctor & Gamble reports that "Today, more than 35 percent of our new products in market have elements that originated from outside P&G."

135 Milton Lehman, *This High Man: The Life of Robert H. Goddard* (New York: Farrar, Strauss, and Co., 1963).

CHAPTER 18
Are You Blinded By Logic?

136 Orzel, *How to Teach Relativity to Your Dog*, 175, 183.

137 Ibid., 282–285.

138 In order to get there, they have to flow through a piece of wire called a conductor. The conductor lights up a filament as the electrical current flows through it from the negative end of the battery to the positive end. The filament glows and this gives us light.

139 All of this, of course, confirms the lesson I learned in the Amazon jungle—the universe cannot exist in a state of imbalance.

140 Capra, *The Tao of Physics*, 292.

141 Bramly, *Leonardo*.

142 Ibid.

CHAPTER 19
Why Do Outsiders See More Solutions?

143 Meyers, *Happy Accidents*, 10.

144 Ibid., 5.

145 Ibid. 102.

146 Ibid., 103.

147 Ibid., 113.

CHAPTER 20
Can You See What You're Not Looking For?

148 Roberts, Serendipity, 125.

149 Meyers, *Happy Accidents*, 79.

150 Ibid., 313.

151 Ibid., at 95.

152 Ibid.

153 Koestler, *Sleepwalkers*, 262.

154 Meyers, *Happy Accidents*, 108.

155 Ibid., 235.

156 Ibid., 7, 24.

157 Ibid., 19, 23.

158 Albert Szent Gyorgyi, *Bioenergetics*, (New York: Academic Press, 1957), 57.

159   Branson, *Losing My Virginity,* 407.

160   Meyers, *Happy Accidents,* 25.

161   Ibid., 185.

162   Ibid., xiii.

163   Sir Alexander Fleming's speech at the Nobel Banquet in Stockholm (December 10, 1945).

164   Meyers, *Happy Accidents,* 238.

165   Steve Lohr, "H. Edward Roberts, PC Pioneer, Dies at 68," *New York Times,* (April 2, 2010).

166   Meyers, *Happy Accidents,* 81.

CHAPTER 21
When Is it Okay to Be Addicted?

167   Ibid., 158.

168   Cathcart, *The Fly in the Cathedral,* 271.

169   Meyers, Happy Accidents, 71–72.

170   Doidge, *The Brain That Changes Itself,* 115.

171   Koestler, *The Act of Creation,* 502.

172   David Dobbs, "Restless Genes," *National Geographic* (January 2013).

173   A typical Formula One race has a global TV viewing audience of approximately 527 million people, and generates billions of dollars in revenue. Red achieved his goal on November 16, 17, 18, 2012 when he successfully hosted his first Formula One race in Austin, Texas. He sold 276,000 tickets to that event, the most tickets ever sold to a single sporting event in American history. Not being satisfied with just one home run, he did it again in November 2013.

174   Branson, *Losing My Virginity,* 186, 193, 194.

175   Graham Farmelo, *It Must Be Beautiful: Great Equations of Modern Science* (London: Granta Publications, 2002).

176   Imelda Marcos was the wife of Ferdinand Marcos, the President of the Philippines. In 1986, they were forced into exile based on allegations of corruption.

CHAPTER 22
How Do You Get Off the Hamster Wheel?

177   To carry the analogy a little further, a legendary innovator would ask, "Why exactly are we looking for a needle? Is it so we can sew two pieces of cloth together? What other ways are there to hold two pieces of cloth together?" And while he's contemplating the problem, he might just take a walk through the woods and come back with cockle burs on his socks. Legendary entrepreneurs and innovators always challenge all assumptions—sometimes for no apparent reason than to be difficult. They always ask *why,* and more importantly, *why not.*

178 Bramly, *Leonardo*, 205.

179 *Critical Choices That Change Lives: How Heroes Turn Tragedy Into Triumph.* Download the first chapter free at: www.CriticalChoices.com

Part III: Now Look Around You

CHAPTER 24
What If You're Out of Options?

180 Remember, back then, there were no cameras, no pictures, no TV's, no CNN, no internet, and no Facebook. So, the king wasn't sure what David looked like.

181 Bramly, *Leonardo*, 259.

182 Branson, *Losing My Virginity,* 245.

183 Ibid., 242-246.

184 Mihaly Csikszentmihalyi, *Creativity* (New York: Harper Collins 1996), 116.

185 Chrysikou, "Your Creative Brain at Work."

CHAPTER 25
What If You Could Change Your Brain?

186 Doidge, *The Brain That Changes Itself,* 16.

187 Ibid., 21.

188 Ibid., 23.

189 Ibid., 16.

190 Ibid., 57-58.

191 Ibid., 35.

192 Ibid., 218.

193 This another example of the dangers of letting our analogies become our truth. The old analogy was blinding us to the truth of what was actually happening in the brain.

194 Ibid., 43.

195 Ibid., 59

196 Ibid., 201.

197 Ibid., 203–204.

198 Ibid., 205

199 Ibid., 207, 369.

200 Ibid., 213.

201 Benedict Carey, "Paralyzed, Moving a Robot With Their Minds," *New York Times* (May 16, 2012).

202 Doidge, *The Brain That Changes Itself* , 87, 252.

203 Ibid., 252–257.

204 Ibid., at 252.

205 I laughed out at the theater when I saw *The Bourne Legacy*. In it, the hero has been taking certain super-secret pills manufactured by a large and evil pharmaceutical company working in secret with the CIA. When he asks the chemist what the pills do, she said, "It creates super intelligence by causing the brain to grow more neurons through a process called neurogenesis." People in the theater turned around and stared at me. It wasn't supposed to be funny. I just thought it was hysterical that Hollywood thinks we need a super-secret pill to accomplish what history has proven that we can do through the sheer force of our will, discipline, and hard work. It's called neurogenesis—and it works.

206 Ibid., 252.

207 Ibid., 255.

208 Ibid., 257.

209 Michael Jordan was actually cut from his high school basketball team.

210 Doidge, *The Brain That Changes Itself*, 288–291.

211 Ibid., 289.

212 Ibid., 303.

213 Ibid.

214 Ibid.

215 Ibid., 304.

CHAPTER 26

When Is it Okay to Be Obsessed?

216 Jim Rogers, *Investment Biker*, (New York: Random House, 1994).

217 Lauder, *Estée: A Success Story*, 24.

218 Gertner, *The Idea Factory*, 11.

219 Meyers, *Happy Accidents*, 62.

220 Ibid., 196.

221 Joe Nocera, "Capturing the Facebook Obsession," *New York Times* (October 15, 2010).

222 John D. Gartner, *The Hypomanic Edge* (New York: Simon & Schuster, 2005), 29.

223 But remember to take periodic breaks. The most brilliant solutions may not come to you until you are in a period of rest—after all the hard work.

224 I have cited many more examples in this book where the person did not invest that much time and effort in order to succeed. But they were driven by a powerful obsession.

225 Ahmad Rashad interview of Michael Jordan, *Full 1 on 1*, NBA TV, 2013.

226 This doesn't mean you can't get "pretty good" at what you do, and even earn a living doing it. Indeed, most people in society go to work every day and do a "pretty good" job at things they are not all that excited about.

227 Gartner, *The Hypomanic Edge,* 18.

228 Chastel, *The Genius of Leonardo da Vinci,* 78.

229 His two students, Tsung-Dao Lee and Chen-Ning Franklin Yang, each won the Nobel Prize in physics in 1957.

CHAPTER 27
What's Your Big Enough Reason Why?

230 Victor Villasenor, *Rain of Gold* (New York: Random House, 1991), 119–126.

231 Hall of Fame Acceptance Speech.

232 I have highlighted a few words and phrases that leapt out at me when I first saw him give this speech.

233 Obsession reminds us that we can have anything we want, but not *everything* we want.

CHAPTER 28
Is There a Way to Level the Playing Field?

234 His book, *Cooked,* is one of the best stories about overcoming I have ever read. Jeff Henderson, *Cooked: My Journey From the Streets to the Stove* (New York: Harper Collins, 2007).

235 Koestler, *The Act of Creation,* 708.

236 To dig deeper into the Jewish foundations of Hollywood, read *An Empire of Their Own* by Neal Gabler. *See* Neal Gabler, *An Empire of Their Own: How the Jews Invented Hollywood* (New York: Random House, 1988).

237 Imagine if you knew your boyfriend or husband had a gaggle of mistresses. It never seemed to bother Coco Chanel. These were wealthy and glamorous young women that a poor orphan girl would never meet otherwise. She turned weakness into strength. Those women became the foundation of her worldwide empire. Water does not seek "the" path of least resistance. It seeks "all" the paths of least resistance.

238 Axel Madsen, *Chanel: A Woman of Her Own* (New York: Henry Holt & Co., 1990), 69.

239 Ibid., 161.

CHAPTER 29
Can You Create Value Out of Thin Air?

240 Incidentally, no other species finds any value in gold, silver or diamonds. You can't eat it. You can't plant it. You can't mate with it. It does not make the best protective armor because it's too soft. It makes for lousy tips of spears and arrows.

241 Michalko, *Cracking Creativity*, 235.

242 Luke 6:38. (NIV)

243 If matter is energy in motion, and money is matter, then money is just energy in motion. That means you can never run out of money because you are constantly surrounded by energy in motion. In honor of Einstein, the formula I have created for this is: $\$ = Mc^2$.

CHAPTER 30

What Are You Willing to Walk Away From?

244 Eventually, the airline expanded, and now flies all over the country.

245 When Herb Kelleher first read this dialogue, he laughed out loud and told me, "You nailed it Dan!"

246 Guller also owns bars and restaurants under the names Parish; 508 Tequila Bar; Chicago House; Zorro; Pelon's TexMex; 609 Trinity; Historic Scoot Inn; Parish Underground; and Guller Hall.

CHAPTER 31

What Solutions Are All Around You Right Now?

247 Orzel, *How to Teach Relativity to Your Dog*, 236, 261.

248 Ibid., 31, 51, 131.

249 To see what is revealed in this single dot in the night sky, simply google "Hubble Ultra Deep Field."

250 Orzel, *How to Teach Relativity to Your Dog*, 31, 51, 131.

251 H.G. Wells, "The Discovery of Our Future," *Nature*, 65, 326 (1902).

Selected Bibliography

Anderson, Paul Scott. "Key Step in Evolution Replicated by Scientists With Yeast." *Universe Today*, January 23, 2012.

Andreas, Steve and Faulkner, Charles. *NLP: The New Technology of Achievement*. New York: William Morrow and Co., 1994.

Ariely, Dan. *Predictably Irrational: The Hidden Forces That Shape Our Decisions*. New York: Harper Collins, 2008.

Bramly, Serge. *Leonardo: Discovering The Life of Leonoardo Da Vinci*. New York: Harper Collins, 1991.

Branson, Richard. *Losing My Virginity*. New York: Crown Business, 1998.

Butterfield, Herbert. *The Origins of Modern Science*. New York: The Free Press, 1957.

Capra, Fritjof. *The Tao of Physics*. Boston: Shambhala Publications, Inc., 1975.

Carey, Benedict. "Paralyzed, Moving a Robot With Their Minds." *New York Times*, May 16, 2012.

Carey, Benedict. "More Expensive Placebos Bring More Relief." *New York Times*, March 5, 2008.

Cathcart, Brian. *The Fly in the Cathedral*. Great Britain: Penguin Group, 2004.

Chastel, Andre. *The Genius of Leonardo Da Vinci*. New York: The Orion Press, 1961.

Chrysikou, Evangelina G. "Your Creative Brain at Work." *Scientific Mind*, July/August 2012.

Csikszentmihalyi, Mihaly. *Creativity*. New York: Harper Collins, 1996.

Dobbs, David. "Restless Genes." *National Geographic,* January, 2013.

Doidge, Norman, M.D. *The Brain That Changes Itself*. New York: Penguin Group, 2007.

Donnerer, Josef, and Lembeck, Fred. *The Chemical Languages of the Nervous System*. London: Karger Publishers, 2006.

Farmelo, Graham. *It Must Be Beautiful: Great Equations of Modern Science*. London: Granta Publications, 2002.

Flatow, Ira. *They All Laughed*. New York: Harper Collins, 1992.

Flores, Graciela. "Paying for Pleasure." *Scientific American Mind,* April/May 2008.

Gabler, Neal. *An Empire of Their Own: How the Jews Invented Hollywood*. New York: Random House, 1988.

Gardner, B.T. and Gardner, R.A. "Comparing the Early Utterances of Child and Chimpanzee." Minnesota Symposium in Child Psychology. Minneapolis: University of Minnesota Press, 1974.

Gartner, John, D. *The Hypomanic Edge*. New York: Simon & Schuster, 2005.

Gertner, John. *The Idea Factory: Bell Labs and the Great Age of American Innovation*. New York: Penguin Group, 2012.

Godwin, Peter. *Mukiwa: A White Boy In Africa*. New York: Harper Collins, 1996.

Graham, Farmelo, Dr. *It Must Be Beautiful: Great Equations of Modern Science*. London: Grant Books, 2002.

Gray, Paul. "Alan Turing—Time 100 People of the Century." *Time Magazine*, March 1999.

Gunderson, Gerald. *The Wealth Creators*. New York: Dutton, 1989.

Gwynne, S. C. *Empire of the Summer Moon*. New York: Scribner, 2010.

Gyorgyi, Albert Szent. *Bioenergetics*. New York: Academic Press, 1957.

Hawking, Stephen. *The Grand Design*. New York: Bantam Books, 2010.

Harrington, Anne. *The Placebo Effect: An Interdisciplinary Exploration*. Cambridge: Harvard University Press, 1997).

Henderson, Jeff. *Cooked: My Journey From the Streets to the Stove*. New York: Harper Collins, 2007.

Kaplan, Robert. *The Nothing That Is: A Natural History of Zero*. Oxford University Press, 2000.

Keller, Helen. *The Story of My Life*. London: Hodder & Stoughton, 1959.

Kinney, Thomas A. *The Carriage Trade*. Baltimore: The Johns Hopkins University Press, 2004.

Klinger, David. *Into the Kill Zone: A Cop's Eye View of Deadly Force*. San Francisco: Jossey-Bass, 2004.

Koestler, Arthur. *The Sleepwalkers: A History of Man's Changing Vision of the Universe*. London: Penguin Group, 1959.

Koestler, Arthur. *The Act of Creation*. New York: Dell Publishing Co., 1964.

Kohler, Wolfgang. *The Mentality of Apes*. London: Pelican Books 1931.

Kolata, Gina. "A Little Deception Helps Push Athletes to the Limit." *New York Times*, Sept. 19, 2011.

Kosslyn, Stephen M., and Miller, G. Wayne. "A New Map of How We Think: Top Brain/Bottom Brain." *Wall Street Journal*, October 18, 2013.

Lauder, Estée. *Estée: A Success Story*. New York: Random House, Inc. 1985.

Lehman, Milton. *This High Man: The Life of Robert H. Goddard*. New York: Farrar, Strauss, and Co., 1963.

Lipton, Bruce. *The Biology of Belief*. New York: Hay House, Inc., 2005.

Lohr, Steve. "H. Edward Roberts, PC Pioneer, Dies at 68." *New York Times*, April 2, 2010.

Mack, Arien and Rock, Irvin. *Inattentional Blindness*. Cambridge: The MIT Press, 1998.

Madsen, Axel. *Chanel: A Woman of Her Own*. New York: Henry Holt & Co., 1990.

Mayer, Amy. "Rename It, Reuse It." *Scientific American Mind*, July/August 2012.

Meyers, Morton. A. *Happy Accidents*. New York: Arcade Publishing, 2007.

Nacera, Joe. "Capturing the Facebook Obsession." *New York Times*, October 15, 2010.

Michalko, Michael. *Cracking Creativity*. Berkeley: Ten Speed Press, 2001

O'Grady, Scott. *Return With Honor*. New York: Harper Collins, 1995.

Ogburn, William, and Thomas, Dorothy. "Are Inventions Inevitable? A Note On Social Evolution." *Political Science Quarterly*, Vol. 37, No.1 (March 1922).

Orzel, Chad. *How to Teach Relativity to Your Dog*. New York: Basic Books, 2012.

Perrow, Charles. *Normal Accidents*. Princeton: Princeton University Press, 1999.

Rifkin, Glenn. "Ken Olsen, Who Built DEC Into a Power, Dies at 84." *New York Times*, February 7, 2011.

Rigden, John, S. *Einstein, The Standard of Greatness*. Cambridge: First Harvard University Press, 2005

Roberts, Royston M. *Serendipity: Accidental Discoveries in Science*. New York: John Wiley & Sons, Inc.1989.

Rogers, Jim. *The Investment Biker*. New York: Random House, 2003.

Rowland, John. *Understanding the Atom*. London: Gollancz, 1935.

Sagan, Carl. *Cosmos*. New York: Ballantine Books, 1980.

Sagan, Carl. *In the Shadows of Forgotten Ancestors*. New York: Random House, 1992.

Sagan, Carl. *Dragons of Eden*. New York: Tess Press, 2004.

Schultz, Howard. *Pour Your Heart Into It: How Starbucks Built a Company One Cup at A Time*. New York: Hyperion 1997.

Villasenor, Victor. *Rain of Gold*. New York: Random House, 1991.

Wiener, Norbert. *Invention: The Care and Feeding of Ideas*. Massachusetts: MIT Press, 1993.

Index

Achenbach, Joel, 119–20
Achish, King of Gath, 221, 321n180
acid inhibitors, 111
Adam and Eve (biblical figures), 56, 314n48
Ad Council, 210
addiction to discovery, 187–93
advertising, 209–11
Age of Reason, 26
agriculture, 19
Aguilar, Mary Jane, 230
AIDS, 175
airlines, 66–68, 211, 299–301, 324n244
airplane, 20
Alexander, Fran: *Psychosomatic Medicine*, 110–11
Alexandria, ancient, 25
alopecia areata, 286
Altair computer, 185
alternating vs. direct current, 40
Alther, Lisa, 160
Amazon, 48
American Express, 199
American Inventor, 287
Amway, 204–5
amygdala, 54–55
analog computers, 124–25
Anderson, Tom, 20
Andreas, Steve: *NLP: The New Technology of Achievement*, 90
Andreessen, Marc, 251
anesthesia, 22
anger, 55
antibiotics, 111–12, 313n42. *See also* penicillin
apartheid, 278
apes' mentality, 125–28
Apollonius of Perga, 97–98
apoptosis, 53–54
Apple, 50
Archimedes of Syracuse, 90, 123–24, 127, 249
Ariely, Dan: *Predictably Irrational: The Hidden Forces that Shape Our Decisions*, 80
Aristarchus of Samos: *On the Sizes and Distances of the Sun and Moon*, 92, 93–94
Aristotle, 91, 94, 101
Armstrong, Neil, 20
Ash, Mary Kay, 170
Asimov, Isaac, 173
Aspergum, 177
aspirin as a blood thinner, 177

assumptions, challenging, 195–96, 320n177
astronomy, 91–97, 101
Athens, ancient, 25
atoms
    negative/positive charges in, 158
    particles/energy in, 14–15, 22, 311n7
    splitting of, 15, 20, 101, 142–43, 187, 311n7
AT&T, 29
Austin Ventures, 213
Avagadro, Amedeo, 22
Avila, Alejandro, 85
awareness. *See also* focus
    basketball example, 63–64, 314n51
    hearing, 61–62
    heightened, 61–68, 70–71
    jitney service example, 65–66
    by organisms, 53, 58
    salsa music example, 61–62
    self-awareness as the eye of the brain, 56–58, 314n48
    Virgin Atlantic example, 66–68
    vision, 62–64
Axelrod, Julius, 281
Aztecs, 99

Babbage, Charles, 170
Bacall, Lauren, 285–86
Bach-y-Rita, George, 228–30
Bach-y-Rita, Paul, 230–31
Bach-y-Rita, Pedro, 228–30, 236
background noise turned into information, 117–22
bacteria, 53, 111–12, 130, 131, 174, 313n42
balance in nature, 158–59, 319n139
Banister, Roger, 82
Bardeen, John, 49
Barnes & Noble, 65
Barnett, William, 21
Barrero, Joe, 251–52
Barsanti, Eugenio, 21
Bataille, Georges, 160
batteries, 29
Becquerel, Henri, 22
Beethoven, Ludwig van, 141
Begayeva, Karina, 266–67
belief in what you can't see, 9–18
    Army Ranger story, 11–12
    belief as motivation, 10–13
    as a choice, 16–17
    famous examples, 12–13
    gold-mine story, 9–10
    matter and energy, 14–16, 311n7

necessity as the mother of invention, 10–11
    and searching, 10
    subatomic particles, 14–15
    zero, 13–14
beliefs, generally
    challenges to our belief system, 105–6, 317n97
    choice of, 70–71
    expectations influenced by, 70, 72–74, 86–89
    focus's effects on, 70, 72–74, 75–78
beliefs' effects on biology, 79–90
    asthma example, 81
    athlete examples, 81–82
    control of beliefs, 83–85
    distraction's role, 85–87
    football example, 84
    Imperial Margarine example, 79–80
    map vs. territory, 90
    and placebos, 80–81
    and police officers' response to black men, 82
    POW experiments, 83
    repetition's role, 85–86
    sham surgery example, 80
    trial lawyer examples, 83–86
    wine experiment, 79
beliefs' effects on what you see
    astronomy example, 91–97
    embracing new truths, 96–97
    and frustration of holding on to unsupported beliefs, 96, 98
    gravity example, 94, 315n74
    Plato's cave metaphor, 91, 315n72
Bell, Alexander Graham, 13, 15, 19, 39–40, 105, 169
Bell Labs, 49, 142
Benini, Pietro, 21
Benz, Karl, 21, 316n90
benzene molecule, 130–31, 140, *141*
Bergman, Ingrid, 285–86
Bernard, Claude, 182
Bernert, David, 64
betrayal, 266–69
Beveridge, W. I. B., 168
Bezos, Jeff, 170, 222
Biancani, Santorio Giuseppe, 21
Bible, 162–63
Bikinis sports bars, 302–3
Blake, William, 158
Blakely, Sara, 170, 283–84
Blumberg, Baruch, 175–76, 281–82
Boeing, 300
BOOKSTOP, 64–65

327

Invite Dan to Speak At Your Next Event

Dan Castro will dazzle your audience with his message of inspiration and motivation that will have your team laughing, crying, and ready to conquer the world. Dan has received standing ovations at conventions with 12,000 people in attendance.

---

www.DanCastro.com

or Call:

512.732.0111

Is There Hidden Money At Your Feet?

Let us help you find it!

We'll show you:

1.

The **Hidden Money in the Real Estate**
All Around You.

2.

How to Earn a **Consistent 12%** on Your Money.

3.

How To **Swing Trade** Your Way To Riches.

4.

How To **Trade Options** Like the Pros.

5.

Money Making Opportunities Hidden
In Plain Sight.

6.

How To Create **Multiple Streams** of Income.

7.

The Difference Between Income and Wealth.

Ask us your hardest questions.
We'll get them answered.

www.MoneyAtYourFeet.com

Other Books by Dan Castro

CRITICAL CHOICES THAT CHANGE LIVES:
How Heroes Turn Tragedy Into Triumph

Heroes have been turning tragedy into triumph for thousands of years. Learn the patterns that heroes throughout history have followed in order to overcome extreme obstacles.

www.CriticalChoices.com

101 WAYS TO SPOT ELEGANT SOLUTIONS
HIDDEN IN PLAIN SIGHT

The absolute list of reasons why heroes and legends can spot elegant solutions that are invisible to everyone else.

www.HiddenSolutions.com

About the Author

Bloomberg Businessweek calls Dan Castro a "serial entrepreneur." In fact, Dan Castro is an award-winning author, an attorney, and serial entrepreneur who has built a law firm, a real estate brokerage, a property management company, a loan servicing company, a marketing company, a real estate investment company, and a workshop called THE HIDDEN MONEY AT YOUR FEET.

His first book, *Critical Choices That Change Lives* won several awards and is now selling all over the world.

After Dan's first book came out, Fortune 500 companies and non-profits everywhere began asking him to share his insights and wisdom in keynotes and workshops.

Dan Castro and his team of HIDDEN SOLUTION experts from virtually every industry can examine your business practices with fresh eyes and point out obvious solutions and hidden ways to make more money that you may be missing. They can also coach you and teach you how to do what they do.

For more information, go to:
www.DanCastro.com